Edwin M. Schur is Professor of Sociology at New York University, where he also previously served as Chairperson of the Department of Sociology. He is the author of numerous books on deviance and social problems, including CRIMES WITHOUT VICTIMS, LABELING DEVIANT BEHAVIOR, and INTERPRETING DEVIANCE.

THE POLITICS OF DEVIANCE

Stigma Contests and the Uses of Power

Edwin M. Schur

A SPECTRUM BOOK

PRENTICE-HALL, INC., Englewood Cliffs, New Jersey 07632

Library of Congress Cataloging in Publication Data

SCHUR, EDWIN M
   The politics of deviance.

   (A Spectrum Book)
   Includes bibliographies and index.
   1. Deviant behavior.   2. Deviant behavior–
Political aspects.   3. Power (Social sciences)
4. Social problems.   5. Social movements.   I. Title.
HM291.S373 1980   302.5   80-13643
   ISBN   0-13-684753-6
   ISBN   0-13-684746-3 (pbk.)

Editorial/production supervision and interior design by Suse L. Cioffi
Cover design by Ira Shapiro
Manufacturing buyer: Barbara A. Frick

PRENTICE-HALL INTERNATIONAL, INC., *London*
PRENTICE-HALL OF AUSTRALIA PTY. LIMITED, *Sydney*
PRENTICE-HALL OF CANADA, LTD., *Toronto*
PRENTICE-HALL OF INDIA PRIVATE LIMITED, *New Delhi*
PRENTICE-HALL OF JAPAN, INC., *Tokyo*
PRENTICE-HALL OF SOUTHEAST ASIA PTE. LTD., *Singapore*
WHITEHALL BOOKS LIMITED, *Wellington, New Zealand*

To Owen, David, Amy, and Sarah

Contents

2

Containment and Control 66

3

The Struggle to Define 132

4

Mobilizing Protest 190

Conclusion: The Persistence of Stigma Contests 228

Preface

Although sociologists continue to disagree as to which broad theoretical outlook offers the most useful orientation to deviance, most recent work in the field makes one central point clear. Deviance issues are inherently political. They revolve around some people's assessments of other people's behavior. And power is a crucial factor in determining which and whose assessments gain an ascendancy. Deviance policies, likewise, affect the distribution of power and always have some broad political significance. Sociologists can neither hide from these facts under claim of value-neutrality, nor deal adequately with them through the application of simplistic political formulas. On the contrary, they need to explore fully the inevitable political ity of deviance in all its complexity. This book is intended as a start in the direction of such an exploration.

During the Fall of 1978, I taught at New York University a graduate seminar on "The Politics of Deviance," through which I had a chance to try to work out some of the themes developed in this book, and from which I am sure the book has benefited. I would like to thank the students in that seminar—Diane Baillergeon, Susan Feinblatt, Georgia Iatrou, Robert Keeley, Mark Killian, Michael Miranda, George Nikitiades, Aline Nusbacher, Ruth Silverman, and Jeffrey Stein—for many thought-provoking reactions and ideas that are no doubt reflected in this work. I wish also to thank Geri Novasic and Shirley Fields for their typing of the manuscript; and to indicate my indebtedness to Michael Hunter, Denise Hoover, Suse Cioffi, and Shirley Stone at Prentice-Hall for their advice and help in connection with the book's production.

1
chapter

Deviance and Politics

"Who can, in fact, force others to accept their rules and what are the causes of their success? This is of course, a question of political and economic power."

Howard S. Becker
Outsiders *(1963)*

THE NEW POLITICS

Despite a surface fascination with political celebrities and intrigues, Americans have until recently shown little instinct for politics in the deepest sense of the word. Our tradition of individualism has frequently caused us to overlook the institutional sources of social problems and has likewise inhibited us from recognizing collective, interests and organizing to promote change. Our inveterate optimism has bred political inertia and a complacent unawareness of the power configurations and manipulations that necessarily and continuously shape our lives. The oft-noted failure of a socialist or other working-class political movement ever to attain real power in the United States is but one illustration of this broadly apolitical tradition. For most Americans politics has been an episodic (election-time) concern, involving only the two major parties and an assortment of successful and unsuccessful candidates, elected and appointed officials. Furthermore, the dominant view of political figures and activities has been a mildly jaundiced one; we have tended to see politics as a somewhat corrupt game rather than as a locus of deep moral commitment.

1

Today these outlooks are in a state of flux. Over the past few decades, substantively diverse social movements have helped to promote a broadened and more positive political perspective. Especially influential in this regard have been the civil rights and antiwar movements, the contemporary women's movement, and the movements for environmental and consumer protection. Collective efforts to change attitudes, behaviors, and politics in these several spheres have, of course, met with varying degrees of success. But the overall impact has been to produce an expanded definition of basic human rights, to strengthen the demand for public accountability, and to encourage yet other attempts at promoting desired social change through organization and collective action. These movements, furthermore, have not been restricted to or necessarily aligned with either of the major political parties. They have transcended specific election campaigns. And they have rested on, and reinforced, deeply felt moral convictions. As a result, many Americans have come to view political activity in a more favorable light and to realize that politics is a continuous and virtually omnipresent process.

Our ways of talking and thinking about the substantive content of political life have changed accordingly. We are not startled, nowadays, by references to the politics of welfare reform, the politics of health-care delivery, or even sexual politics. Before long, the central theme of this book — the politics of deviance — may similarly become a cultural commonplace. If that does happen, it will partly reflect developing academic outlooks on deviance and politics, but more directly it will be because of significant public situations and activities that link the two domains. As Horowitz and Liebowitz (1968) recognized, the changing relationship between political dissidence and personal "deviance" has involved at least two developments. On the one hand, persons who see themselves as furthering political goals have increasingly felt it necessary to engage in widely disapproved rule-violating acts, ranging from civil disobedience and passive resistance to self-immolation and armed violence. On the other hand, persons whose behaviors or conditions traditionally led to their being treated as deviant have, in recent years, been drawn to organizing politically to advance their collective interests. The best-known example of this trend probably is the gay liberation movement, but recent efforts to organize prisoners and prostitutes, to change drug laws, and to legalize abortion also illustrate this general pattern. Both broad trends may reflect a widening and intensification of overall political consciousness, as a result of which people may be coming to realize that the very process of deviance-defining is political in nature. Such controversial assertions as, "All prisoners are political prisoners," indicate — in somewhat extreme form — the conclusions to which such an outlook may lead.

REINTERPRETING DEVIANCE

Even if one is not prepared to go that far, there is good reason to stress the political aspects of deviance situations. Sociologists do not all agree on a precise definition of the term *deviance*. The most influential perspectives that have emerged recently in the sociology of deviance, however, inevitably lead the analyst to consider deviance a political phenomenon — in the broadest sense of the term. These perspectives have altered the course of deviance studies in at least two important ways. One major change has been in the general focal points for research and analysis; the other has involved the substantive scope of the field. Traditionally, sociologists were preoccupied with deviating behavior and individual deviators. They studied deviance largely in terms of "causation," which they often sought to explain by comparing the supposed deviants and "nondeviants." (This approach presents a great many difficulties, methodological as well as theoretical. Although its major limitations will be apparent as we proceed, no detailed consideration of such shortcomings is possible in this brief essay.) More recently, attention has shifted away from the individual deviator and toward the processes of defining and reacting to deviance.

Interest in why some individuals and not others deviate has not completely disappeared. But many investigators are now convinced that the more sociologically interesting questions concern the definitional and social-reaction processes themselves. How does a type of behavior or condition come to be viewed and treated as "deviant" in the first place? What factors influence the identification of, and reaction to, individual "offenders"? How do these reaction processes actually work? What functions do they serve, for the specific reactors or for society at large? What are the social consequences, for the individuals reacted to in this way, of being treated as "deviant"? Distinctive patterns and processes of definition and reaction are now widely recognized to be the core features exhibited in common by all deviance situations.

It is not easy to specify the "content" of this kind of reaction—which, as we shall see, is better thought of as appearing or being imposed in degree, rather than as being an all-or-nothing, present-or-absent matter. Deviance situations seem to arise when (and to the extent that) people who are in a position to impose their judgments find other people's behavior in one way or another "unsettling" (Suchar 1978, p. 1). The specifics of such reactions and the grounds for them may vary considerably—sometimes incorporating strong moral outrage, at other times reflecting merely feelings of distaste or even pity. Common to all these situations, however, is a process of social typing through which those who, for whatever reason, feel threatened seek to avoid the persons and negate the conditions they find objectionable. To the extent it succeeds, this process depersonalizes the offending individuals—who are treated as mere instances of a discreditable category, rather than as full human beings—thus imposing personal stigma and providing a basis for collective discrimination against them. There is no one generally agreed-upon sociological concept used to describe these processes. For want of a better term, we can say that in such situations certain types of behavior and conditions, as well as particular individuals, are — in varying degrees — *deviantized* (Schur 1979).

Once we see that the key to understanding deviance lies not in specific kinds of acts and individuals but rather in this deviantizing process, then the stage is set for reconsidering as well the range of specific substantive problems in which the deviance sociologist should have an interest. Traditional deviance analysis tended to focus on specific rule-violating acts for which individuals were commonly held morally blameworthy and personally responsible. Thus, study of such behaviors as crime and delinquency, suicide, and drug addiction formed the basis for most theorizing about deviance. Given the recently emphasized focus on definitions and reactions, these standard "forms of deviance" are themselves being interpreted in new ways. But in addition sociologists increasingly point to important elements of similarity between these standard deviance situations and others in which moral blameworthiness is less readily or fully assigned — such as those involving mental illness, mental retardation physical handicaps, deviating conditions or lifestyles (e.g., homosexuality, nudism, and bohemianism), and deviating political or religious beliefs and practices. All of these situations seem to display — in varying ways and degrees — the same basic deviantizing process. Indeed, as we shall see further, strong analogies can also be drawn to the treatment in our society of racial and ethnic minorities and women. Although the substantive detail varies, a common process of stigmatization (employing similar elements of stereotyping, depersonalization, and the like) is present in all of these situations. And by the same token, as already noted, the stigmatized in all of these different categories are likely to organize to counter such stigma — in much the same way and with recourse to many of the same techniques.

These substantive extensions and analogies help us to appreciate more readily the broadly political nature of deviance situations. Politics, according to the classic formulation of Harold Lasswell (1936), has to do with, Who gets what, when, how? Deviance defining represents one key arena within which such distributional outcomes emerge and undergo change. On its face, the Lasswell dictum would seem to point primarily to the allocation and control of economic and (conventionally conceived) political resources. Yet power, the basic stuff of politics, has many aspects and dimensions. At both the individual and collective levels, all of the deviance situations noted above center around the distribution of a certain kind of social power. Although economic, legal, and direct political power may sometimes be involved, what is most essentially at stake in such situations is the power or resource of moral standing or acceptability. Other appropriate terms for this would include propriety, respectability (Douglas 1970), and rectitude (Lasswell and Kaplan 1950, pp. 87–89). Individuals on the receiving end of the deviantizing process face as a result the prospect of a significant lessening of moral standing, and often they vividly experience it. Thus sociologists note that people defined as *deviant* — be they larcenists, drug addicts, "radicals," nudists, or even persons with mental or physical disabilities — all suffer from a "spoiled identity" (Goffman 1963) and must make various efforts to avoid or counteract the social and psychological impact of this stigma (Schur 1979, chap. 5).

By the same token, of course, placing some persons in these disvalued categories necessarily implies valued status for others, the so-called conformists. It is their rules that are applied, their standards that are legitimated, their "respectability" and power that are sustained and reinforced. We can see, then, that the power at stake in deviance-defining directly affects specific individuals and somewhat less directly affects the relative standing of various groups or segments within a society. As a mode of social subordination — one writer has recently used the term *inferiorization* (Adam 1978) — deviantizing is, in effect, a key element in a society's stratification order. At both individual and collective levels, it is a process of putting down those who in some way or other offend. In a sense all those who have been designated deviant comprise, by virtue of such treatment, some kind of have-not class. Since this would include an enormously heterogeneous collection of supposed nonrespectables, however, we should not expect it to act like a class in the "conflict group" sense (Dahrendorf 1959, chap. 6). Indeed, as we shall see, it is not likely that even the subclasses within this broad category (e.g., homosexuals, prisoners, mental patients) will always exhibit the social cohesiveness and consciousness of collective interests that are necessary for concerted and effective political action.

In part, the situation reflects the complicated intersection of this type of moral stratification with other dimensions of the stratification order (economic class, racial and ethnic divisions, and so on), some aspects of which we will be considering below. Describing the social order in terms of the distribution of an element he termed "social honor," Max Weber pointed out that "the social and the economic order are not identical. The economic order is for us merely the way in which economic goods and services are distributed and used. The social order is of course conditioned by the economic order to a high degree, and in its turn, reacts upon it" (Gerth and Mills 1958, p. 181). This comment suggests too an important complexity in the implications and uses of power that will concern us greatly throughout this book. Power, of any sort, is more like a process than an object. From that standpoint, it tends to operate as both cause and effect. Deviance outcomes (individual or collective) thus both reflect and determine configurations of power. Indeed, in a sense it is only by observing their success — which we then attribute to the exercise of preexisting power — that we can determine who the powerful really are. At the same time, however, such success often does help us to predict future outcomes as well. Thus, if the economic and political power of large corporations enables them to influence legislation and administrative policy in a way that protects their interests and insulates then from stigma, it is evident that this achievement confers power as well as reflecting it. Similarly, to cite a different kind of example, if preexisting wealth or professional attainments enable a suddenly handicapped person to maintain relatively favorable self-conceptions despite disvaluation by the nonhandicapped, such success will itself sustain and strengthen his or her resources for coping with future situations.

Much recent deviance sociology has emphasized the other side of this process — documenting, for substantively diverse areas of disvaluation, many of the ways in which powerlessness and vulnerability to stigma can snowball. Despite such self-propelling tendencies in the development and uses of power, however, it would be a serious error to think that every deviance outcome could be considered a foregone conclusion. As we have seen, there are always at least two sides in a deviance situation — that of the reactors and that of those reacted against. Indeed, one of the best ways of thinking about the entire area of deviance is in terms of what might be called *stigma contests*. In these continuing struggles over competing social definitions, it is relative rather than absolute power that counts most. The power of either side may be subject to change, not only through external causes but to an extent by conscious effort. When people engage in organized political activity on deviance issues they are, in fact, intentionally attempting to influence what might otherwise seem an irreversible course of events. They are trying to ensure that a particular balance of power will tip in their favor.

Deviance as a Construct

Before turning more directly to the politicality of deviance, it may be useful to indicate a bit further certain key themes in contemporary deviance analysis that generate a political focus.

As we have seen, recent studies emphasize the processes of social definition and reaction out of which deviance situations arise. The already-classic statement by Becker laid the groundwork for recognizing that deviance in fact is "produced" or "constructed" through such processes:

> . . . *social groups create deviance by making the rules whose infraction constitutes deviance*, and by applying these rules to particular people and labeling them as outsiders. From this point of view, deviance is *not* a quality of the act the person commits, but rather a consequence of the application by others of rules and sanctions to an "offender." The deviant is one to whom that label has successfully been applied; deviant behavior is behavior that people so label. [Becker 1963, p. 9]

Deviance, then, is not some kind of objective and immutable entity *to* which people respond subjectively and *about* which public policies sometimes are instituted. On the contrary, it is *through* social definitions, responses, and policies that particular behaviors, conditions, and individuals acquire their "deviantness" (Schur 1979). The importance of this definitional aspect of deviance should be apparent from the fact that deviance defining shows considerable variability — for example, from culture to culture (see Edgerton 1976), and within any one culture, variability over time. Thus in our own society we are familiar with a good many instances of change in the deviantness attaching to particular behaviors and conditions. For example, recently such behaviors as cigarette smoking and acting like a "white racist" have increased in overall social objectionableness and are more and more likely to be grounds for stigmatizing reactions. On the other hand, marihuana use, premarital intercourse, and being a divorcée, are not as likely as before to be widely and heavily stigmatized.

These examples point up the fact, furthermore, that deviantness usually is not an either-or phenomenon but is instead a matter of degree. There is, to be sure, a considerable amount of public consensus regarding the seriousness of certain major criminal offenses (Peter Rossi et al., 1974; Newman 1976). Nonetheless there are wide ranges of sometimes-problematic behaviors with respect to which responses are simply not so clear, uniform, or stable that we can sensibly describe them as being either deviant or not deviant. Instead, they are subject to highly varying characterizations (not only over time but at any one time, depending on the context and who does the characterizing). A few additional examples will highlight the fact that, quite apart from broad cultural and temporal variability, the very same behavior or condition may—at *any* time—be subject to multiple characterizations. Thus, the same ingestion of chemicals may be viewed and reacted to as drug use or drug abuse. A single pattern of sexual behavior may cause a person to be labeled as sexually active or, alternatively, promiscuous. An offending or upsetting action or incident can provide the basis for such diverse interpretations as eccentricity, instability, and mental illness. Some people might argue that severity of response (i.e., degrees of deviantness read into the situation) tends to correspond to degree of objectionableness or upsettingness. Yet even if we could agree on a way of measuring the latter, such correspondence would not *have* to occur.

More crucial still, claims that it does occur can never really be proved or disproved because the feelings or beliefs that give rise to deviantizing—"objectionableness," "upsettingness," and the like—are precisely that, feelings or beliefs rather than objective conditions or facts. What one person finds objectionable another does not, and there is no way for a scientific "referee" to establish the correctness of either response. The distinction between behaviors and conditions, on the one hand, and the social characterization of these behaviors and conditions, on the other, is then central to the recent perspectives on deviance. In many respects, "what is made of an act socially" (Schur 1971, p. 16; see also Freidson 1965) is the most important and interesting ingredient of any deviance situation. This realization lies behind the declining interest in studying individual deviators with an eye to uncovering "causal factors" and the corresponding wish to study instead, or at least as well, the processes through which such behaviors and individuals are defined and reacted to as deviant. As Erikson has properly emphasized, "Sociologically . . . the critical variable is the social *audience* . . . since it is the audience which eventually decides whether or not any given action or actions will become a visible case of deviation" (Erikson 1962, p. 308). Whether we are primarily focusing on the selection and treatment of individual "offenders," or on the broader social processes through which collective deviance definitions arise and change, we clearly need to transcend simplistic types-of-deviance and types-of-deviants theories. At all levels and in all cases, it is not just what the so-called deviant did but also what other people do that must be examined. We must recognize that — to modify the aphorism about the tango — it takes two to deviance! This is why the recent perspectives on deviance are often termed interactionist (Rubington and Weinberg 1978; Goode 1978); deviance situations develop through an *inter*action between the supposed deviators, on the one hand, and those who seek to impose deviantizing conceptions and processes on the other. The notion of developing situations is itself very important, for it underlines the point that deviance does not so much inhere in any given set of circumstances as it emerges (F. Davis 1963, pp. 10–11) or is actualized (Suchar 1978) through this not fully predictable interaction process. The aforementioned concept of *deviance outcomes* may help us to keep this emergent quality in mind. Just as the prevailing "outcome" at any one stage. (e.g., fate of a perceived deviator, implementation of a deviance policy) has developed out of, and been shaped by, what went before, so too is such an outcome usually tentative, subject to change, likely in turn to evolve into yet another set of circumstances. Since deviance situations are best thought of in terms of such evolving and shifting outcomes, what the outcome will be in any given instance becomes highly problematic. It is because deviance definitions, reactions, and policies are in large degree problematic that broadly political forces come into play.

As noted above, the leeway in these situations for using individual or collective resources in seeking desired goals suggests that any deviance outcome is likely to have evolved out of past power struggles. Similarly, many deviance outcomes reflect ongoing power struggles or will give rise to future ones. In these stigma contests, we see clearly the central role of social conflict in shaping deviance situations. Indeed, one observer has gone so far as to assert: "Deviance is the name of the conflict game in which individuals or loosely organized small groups with little power are strongly feared by a well-organized, sizable minority or majority who have a large amount of power" (Lofland 1969, p. 14). This statement refers primarily to collective struggles over deviance definitions, but as several of the examples cited earlier indicate, power differentials are also very important in affecting what happens to specific individuals who may be subject to stigma. Indeed, it is precisely because any one such individual usually holds relatively little power to withstand strong deviantizing pressures that collective organization to influence deviance-defining comes about.

The Deviantizing Process

A great deal of recent research and theorizing on deviance has documented this typical vulnerability of the individual perceived deviator. The reference to the "perceived" deviator is important because a person can be reacted to, even "processed" as deviant, regardless of whether he or she actually committed the objectionable act. Here, as in the collective perception of threat, it is the perception that counts. At an extreme, deviance processing can even go beyond "false accusation" of particular individuals for acts that did occur and involve processing for totally imaginary "violations." Witchcraft trials and Stalinist purges have been cited to illustrate this point (Currie 1968; Connor 1972). As the reference earlier to the often-snowballing nature of power-lessness suggests, sociologists have shown that once set in motion the deviantizing process develops a momentum of its own. Through self-fulfilling, self-reinforcing, and self-propelling processes, a powerful tendency toward deviance amplification (Schur 1979, chap. 4) comes into being. Stigma successfully imposed lowers the individual's confidence and self-esteem, restricts his or her opportunities, sets the stage for "engulfment" (Schur 1971, pp. 69-81) in the stigmatized role, and generates the likelihood of further, and intensified, stigmatization.

That is so in part because stigmatized statuses and identities tend to carry a "master status" quality (Becker 1963, pp. 33–34). When an individual is assigned a deviant status this identification (including the myriad stereotypes about "that kind of person" that usually are associated with it) deeply governs other people's perceptions of the perceived offender. As Becker notes, the deviant status tends to "override all other statuses." The offending individual is no longer just another person. Rather, he or she is now a thief, an addict, a hooker, a cripple. These categorizations and the depersonalized response they imply form the basis for the insidious process of *retrospective interpretation* through which other people "reread" the character of the perceived deviant. Among the most dramatic examples of this rereading phenomenon are the "status degradation ceremonies" discussed by Garfinkel (1956). Official processing, as in criminal trials and mental commitment hearings, signals dramatically the processed individual's abrupt and substantial change of status. (It is partly because our society provides few "status elevation ceremonies" for the formerly deviantized that stigma imposed in this and other ways is so hard to shed.) But retrospective interpretation is not restricted to official proceedings of this sort. It is, rather, a deep-seated tendency built into the deviantizing process at all levels of social interaction.

In a well-known study of students' reactions to acquaintances they discovered or suspected were homosexual, Kitsuse found that his respondents typically reinterpreted such persons' earlier behavior in the light of this newly perceived deviant status.

> The subjects indicate that they reviewed their past interactions with the individuals in question, searching for subtle cues and nuances of behavior which might give further evidence of the alleged deviance. This retrospective reading generally provided the subjects with just such evidence to support the conclusion that "this is what was going on all the time." [Kitsuse 1962, p. 253]

Members of the so-called helping professions may also reread the character of their clients in much the same way. The case histories and records of patients in mental hospitals, Goffman suggests, do not always entail a comprehensive and nonselective recording of all life occurrences but instead seem to serve the function of showing "the ways in which the patient is sick and the reasons why it was right to commit him and is right currently to keep him committed, and this is done by extracting from his whole life course a list of those incidents that have or might have had 'symptomatic' significance" (Goffman, 1961, pp. 155–156). As Lofland has argued, a need for perceptual consistency (in terms of the stereotypical notions people have about various kinds of problematic behaviors) seems to lie behind these reinterpretation or "biographical reconstruction" processes: "There must be a *special* history that *specially* explains current imputed identity. Relative to deviance, the *present evil* of current character must be related to *past evil* that can be discovered in biography" (Lofland 1966, p. 150). Goffman's further observation that anyone's life history or current behavior could provide a basis for such selective interpretation was borne out in Rosenhan's startling *pseudopatient* study (Rosenhan 1973). When confederates of the researcher, who were not mentally ill, managed to obtain admission to mental hospitals, no matter how normally they acted staff members routinely responded to them in terms of their imputed condition of mental illness. Their perfectly sensible questions were ignored, their quite ordinary actions past and present were interpreted as symptoms of underlying psychopathology, and even when they finally obtained release their supposed disturbances were simply described as being in remission.

Even the relatively secure research-confederate pseudopatients in the Rosenhan study, in the wake of the uniform response to them as patients only, experienced strong feelings of powerlessness and depersonalization. It is hardly surprising, then, if other persons (i.e., nonresearchers) subjected to deviantizing responses — persons who typically have few resources enabling them to withstand the effects and whose real life chances are usually as a result badly impaired — suffer a severe loss of self-esteem as well as a restriction of their social options. Quite simply, it is very difficult to maintain a favorable view of yourself if other people see you in a negative light and treat you accordingly. As depersonalization increases and the response of others to you is primarily in terms of the deviantized status, it becomes difficult not to become convinced yourself that such status provides your main identity. At an extreme, the heavily deviantized person may come to see himself or herself as "nothing but" an instance of the stigmatized category — be it a rapist, a corrupt official, an alcoholic, a homosexual, or a midget. We must note too, in this connection, that it is the stigmatizing quality of the response — whatever the motivation underlying it may be — that triggers these self-fulfilling, self-derogating processes. Thus, "The blind person comes to feel that he is not completely accepted as a mature, responsible person. As a second-class citizen, he must deal with the eroding sense of inadequacy that inevitably accompanies that status" (Scott 1969, p. 37).

As suggested above, such processes are by no means uniform, absolute, or irreversible. Individuals vary in the resources and techniques they personally can use to avoid or offset stigma (details of such techniques cannot be considered here) and also in their access to opportunities to join with others in mounting a collective response to deviantizing. Furthermore, there is considerable variability in the exposure to and nature of the deviantizing responses and pressures themselves. Generally it can be said, however, that "other things being equal, the greater the *consistency, duration* and *intensity* with which a definition is promoted by Others about an Actor, the greater the likelihood that an Actor will embrace that definition as applicable to himself" (Lofland 1966, p. 121). Lemert highlighted this probability of self-propelling stigma reinforcement by suggesting a sequence in which initial or "primary" deviation might, under the pressure of negative reaction, increasingly lead to "secondary" deviation: "When a person begins to employ his deviant behavior or a role based upon it as a means of defense, attack, or adjustment to the overt and covert problems created by the consequent societal reaction to him [i.e., to his initial deviating], his deviation is secondary" (Lemert 1951, p. 76). At a theoretical extreme there might be "ultimate acceptance" by the perceived offender of "deviant social status and efforts at adjustment on the basis of the associated role" (ibid. p. 77). While such acceptance is in fact rarely total, the very substantial engulfment in deviant self-images and roles that typically does evolve in these situations makes Lemert's concept very important.

The many practical role restrictions that offending individuals may experience interact with and heighten the impact of attitudinal rejection. Thus, the publicly identified homosexual may face not only interpersonal scorn and humiliation but also limited work opportunities and economic prospects, obstacles to residing in a desired location, difficulties in joining various organizations, routine harassment, let alone inadequate protection, by the police, and many other practical problems. Combined with the general tendency among the dominant heterosexual population to respond to homosexuals primarily if not exclusively "as" homosexuals, these difficulties often make self-segregation seem a logical protective and morale-enhancing step. Along with degrees of segregation imposed from without, this may lead to involvement in and preoccupation with "the gay world" beyond the extent that might—in the absence of such pressures—seem "natural" (Altman 1973, chaps. 2,3, and 7). As we are going to see below, this particular situation happens at present to be undergoing considerable change under the impact of the gay liberation movement.

Beyond the "Labeling" Controversy

Studies that have developed and applied some of these recent perspectives on deviance and that have focused especially on what is here called the deviantizing process are usually referred to as incorporating the "labeling" perspective (as per Becker's "deviant behavior is behavior that people so label"). Recently a great deal of sociological controversy has centered on the validity and limits of that perspective. (For a variety of viewpoints see Schur 1971; Hawkins and Tiedeman 1975; Gove, ed., 1975; Suchar 1978; Schur 1979.) It is not necessary, for our purposes, to thoroughly review and evaluate all of the arguments involved in this dispute. A few, however, call for brief comment here, and we will touch on some others in later sections of the book. At least some of the criticisms of the labeling orientation rest on a misunderstanding, or unnecessarily restrictive interpretation, of what that perspective is all about. In this regard, the very popularity of the term *labeling* has been unfortunate, for often it has taken on very narrow connotations. Particularly for some of the critics, labeling seems to refer to one thing only—the alleged unfavorable consequences produced by direct negative labeling of specific individuals, the process that was briefly sketched out in the section above on deviantizing. Yet as our entire discussion so far should have made clear, this direct interpersonal deviantizing process—as it is revealed directly in behavioral and social psychological consequences—is but one aspect, albeit an extremely important one, of the recently emphasized social reactions or definitional perspective. What that orientation more broadly points to is the fact that at every level of social life — in personal interaction, in the processing of individuals by designated (social control) organizations, and in the generation of broad deviance conceptualizations and classifications at the societal level — deviance is always a social construction, brought about through a characteristic process of social definition and reaction. In all instances, and whatever substantive behavior or condition is involved, a necessary condition for the very existence of deviance is the imputation or assignment of "deviantness." This distinctive complex of social meanings and the defining-reacting process through which it is applied are the features we find to be common to all deviance situations.

Critics who treat the labeling orientation as though it were little more than a formal theory about the individual causation of deviating acts, a theory they insist must be quantitatively tested and assessed relative to the supposedly alternative traditional theories of causation, thus ignore the perspective's broader significance. Similarly misguided are critics who treat the approach as being narrowly social-psychological in its interests, some of them going on to argue as well that it is therefore an essentially apolitical orientation. In fact, and as we have already discussed in very general terms, by providing a broad interpretive outlook on deviance-defining as it occurs at different levels of the social order, a reactions or definitional perspective inevitably highlights many aspects of deviance situations that both reflect political processes and are subject to pressure and influence through concerted political action. (See the different focal points for analysis in "A Paradigm for Studying Deviance Situations," in Schur 1979, pp. 507–520.) The underlying power factor in all deviance-defining has been indicated above. We shall be returning to that key point, and to many specific examples of the diverse political elements in deviance situations, throughout this book. At this stage, however, it may be useful to indicate very briefly some further ways in which the concerns of a broad reactions focus help to underline the politicality of deviance.

One such concern is with the amplification of deviance by the mass media. The media affect deviance-defining at various levels through reinforcement of deviance stereotypes and selective depiction of various events. As Scheff has noted (1966, pp. 67–80), the frequent references to "an ex-mental patient" in reporting on incidents of violent crime promotes distorted public impressions about both the consequences of mental illness and the causes of violence. The equally common references to "an ex-convict on parole" similarly encourage public misunderstandings. (In both cases it is the selectivity of the reporting that creates the false impression — the media cite neither meritorious actions of ex-mental patients and ex-convicts when they occur nor the involvement of "non-ex-mental patients" or "non-ex-convicts" in current crime incidents.) As one British study of media references to high delinquency rates in a Glasgow neighborhood showed (Armstrong and Wilson 1973), media coverage of local situations can trigger self-fulfilling cycles of community fear, stepped-up policing, and stigma amplification. More generally, media coverage becomes a key element, shaping and interacting with public attitudes and social-control efforts in connection with any and all perceived local or national "crime waves." (See Fishman 1978.) Overall, it should be emphasized that since deviance by definition represents that which the dominant majority finds unsettling and contaminating and therefore seeks to avoid, a great many of our impressions about, and attitudes toward, specific deviance issues necessarily derive from the media. These public conceptions usually have important public-policy implications, and as a consequence the influence or control of media content can become a key resource for those engaged in large-scale stigma contests.

Another way in which the focus on definition and response calls attention to potential arenas of political action is through its concentration on organizations that process deviance. In line with the sociological turn away from deviating acts and individuals and toward deviantizing reactions, the role of social-control agents and agencies in influencing deviance outcomes has come to the fore. (See Schur 1979, chap. 6; also Hawkins and Tiedeman 1975, chaps. 5–8.) Many labeling-oriented studies have documented the selective or routinized intervention that characterizes much deviance processing and the fact that these tendencies are often grounded in, and facilitated through, the stereotypes or "typifications" held and developed by control agents. (See, for example, Piliavin and Briar 1964; Sudnow 1965; Scheff 1966; Mercer 1973.) Obviously such processing fatefully affects the lives of the individuals who are processed. Equally significant is the fact, perceptively noted by Kitsuse and Cicourel (1963), that how these processing organizations treat deviance and the kinds of information they put out largely determine public conceptions regarding the general nature and dimensions of deviance problems and the characteristics and social distribution of the so-called deviants.

As many of the recent control-agency studies have shown, furthermore, these deviance outcomes often reflect the emerging needs of the organization itself — to develop a smooth-working processing system, to maintain community demand for, and support of, its policies and programs, and to operate in relation to other organizations and additional outside forces, including especially sources of funding and legitimation. Many social-control organizations are state agencies or receive governmental funding and certification. Others may be subject to governmental regulation. Given the importance for their general standing and day-to-day work operations of public policy and funding priorities, most agencies that deal with deviance — private organizations as well as public, and regardless of specific ideology or professional standing — inevitably find themselves thrust into the maelstrom of political life (Emerson 1969; Scott 1969; and see also Dickson 1968). A corresponding point, implied by comments above and brought out by some of the same deviance studies, is that private or state control organizations may develop strong vested interests in particular public policies and may even actively engage in political efforts to advance and protect these interests. These remarks should indicate too that the state itself clearly plays a significant role, direct or indirect, in virtually all of the broad deviance situations (e.g., "the drug problem," "the war against crime," "treatment of the mentally ill") that preoccupy the citizenry in a modern society. As we shall see below, there is considerable disagreement regarding the precise nature, extent, and overall implications of this role. That the state must in some way be taken into account in any general interpretation of deviance defining does, however, seem indisputable.

Collective Definition

Finally, there has been one other broad political thrust in the recent approaches to deviance. It has resulted from their direct attention to processes and patterns of collective definition at the societal level. This has pushed sociological analysis in a number of different, but complementary, directions. One has to do with the general functions that the very process of deviance defining — of any sort, whatever form it takes — may serve for the collectivity itself. The major concept arising out of this work has been *boundary maintenance*. Deviance defining contributes to social cohesion and reinforces the dominant standards in a society by establishing social and moral limits. As Erikson comments:

> The deviant is a person whose activities have moved outside the margins of the group, and when the community calls him to account for that vagrancy it is making a statement about the nature and placement of its boundaries. It is declaring how much variability and diversity can be tolerated within the group before it begins to lose its distinctive shape, its unique identity. [Erikson 1966, p. 11]

Interpretations of this sort show how some strands of the definitional, or reactions, perspective draw on, rather than break with, the tradition of "functionalist" theory in sociology. (See Durkheim 1893, 1933; Coser 1962; Erikson 1962.)

Another direction that sociological analysis has taken, and which also represents a link between functionalism and recent deviance theory, is seen in works that explore the particular forms of deviance-defining in a given society in relation to its dominant value patterns and social arrangements. From this "mirror image" aspect (see Bell 1961; also Davis 1937) we begin to see that in many respects a society has "the deviance it deserves" (Schur 1979, pp. 71–73). Each society displays, at a given time, a particular set of "deviances" that in many complex ways reflect the other features of that social system. A key point, properly emphasized by Erikson (1966), is that these patterns of deviance especially reflect a society's major preoccupations and fears. Just as fear of witches makes it more likely that one will encounter them, so too a society preoccupied with sex is likely to have a great deal of sexual deviance, and a society vigilantly on guard against political deviation will experience it in high degree. Thus too, the further point developed by Erikson and others that the amount and deployment of social-control resources (e.g., the extent of policing in an area, the number of mental-hospital beds, the intensity of efforts to curb prostitution) help to determine deviance outcomes. These functional ties between *control* and *deviance* represent a key theme in the reactions perspective, pointing out that the self-fulfilling prophecy mechanisms operate not only in the deviantizing of individuals but on broader levels as well. A given society, then, is likely to have the kinds of deviance it fears and perhaps even the amounts of deviance that it seeks out.

A third major focal point for studies of collective definition has to do with the processes through which, and conditions under which, particular deviance categories develop and change. In this connection, sociologists have become extremely interested in the "natural history" of social problems (Spector and Kitsuse 1977). Whether or not they will succeed in generalizing about common sequences through which all perceived social problems develop, it is quite clear that each such perceived problem goes through a specific course of development, the exploration of which may be very enlightening. Two characteristic and interrelated features of the developmental process have been highlighted in the recent studies. One is the fact that at certain times a particular substantive type of deviance may be "discovered" or "invented" — in the sense that a totally new deviance category is generated. This is not to say that such a new definition has literally created the problematic behavior itself, though as we saw earlier, the extreme cases of witchcraft trials and the Stalinist purges came close to that. Rather, the point is that the new collective characterization of the behavior has extremely important social consequences. Thus, the conceptualization, dimensions, and ways of dealing with the perceived problem are all affected — indeed, it is usually as part of this process that the behavior is first collectively defined as *being* a distinct, classifiable problem. That is what happened, for example, when the sociolegal classification of "juvenile delinquency" was created through passage of the first juvenile court act (Platt 1969). Recent examples include the "discovery" of hyperkinesis (Conrad 1975; also Schrag and Divoky 1976), and child abuse (Pfohl 1977). Sociohistorical analysis has become an important tool, then, for completely understanding any type of deviance-defining at the collective level.

In this book the historical dimension will not be a primary focus. We are going to be more directly concerned here with the key features of stigma contests in contemporary American society. Whether we examine deviance situations from a historical standpoint or by exploring their currently manifested aspects, a second key aspect of collective definition becomes central. This aspect is *moral enterprise* (Becker 1963, chaps. 7 and 8). Although trends in deviance-defining may reflect broader patterns of social change, the process always requires a degree of initiative — specific individuals and groups must promote or resist particular ways of conceptualizing deviance and policies toward it. Hence the inevitable links between deviance, political action, and social change. We have seen that deviance struggles involve competition over relative moral standing. Usually, Becker's terms *moral entrepreneur* and *moral crusade* are used in reference to efforts to impose or extend deviance definitions, while the aforementioned idea of *politicization of deviance* is applied to collective attempts to resist or reduce such deviance defining. Yet, as we shall see repeatedly in the pages that follow, these terms really cut both ways. Both sides in a stigma contest are seeking moral dominance; both may try to use political means toward that end.

The concept of *perceived threat* provides a key link between the overall or basic boundary-maintaining function of deviance defining and the emergence of particular collective definitions of deviance within specific social contexts. Changes in collectively experienced threat, of whatever sort, seem to underlie both abrupt shifts and general trends in deviance defining. As emphasized earlier in this chapter, it is the feeling that behaviors, conditions, or individuals are in some way threatening that triggers the personal or collective initiatives that propel stigma contests. Such perception can grow without any actual increase in the perceived deviation itself. Thus in an ingenious laboratory experiment, Lauderdale (1976) found that when the deviation from group norms by research confederates planted within experimental groups was held constant, negative reactions to these "deviants" on the part of other group members varied along with the introduction of an external "threat" element (reason to believe the group's work might be terminated). Lauderdale points out that "moral boundaries of a social system move independently of the actual behavior of individuals defined as 'deviant' by the system" (Lauderdale 1976, p. 660).

In trying to understand deviance situations, therefore, we must always address the crucial issue of perceived threat. Who feels threatened? By whom or what? In what ways and under what conditions. What can those who feel threatened do about it? How can their efforts to resist threat, in turn, be resisted and opposed by the perceived deviants? Recognizing the importance of the threat element necessarily brings us face to face with the question of interests. On this matter, regardless of claims to the contrary, and although they undoubtedly may develop the point in different ways, reactions theorists, and even functionalists, share a basic understanding with Marxists and self-proclaimed radical sociologists. To ask who is threatened is to ask whose interests are at stake. Likewise, sophisticated functionalists have emphasized that — while all existing social arrangements have functional ties with other aspects of the system in which they appear — any given arrangement is going to be a good deal more "functional" (in the positive sense) for some people than for others. So we need always to ask, functional for whom? Particularly in the designation of social problems and the selection of favored policies, functionalism and the reactions approach both emphasize that people's judgments and priorities are bound to differ in socially patterned ways. (See Merton 1976.) As we are going to see in much of the discussion that follows, where mainstream sociologists and some of their radical critics do tend to disagree is on the issue of whether *all* deviance outcomes can be attributed *exclusively* to the control imposed and exercised by a single identifiable and cohesive ruling elite. The argument to be developed in this book is that deviance issues, viewed collectively, are more complex than that. The multiplicity of interests at stake and the problems on every side, and with respect to each issue, of generating cohesive support and mobilizing collective action, make the monolithic elite model of a deviance-defining overly simplistic.

DIMENSIONS OF POLITICALITY

We have already seen that, in the broadest sense, deviance is an inherently political issue. By definition, since they are modes of disvaluing and discrediting, the designation of deviance and the deviantizing of individuals involve the exercise of power and affect the subsequent distribution of power. Furthermore, as Becker has noted:

> In addition to recognizing that deviance is created by the responses of people to particular kinds of behavior, by the labeling of that behavior as deviant, we must also keep in mind that the rules created and maintained by such labeling are not universally agreed to. Instead, they are the object of conflict and disagreement, part of the political process of society. [Becker 1963, p. 18]

Although sociologists have sometimes debated the merits of a "conflict approach" in this area, once one recognizes deviance to be a matter of social definitions and reactions there is no need to continue that debate. Public disagreement on standards of moral evaluation and on their specific uses make clear that what the deviance analyst is most essentially concerned with is in fact a form of social conflict.

Precisely who is in conflict with whom, and just which and how many interests are at stake in a given deviance situation, will not always be self-evident. Nor is it usually a foregone conclusion by what means the conflict will be carried out, or with what consequences. Even the general types of interests involved, let alone the more specific ones, vary considerably. As the comments earlier about power and deviance outcomes indicated, the relevant interests may be economic, narrowly political, or primarily symbolic. They may be individual or collective, obvious or subtle, openly professed or latent and not even consciously recognized. As the many examples to be developed in this book will show, in any given deviance situation or broader problem area we will often find various combinations of these different types of interest at work. Complicating matters still further is the fact that individuals and groups frequently have ambiguous or multiple interests relative to a particular deviance issue. From this it follows that in collective deviance struggles individual allegiances and degrees of commitment, group mobilization and cohesion, and the formation of general alliances and working coalitions all tend to be variable and uncertain.

In exploring stigma contests we also need to keep in mind that they can be played out at several different levels of social life and in a variety of institutionally influenced contexts. Table 1 offers a typology of the political dimensions of deviance, which attempts to depict in very broad terms this multilevel, multicontext feature. With respect to any substantive deviance category, the power elements and struggles can appear in varying degrees on any or all levels. A particular level will be more important — both to the participants themselves and for purposes of sociological interpretation — in one substantive area, less so in another. To an extent, the inherent power element in deviance defining implies that some kind of "intrinsic politics" is always present, even if it hasn't been widely recognized. The women's movement has brought that out, for example, by referring to the "personal politics" of various patterns of sexist interaction — which could also be seen as involving the deviantizing of women. The situated politics of deviance may involve

TABLE 1

A Typology of Political Dimensions

I. The Micropolitics of Deviance
   A. Intrinsic
   B. Situated
II. The Institutional Politics of Deivance
   A. General
   B. Organizational
   C. Professional
III. The Collective Politics of Deviance
   A. Conceptual
   B. Official

any number of things. Passage of a specific drug law, police harassment of homosexuals in a given locale, mental commitment proceedings in a particular court, determinations of suicide by a given medical examiner, defensive adaptations of prostitutes, the programs of an organization to assist the physically handicapped — all of these have a "situated" character and require analysis of the power, or political, interplay partly in those terms.

Although all kinds of deviantizing must have some intrinsic and situated aspects, there is likely to be considerable variation among them in the extent to which they also develop openly or actively at the broader social levels indicated by dimensions II and III in the table. Indeed, it may be useful for some purposes to picture a kind of continuum of degrees of politicization, with situations ranging from the less-overtly politicized ones dominated by category I features to more highly politicized ones, where many of the category II and category III features are evident. Much of the discussion and illustrative material to follow will point up such variation and consider some of its sources. We shall also examine specific examples of the several subcategories listed in the table. As we shall see, the politics of deviance may at times significantly involve the general institutions of a society (e.g., family and sex-role differentiation, religion, education). In many instances a dispute will crucially affect or be influenced by organizations that deal with deviance (e.g., mental hospitals, the juvenile court, the police), and sometimes the role and jurisdiction of major recognized professions (e.g., psychiatry, law) will be at stake. The extent to which collective conceptions regarding a perceived deviation become generalized throughout the society at large and the enactment of official policies toward it are potentially important, but similarly variable, foci of political concern and struggle.

As should be apparent, the different levels are not mutually exclusive but instead indicate elements that typically overlap and interact in their operation. In a sense, the broader collective dimensions reflect the sum total of all that goes on at the situated and personal levels, and vice versa. As in all of social and political life, "the individual, the microsocial, and the macrosocial levels together make up social reality. None has necessary existential or explanatory priority" (Lehman 1977, p. 10). In this book, we are going to devote primary attention to the institutional and collective politics of deviance, but especially in considering various substantive illustrations, microsociological elements will be touched on as well.

Politics is sometimes said to be the art of the possible. The politics of deviance reflects such a constraint, revealing an amalgam of moral principles, gut reactions, and realistic goal seeking. What is possible for individuals and groups participating in stigma contests keeps changing, in part through their own continuing efforts to maximize resources, manipulate key symbols, monopolize decision making, and in general gain and wield social power. In the discussion and examples that follow, we are going to be examining many such efforts and attempting to make some tentative generalizations about them. It will be particularly apparent that on most major deviance issues public definitions and policies are indeed — as the aforementioned theorizing suggests — subject to continuous fluctuation. This should convince us that, by virtue of the power and conflict elements shaping deviance outcomes, the politics of deviance is inextricably bound up with social change. While major changes in a society help to determine the course of deviance struggles, such struggles at the same time themselves contribute to the changing nature of our society — crucially affecting the way we live.

EXAMPLE 1. *Politicality Revealed: Psychiatry and Mental Illness*

As in the case of deviance in general, a combination of academic work and public debate has spurred recognition of the political aspects of psychiatry and mental illness. Among the most important general themes that have emerged in the course of this recognition are the following: "Mental illness" is first and foremost a designation, a way of characterizing and classifying behavior. As a consequence, it necessarily involves an element of evaluation. For the most part, standards of mental health and illness are not fixed scientific ones, but rather they entail judgments that often may vary along sociocultural lines. Not surprisingly, then, psychiatric diagnoses are themselves uncertain and highly variable; and since they usually refer to social behavior rather than organic illness, the relevance of medical criteria is not always clear. These diagnoses, furthermore, convey as well as incorporate social judgments. Mental illness designations are highly stigmatizing and thus impose reductions in power and social standing. By the same token their imposition constitutes a wielding of social power. Because psychiatric diagnosis is inherently evaluative and hence in a way necessarily arbitrary, application of the mental illness designation is, if unchecked, almost infinitely expandable. Therefore, despite the undoubted benefits that voluntary psychotherapy may confer, and notwithstanding the good intentions of most therapists, compulsory impositions of psychiatric "help" represent a significant mode of social control. Particularly when the state becomes implicated in its public uses, psychiatry may become a potent tool for controlling any or all individuals and groups deemed to threaten or undermine the (political as well as social or cultural) status quo.

These outlooks have been brewing for some time, partly as a result of diverse lines of analysis developed by social scientists and social critics — including some members of the psychiatric profession itself. In a classic essay, sociologist Kingsley Davis (1938) suggested that the then-emerging "mental hygiene" movement employed evaluative criteria closely linked to the American social-class system — incorporating, in particular, the dominant Protestant work ethic that called for "prudence, rationality, and foresight." Hollingshead and Redlich (1958), in their major study of the social-class distribution of psychiatric patients in New Haven, found that both diagnosis and treatment varied systematically according to social-class membership. Diagnoses of psychotic conditions and use of custodial and physical treatment (mental hospitalization, electric shock, and the like) predominated for the lower-class patients, whereas those of higher status were more likely to be diagnosed as neurotic and to receive the more sophisticated and individualized therapies. The researchers believed that systematically varying reactions by therapists to persons of the different social strata helped to account for such treatment outcomes.

Additional power and political aspects of psychiatry were implied by early studies of the wide-ranging application of mental illness models. In his critique of psychiatric theories of drug addiction, Lindesmith (1940) emphasized the circularity and lack of specificity that often characterized the diagnosis of addicts. He concluded that persons known to be addicted were judged in advance (psychiatrists presuming underlying psychic disturbance in such cases) and that whatever personality characteristics these persons displayed — and however contradictory these might be, from one case to another — were then taken to be indicators of psychopathology. An early study by Sutherland (1950) similarly highlighted the questionable application of the amorphous "psychopath" diagnosis to a range of sexual offenses. Sutherland's work is especially pertinent here, because he examined the natural history, or sequence of typical stages, underlying the passage of special "sexual psychopath" laws in numerous jurisdictions. Community fear aroused through a few serious sex crimes, "agitated activity" in connection with that fear, and appointment of a committee to study the problem and make recommendations always preceded the legal enactments Sutherland studied. Thus, a new deviance category employing vague mental illness concepts emerged through a process of changing community definition and response.

For many years, sociologists had been pursuing another line of relevant research by studying the mental hospital in organizational terms and internally as a social system. Many of these studies depicted the implicit politics of interaction between staff and patients and the substantial powerlessness of the latter. A high point in this body of work, one which in a sense combined traditional social-system perspectives with the evolving interactionist focus on deviance, was Erving Goffman's book *Asylums* (1961). Goffman saw that the mental hospital was but one instance of a more general type of setting he termed the *total institution* (other examples would be prisons, concentration camps, military barracks). In such a setting the individual is subjected to all-enveloping control and undergoes a ritual "mortification" process through which his or her old identity is stripped away and a new basic (patient or inmate) identity imposed. Both in the path toward admission to a hospital — here Goffman wrote of a "betrayal funnel" — and within the institution, processes of interaction with other persons vitally influence the course of the patient's "moral career." While professional staff profess to a helping or serving orientation, much that occurs in the hospital seems to belie this "service model." Goffman asserts that "to be made a patient is to be remade into a serviceable object, the irony being that so little service is available once this is done" (1961, p. 379). Nor are those on the outside totally without interest in this deviance processing: "Mental patients can find themselves crushed by the weight of a service ideal that [through its application in other contexts] eases life for the rest of us" (ibid., p. 386).

Since his main aim apparently was to identify and analyze a general type of social institution, Goffman did not specifically develop the political implications of his study. Nonetheless, it has had considerable public influence — being drawn on constantly by critics of the mental hospital, provoking modification of treatment programs, and helping to spark a movement for deinstitutionalization — i.e. putting fewer persons in mental hospitals and releasing those unnecessarily incarcerated. Foucault, in a work to be discussed later in this book, has more pointedly suggested that such total institutions can be seen as symbols or symptoms of repressive and depersonalizing social systems in general. At the very least, it is clear that mental hospitals keep a great many disturbing, if not disturbed, people under strict control. As already noted, the Rosenhan (1973) pseudopatient study starkly demonstrated the powerful effect on inmates of being treated virtually as nonpersons and the almost complete powerlessness of these individuals to resist such characterization.

The very fact, furthermore, that Rosenhan could for all practical purposes "produce" mental patients through research subterfuge underlines the point that mental illness is, above all and whatever else, a perceptual and social designation or characterization — rather than a mode of behavior or condition intrinsic to, and revealed in, particular kinds of individuals. Numerous studies have explored aspects of this characterizing process, showing how mental illness outcomes invariably develop through processes of social interaction and changing "definitions of the situation." In some well-known research (Yarrow et al. 1955) on the interaction between wives and husbands that led to mental hospitalization of the husbands, the investigators traced out a process in which the wives at first attempted to "normalize" the husbands' eccentric behavior (discount it, find rational explanations for it) but gradually and increasingly came to redefine the situation in mental illness terms. One sociologist (Gove 1975, p. 39) sees this finding as proof that people are not glibly or arbitrarily labeled mentally ill. He claims it shows that only those really sick and "impossible to deal with" are hospitalized. A more significant implication of the study, however, is the central and necessary role of interpersonal reactions and redefinition in the decision to hospitalize. (See discussion in Schur 1979, pp. 175–177.) If the wives had continued to normalize the husbands' eccentricity, or for whatever reason had felt compelled to accept it, the outcomes would have been very different. Power differentials — in the form of resources for coping, ability to compel acquiescence, and so on — seem to lie beneath the surface of such an interaction process.

Even in voluntary psychotherapy, one writer (Scheff 1968) has suggested, the situation may be influenced by latent power elements. Thus, a subtle form of "negotiation" may occur with respect to defining just what kind of a problem it is that the patient has and what the ground rules for the therapy will be. As Scheff notes the therapist invariably has greater power to influence this outcome, "principally because he is well trained, secure, and self-confident in his role in the transaction, whereas the client is untutored, anxious, and uncertain about his role" (p. 6). Studies of mental illness designating within work settings also reveal that an interaction process usually is involved. Lemert (1962) found that the identification of paranoid individuals within an organization often occurred as part of an evolving process during which the persons involved were in fact being isolated and excluded or manipulated by coworkers, even if their perceptions regarding this treatment ultimately became exaggerated and distorted. More recently Goffman has suggested (1972, pp. 355–357) that mental symptoms as seen within an organizational context arise when group members perceive an actor's behavior as involving "willful situational improprieties," or an unwillingness to "keep his place." Such behavior is defined as mental illness because it "must create organizational havoc and havoc in the minds of members." Again, the relative power positions of persons in a situation of this sort appear likely to influence such outcomes.

In his effort to present a more general reactions-oriented theory, Scheff (1966) has referred to mental illness as consisting of "residual rule breaking" — acts people find objectionable or upsetting but which they cannot easily fit into some other standard conceptual category. Social response patterns, often built around mental illness stereotypes that condition both interpersonal reaction and organizational processing of such residual deviators, determine whether a mental illness definition of the situation becomes "stabilized." If it does, or to the extent it does, not only the reactions of others but even the deviator's own self-conceptions may reflect this characterization. Some of the research that led Scheff to these conclusions represents part of a recent multifaceted development that reaches beyond the mental illness issue, and which might be termed the unmasking of euphemism with respect to deviance processing. (For similar developments in the area of juvenile justice, see Schur 1979, pp. 461–468.)

In this connection, two major themes have been emerging. The first is that authoritative efforts to do something *for* people believed to have or to pose problems, typically involve doing something *to* them as well. From this standpoint, the well-intentioned helping professions may in fact often be serving as agents of social control. (See Gaylin et al. 1978; also Rosenheim 1976; Allen 1964; Piven and Cloward 1971; Freidson 1971; Illich 1976.) The second, related recognition has been that supposedly nonstigmatizing legal and administrative procedures established to facilitate these efforts — juvenile court, civil commitment to mental hospital, civil commitment to drug treatment programs, administrative regulation of welfare benefits — not only are, in fact, stigmatizing but also typically involve a failure to safeguard the processed individuals' basic constitutional rights. For the area of mental illness, Scheff's research on mental commitment proceedings (Scheff 1968, chap. 5), disclosed a pattern of harshly routinized commitment in which judges unhesitatingly followed the recommendations of court-appointed medical evaluators — recommendations based on scant observation and an apparent desire to err on the side of "safety" by almost always presuming illness. The evaluation interviews "ranged in length from 5 minutes to 17 minutes, with the mean time being 10.2 minutes" (ibid. 1968, p. 144). Both in these commitment proceedings and in hospital release proceedings, which Scheff also studied, the actual medical condition of the processed person — as objectively determined by Scheff and his research team, partly by questioning the medical staff themselves — rarely appeared to determine the outcome. Scheff concluded that "there is a large proportion of the patient population, 43 percent, whose presence in the hospital cannot readily be explained in terms of their psychiatric condition" (ibid., pp. 167–168).

During the past two decades a few renegade psychiatrists have, along with some very active civil liberties lawyers, contributed even more directly than the social researchers to making psychiatric power an issue of public controversy. Preeminent among the psychiatrists has been Thomas Szasz, who is perhaps best known for his provocative insistence that mental illness is a myth (Szasz 1961). Although Szasz's ideas have been hotly contested by many of his professional colleagues, his writings have strongly influenced reformers and activists as well as researchers and even some mental health practitioners. According to Szasz, "mental illness" really refers to "problems of living" — social situations that inevitably have moral implications as well, and the assessment of which therefore cannot be made according to standard medical criteria. Psychiatric diagnosis, he insists, necessarily involves making judgments and imposing classifications and, as such, constitutes a powerful mode of social control. The uses of psychiatry, Szasz believes, must be kept limited, private, and voluntary, in order to protect individual liberty and prevent the growth of "the therapeutic state" (Szasz 1963; see also Kittrie 1971; Foucault 1977). Szasz has been particularly vocal in condemning psychiatrists' acceptance of various roles in our legal system — as when they provide alleged medical testimony in criminal trials or participate in involuntary commitment proceedings. In such situations and others where psychiatrists are called on to determine what should happen to people, they are — in Szasz's view — asked to go beyond their legitimate helping role. Medical terminology is used to shield the fact that they are inevitably taking sides in social and ultimately moral disputes.

By questioning the scientific status and even the appropriateness of key psychiatric determinations — such as those of social "dangerousness" — and by documenting through case studies the role of psychiatry in specific instances of mental commitment that may have violated legal standards of due process or may have been completely unnecessary, Szasz has helped to provide a basis for challenging the legality of various uses of psychiatric power (Szasz 1963, 1965). The widely read British psychiatrist-writer, R.D. Laing, while not so directly concerned with legal issues, has also contributed to the growth of some of the same general outlooks. He has argued, for example, that "in the context of our present pervasive madness that we call normality, sanity, freedom, all our frames of reference are ambiguous and equivocal," and has further stated, "The standard psychiatric patient is a function of the standard psychiatrist, and of the standard mental hospital" (Laing 1965, pp. 11, 28).

The writings of Szasz and Laing and research such as that of Goffman and Scheff have been drawn on as support by civil liberties lawyers working to protect the rights of prospective, current, and former mental patients. This developing legal campaign has reflected the more general substantive broadening of politics in America noted in the beginning of this book. In recent years for example, the American Civil Liberties Union has widened the substantive application of its traditional efforts to protect individual rights and ensure due process of law. It has litigated specific cases and made more general assessments of the law in such areas as the rights of prisoners, the rights of mentally retarded persons, the rights of the poor, and the rights of gay people as well as the rights of mental patients. (Those are some of the topics in its current mass-marketed handbook series.) Such efforts in the mental illness field have resulted in quite a few changes in procedures relating to mental commitment, review and appeal, and release, and have increased public awareness of various denials of rights to institutionalized and released mental patients. There have been a few landmark court decisions, such as that in the *Donaldson* case *(O'Connor v. Donaldson,* 1975). Ruling unconstitutional the nearly fifteen-year incarceration of a harmless patient, which had allegedly been for his own good, the U.S. Supreme Court stated:

> A finding of "mental illness" alone cannot justify a State's locking a person up against his will and keeping him indefinitely in simple custodial confinement. Assuming that term can be given a reasonably precise content and that the "mentally ill" can be identified with reasonable accuracy, there is still no basis for confining such persons involuntarily if they are dangerous to no one and can live safely in freedom. [as quoted in Ennis and Emery 1978, p. 38]

The legal fight to protect the rights of patients while they are within mental institutions — for example, to refuse certain kinds of unwanted treatment — has not yet met with comparable success. The authoritative ACLU report on rights of mental patients states:

> Generally, mental hospitals neither inform patients about the risks and benefits of drugs nor respect a patient's refusal to take drugs. Drugs are routinely forced on patients by "shooting" them with a needle while they are physically restrained. Some patients struggle; others learn resistance is in vain. Much of the physical abuse of patients in mental hospitals occurs during these incidents.

> Of course the law protects "normal" patients from unwanted drugs. Everyone but mental patients can refuse any drug he does not want, and doctors have a duty to inform "general" patients of the likely effects of drugs before they consent to drug therapy. Several courts have recognized a similar right for mental patients in many situations. [Ennis and Emery 1978, p. 141]

Encouraged by the recent civil liberties effort in this area, and to an extent strengthening and reinforcing it, some former mental patients have attempted to organize collectively and to join forces with disaffected therapists to form a radical mental health movement (Agel et al. 1973; Severo 1978). The combination of geographical separation, diversity of outlooks on questions of therapy, and uncertainty or disagreement regarding the proposed movement's relation to other radical movements appears so far to have limited its direct impact. (We will be considering further, in chapter 4, the general problems of mobilization and support that invariably face nascent protest movements of this sort.) Remarking that the organization of this particular protest "remains fragile, even in its militancy," one investigating journalist nonetheless recently stated, "It remains unclear how many people are involved. But at least thousands of past and present mental patients are participating in what they regard as their liberation movement, a nonviolent effort that has attracted people of all ages and has an orientation that is essentially middle-class" (Severo 1978, p. D14).

More significant, perhaps, in propelling the politicization of psychiatry and mental illness have been the movements for women's and homosexuals' liberation. Psychiatry has been attacked by women's liberationists on a number of grounds — for adopting and perpetuating untenable theories of basic female passivity and dependence; for overdiagnosing women's problems as being personal rather than institutional in nature; for treating women as though they should, in all situations, be the ones to "adjust." (See Weisstein 1972; Chesler 1972; Ehrenreich and English 1973.) Even if these critiques have not yet led to substantial changes in psychiatric practice, they have publicly exposed the previously latent gender politics of psychiatry. As two activist writers have put it, "The medical system is not just a service industry. It is a powerful instrument of social control, replacing organized religion as a prime source of sexist ideology and an enforcer of sex roles" (Ehrenreich and English 1973, p. 83). Exerting influence in combination with the more general movement for public accountability of the medical profession as regards inequities in the delivery of health care, the feminist challenge has meant that psychiatry, like all of medicine, is increasingly subject to political as well as personal scrutiny.

A similar recognition that much psychiatric thinking and practice have been in opposition to their collective interests has led to stepped-up critiques of psychiatry by gay activists. Actually, the standard psychopathology assumption with respect to homosexuality has for some time been in dispute. In an important experimental study (Hooker 1963), when standard psychological tests were administered to homosexuals drawn from the public at large (the subjects were neither in psychotherapy nor in trouble with the law) and the results examined blind (by psychologists who did not know of the subjects' homosexuality), no greater indications of psychopathology were found than among the test results of carefully selected nonhomosexual, control subjects. Though many therapists used to consider "conversion" to heterosexuality the major or only appropriate goal in treating homosexual patients, there was never unanimity on this point and recently opposition to it has grown even within psychiatry. (See Marmor 1965; Hoffman 1969; Weinberg, 1972.) A crucial development has been the increased unwillingness of homosexuals themselves to accept the notion that they are necessarily sick. Although a sickness definition of their condition may previously have been seen as preferable to one that labeled them immoral, the former is now also being widely recognized as oppressive in its consequences. One advocate of gay rights has stated:

> The use of the sickness designation serves much the same purpose in keeping homosexuals subordinate as did the older anthropological studies purporting to show that, in one way or another, the Negro was intellectually and otherwise inferior.

In short, homosexuals have, in effect, been *defined* into sickness by a mixture of moral, cultural, social, and theological value judgments, cloaked and camouflaged in the language of science. [Kameny 1971, p. 61]

Intraprofessional and extraprofessional opposition to overdiagnosis of psychopathology came to a head in the early 1970s when the American Psychiatric Association undertook a reconsideration of the relevant provisions of its standard diagnostic manual. In a much-disputed decision (see discussion in Spector and Kitsuse 1977, pp. 17–20), the association finally in 1973 deleted homosexuality from its published list of sexual disorders. The term *sexual orientation disturbance* was substituted, with commentary indicating that homosexuals might experience disturbance in connection with such orientation but that homosexuality per se was not to be viewed as a psychiatric disorder.

In the wake of all the aforementioned research and public activity relating to diverse aspects of psychiatry and mental illness, major political issues persist. Despite all the criticisms of extending psychiatric diagnosis into substantively inappropriate areas, the tendency to view various problematic social conditions as psychiatric problems has not fully abated. A good example is the current use of the rubric "learning disabilities" to cover a range of troublesome behaviors on the part of schoolchildren. Condemning the allegedly predictive screening efforts, and the widespread administration of tranquilizers and other drugs, practices associated with this trend, Schrag and Divoky (1976, p. 14) assert that "the techniques of medicine are used extensively to serve the purposes of social control." (See also Conrad 1975.) The conversion of social deviation into medical disturbance, they argue further, legitimizes and enlarges "the power of institutions over individuals," and at the same time provides a "bonanza" for a wide range of specialized staff, program administrators, and pharmaceutic manufacturers (Schrag and Divoky 1976, pp. 16, 69). Exposés such as theirs and the growing general interest in collective action to advance children's rights should help to keep this recent trend a matter of public controversy. Another extension of psychiatry that is likely to face continuing challenge (in this instance, from opponents of "ageism") concerns treatment of the elderly. Investigative reporting on nursing homes and disclosures of the extent to which our society simply "warehouses" old people both in those institutions and in state mental hospitals have uncovered a situation that Americans earlier had tried hard to ignore. Psychiatry often helped to protect the nonelderly from confronting these facts. One socially conscious member of the profession has stated, "If a psychiatrist treats the unhappiness of the older person as an illness, he may help to justify society's unwillingness to treat that person decently" (Halleck 1972, p. 131).

Partly because of critiques of conventional psychiatric therapies and institutions, the "community mental health" movement has been heralded as a major advance. There is considerable controversy about this popular approach — the political implications of which are not entirely clear. On the one hand, it reflects a commendable desire to extend help in the local community setting to people who might not otherwise readily obtain it, and also a well-intended wish to head off psychological disturbance in an effort to eliminate the need for long-term treatment or even hospitalization. On the other hand, critics see the central notion of community outreach in a different light — as an aggressive, unasked-for seeking out of "cases," in which many social problems and situations may be treated as psychiatric problems, a development that has dangerous potential for extensive social control (Leifer 1966; Szasz, 1970). A recent study of psychiatric emergency teams (PET) doing crisis-intervention work out of a community mental health center in California, found that PET workers themselves often questioned the helping nature of their efforts.

> In many instances, when unable to do something for a client, PET workers ended up doing something to him; that is, they

found themselves acting in opposition to the client's explicitly stated desires, in ways [primarily, ordering mental hospitalization] in which both PET and client felt were not likely to result in a qualitative up-grading of the client's life, and which often involved deception, coercion and constraint. [Emerson and Pollner 1976, p. 249]

Tied to the community mental health effort, through aftercare and noninstitutional treatment programs, is the policy of deinstitutionalization. Following court decisions such as that in the *Donaldson* case and others requiring upgrading of institutional conditions, and in the face of mounting hospital costs, various states have recently speeded up an already-existing trend toward a decline in the hospitalization of mental patients. A recent survey notes, "Mental hospital populations in the United States are now well under half their 1955 levels, having declined over a twenty-year period (1955–1974) by more than sixty percent. The initially moderate yearly decline has accelerated markedly in recent years, with almost half the recorded fall (154,400 out of a total of 343,300) taking place since 1969" (Scull 1977, p. 68). In New York City, a recent state policy of placing patients in "the least restrictive setting" possible has meant the release of large numbers of previously incarcerated persons, many of whom have been placed in single-room-occupancy buildings, often located in deteriorating residential neighborhoods. Of the controversy this policy has evoked, a journalist recently wrote, "Smoldering community resentment against the state's deinstitutionalization program has reached a flash point. Irate community groups and local officials contend that the state has actually been 'dumping' thousands of chronic mental patients into their communities without providing for their after-care [Sullivan 1978; see also Witten et al. 1977].

Deinstitutionalization provides an illustration of how complex the set of interests at stake in a particular deviance policy dispute may be. A leading student of the trend cites the state's interest in controlling soaring costs as "the primary factor underlying the move towards decarceration" (Scull 1977, p. 140). Noting that fiscal conservatives have joined with welfare-oriented liberals to support deinstitutionalization, the same writer suggests that cost savings explain "the curious political alliance" favoring this policy (ibid., p. 147). At the same time, the labor movement — which might ordinarily be expected to support efforts to release and help the typically downtrodden state hospital patients — has apparently been torn because of its economic interest in preserving hospital jobs. In 1977 a major national union that includes hospital workers (the American Federation of State, County and Municipal Employees) ran large newspaper advertisements condemning deinstitutionalization of mental patients — ostensibly in support of "the dignity of the mentally ill through real care, not empty promises" *(New York Times*, May 22, 1977, p. E5). Ordinary taxpayers, who might expect ultimately to benefit economically from deinstitutionalization, may likewise have conflicting interests — particularly if mental patients are being released to their particular neighborhoods. Additional economic interests also come into the picture because of the potential for private profit that decarceration produces. Thus Scull has noted, "There have appeared whole chains of enterprises seeking to capitalize on this emerging market, ranging from privately run drug treatment franchises to fair sized corporations sprawled across several states dealing with derelicts and discharged mental patients" (Scull 1977, p. 150). In a news story about a specific dispute over a community-based program for released mental patients on New York City's upper West Side, it was reported,

> In the Bridge and Brewster case, there is also the added question of the motive of the building's operators. Some people, including Henry J. Stern, the Liberal Councilman at Large for Manhattan, have charged that the plan is a "real estate scheme" designed to allow the lessees to convert the building into a government-supported operation. The lessees have denied that such a plan exists" (Meislin 1976).

A final aspect of psychiatry that may continue to provoke public controversy is its broad potential as a device for direct control of clearly political deviation. This has been another major theme in the writings of Szasz, who has cited both the political uses of psychiatry in the Soviet Union and some possibly similar incidents in the United States. He has discussed especially the long-term incarceration of the pro-Fascist poet Ezra Pound and the temporary hospitalization of right-wing General Edwin Walker, claiming that both incidents were politically motivated (Szasz 1963, 1965). Recently increased disclosures of the use of mental hospitalization as a major device for curbing political dissidence in the Soviet Union (Bloch and Reddaway 1977; see also Spector and Kitsuse 1977, chap. 6) do lend credence to the argument that there is always a potential for governmental use of psychiatry in direct furtherance of political ends. Yet probably few observers (even among those sympathetic to many of his other arguments) would agree with Szasz that the situation in the United States today presents an imminent danger in this regard, any more than they would accept the extreme antipathy to publicly provided social services that his condemnation of institutional psychiatry has sometimes led him to express.

EXAMPLE 2. *Politics Intensified: The Abortion Conflict*

The intrinsic sexual politics of abortion have long been apparent to feminists. Over the years, the impact has been deeply felt, if not always openly analyzed, by the millions of women who needed to terminate a pregnancy. Women's vulnerability and dependence, their low social power relative to men, were until recently reflected in virtually all aspects of the abortion situation: the passage of restrictive laws — usually by men, who dominated legislatures; the women's need to take total responsibility for dealing with unwanted pregnancies — since husbands and lovers often proffered little help or support; the control of legal procedures by the medical profession — requiring the woman to plead with male doctors for an operation; the vulnerability at the hands of the illegal practitioner, who was also usually a male. Simone de Beauvoir was eloquent on the subject in her classic work, *The Second Sex* (1957), where she commented particularly on "the hypocrisy of the masculine moral code":

> Men universally forbid abortion, but individually they accept it as a convenient solution of a problem; they are able to contradict themselves with careless cynicism. But woman feels these contradictions in her wounded flesh; she is as a rule too timid for open revolt against masculine bad faith; she regards herself as the victim of an injustice that makes her a criminal against her will, and at the same time she feels soiled and humiliated. [de Beauvoir 1953, p. 491]

In some ways, the recent overt and virulent controversy over American abortion policies represents a culmination of longstanding efforts to promote sociolegal change (Sarvis and Rodman 1974; Humphries 1977) and also reflects broader social trends relating to sexual behavior, population, the family, and the status of women. (See Rossi 1966; Schur 1968.) Yet the intensity and public nature of the current conflict signify as well the force of rapidly and greatly heightened direct politicization efforts on both sides of the issue. The controversial 1973 decision by the U.S. Supreme Court in the case of *Roe* v. *Wade*, seeking to resolve previous disputes, actually became a major factor in producing this intensification — for it galvanized into concerted and organized action the opponents of the already well advanced liberalization of abortion laws.

In that decision, the court ruled that during the first three months of pregnancy, the abortion decision reached by a woman and her physician is not subject to state interference; that with respect to the second three months, the state may, in order to promote the health of the mother, regulate abortion procedures — for example, by specifying where abortions may and may not be performed; and that for the third trimester (when the fetus has attained viability — capacity for independent life) the state may regulate and even proscribe abortion except when it is necessary to preserve the life or health of the mother. (See Sarvis and Rodman 1974, chap. 4; Lader 1973, pp. 244–245.) As Sarvis and Rodman (1974, p. 66) have noted, the decision "dramatically and drastically altered the legal situation." Before examining various aspects of the intense politicization that ensued, it may be useful to sketch out briefly some of the immediate background to this pivotal court ruling.

As of the mid-1950s — and for the most part dating back to the 1800s — statutes in most American states made all abortion illegal unless "necessary to preserve the life of the mother." Given medical advances that had by then occurred, it was in fact exceedingly rare that a condition arising during pregnancy would seriously threaten the mother's life (A. F. Guttmacher, in Rosen 1954, p. 12). From a medical standpoint, therefore, the legal criterion these laws set forth was no longer very meaningful. At the same time, certain recently recognized conditions that many doctors saw as justifying abortion were not covered by the exception written into these statutes. Two notable examples were German measles early in pregnancy — known since 1941 to give rise to a substantial risk of fetal abnormality — and risks created by certain drugs taken by the mother during pregnancy — as eventually dramatized by the many impaired children whose mothers had used the drug thalidomide while pregnant. During this period, then, the legal standing of even hospital-performed abortions was usually unclear or shaky.

Understandably, physicians were extremely cautious about approving terminations of pregnancy. Hospitals often did make an exception in German measles cases; abortions were also sometimes granted on psychiatric grounds, though strong evidence that if the abortion was not performed, the mother was likely to commit suicide — hence posing the "necessary to preserve the mother's life" situation — was required for such intervention. When hospitals did authorize abortions, they rarely encountered direct legal interference. Yet the ever-present possibility of such interference led to caution; not even for pregnancy through rape or incest was abortion permitted by law. More general considerations of the mother's overall health and socioeconomic welfare, while no doubt taken into account by physicians to the extent possible, clearly did not alone constitute legal grounds for terminating a pregnancy. It was around this time that many American hospitals established special boards and routine procedures for the processing of therapeutic-abortion applications. These mechanisms clearly reflected medical concern about the legal status of abortion decisions, and they also served to formalize and diffuse responsibility for denying individual abortion requests. From the standpoint of abortion seekers, however, the system was confusing, intimidating, and offensive in requiring them to justify their need of medical help. As one account suggested, under the abortion-board scheme "the patient becomes the pawn in a bureaucracy often more intent on protecting hospital status than meeting critical human needs" (Lader 1966, p. 30). Whatever the subjective reactions of the various participants may have been, the objective consequences of the board system were readily apparent. All available evidence indicates that during this period the boards contributed significantly to a sharp decline in the performance of hospital abortions (see Schur 1968, pp. 138–139), and there is some indication too that in effect if not in intent this system discriminated against the poor (Lader 1966, pp. 29–30).

The fact that relatively few abortions were performed in hospitals did not, of course, mean that women were not having unwanted pregnancies terminated. There was, obviously, no way of determining precisely the magnitude of illegal abortion. An estimate made by a statistical committee of abortion experts in 1955 placed the annual number of induced abortions in the United States anywhere between 200,000 and 1,200,000 (Calderone 1958, p. 180). Of these, only around 8,000 were hospital-authorized terminations. Restrictive laws were merely diverting an enormous demand from legal to illegal channels. As published accounts increasingly documented (for example, Schur 1955; Calderone 1958; Schur 1965; Lader 1966) these laws were in fact largely responsible for the thriving black market in abortions. Because the securing of an illegal abortion was a "consensual transaction" that rarely produced a citizen complainant to initiate enforcement activity and provide evidence, illicit abortionists were difficult to prosecute. Legal restrictions on obtaining the relatively scarce service they provided buttressed the economic incentives for black market practice, establishing what one writer (Packer 1968) called a crime tariff — an economic market situation in which illicit practitioners willing to take some legal risks were in an almost monopolistic position and could charge whatever the traffic would bear.

Given that this illegal practice attracted persons varying greatly in training, competence, conscientiousness, and general ethical concern — and that the abortions were in almost all cases necessarily performed under less than optimal conditions — it is hardly surprising that medical complications and even deaths from these operations were widespread. Estimates of abortion deaths ranged as high as 10,000 annually; writing in 1966, Lader reported that "deaths from abortion have doubled in New York City in the last decade. The principal victims are the deprived minority groups" (Lader 1966, p. 66). Recourse to the underground abortionist was more often than not preceded by various attempts at self-induced termination of the pregnancy, usually by methods that (whether manual or chemical) were unlikely to be effective unless undertaken in such a manner that they would also be extremely dangerous. When these attempts failed and women sought out the black market, they faced not only physical dangers but also the likelihood of financial and even sexual exploitation, and often the need to deal with unsavory and unscrupulous individuals in secret and under sordid conditions.

The potential for psychological disturbance involving severe postabortion shame and guilt — which comparative studies showed was not high in countries that widely permitted safe, legal, hospital abortions — was very great under these circumstances.

These adverse consequences of criminalizing abortion were emphasized in the developing open critique of the American laws that began to accelerate in the 1950s and became even stronger in the next decade. Initially, this critique was spearheaded by individual physicians and legal analysts, who highlighted both the medical inadequacy and the social inequity that these laws entailed. A key theme that emerged had to do with the social-class politics of abortion. It soon came to be widely recognized that making abortion a crime imposed special hardship on poor women. Under conditions of illegality, socioeconomic status becomes a major determinant of the quality of abortion services a woman obtains, and hence of the risks she runs. The educated and relatively affluent woman usually has a good chance of locating a skilled medically trained practitioner, even if she may have to pursue at length various informal information networks in order to do so (Lee 1969). Lower-class women will more likely end up with the lower-priced operatives, who are often both untrained and unscrupulous. Thus, these women are at least doubly disadvantaged. Not only are they likely to be in a relatively weak position with respect to finding out about and pursuing any available opportunities for a legal, hospital abortion, but they are also highly vulnerable in the black market situation. Furthermore, since many of them seek abortion in the first place precisely because of inadequate resources for raising a large family, the socioeconomic disparity in access to safe abortion often compounds an already deep-seated situation of dependency and despair. The current restrictions on public funding of abortions for the poor (see below) point up the fact that revision of the statutory grounds for legal abortion does not by itself provide a full solution to this problem.

At this stage in the evolving liberalization trend—the late 1950s—the professional politics of abortion remained unclear, owing to the complex situation in which medical practitioners found themselves. On the one hand, it was becoming evident that hundreds of thousands of women were failing to receive the competent medical services they desired, and that when rejected by licensed physicians, they almost invariably turned to unauthorized and often incompetent operatives. On the other hand, many physicians no doubt continued to view abortion as running counter to their healing and life-preserving role and were content to leave this undesired patient population to the illicit market. At the same time, however, the medical profession's jurisdiction or authority to make the crucial decisions with respect to abortion was being impaired by the laws. A special irony in the situation was that what constituted a *therapeutic abortion* —the term generally applied to any hospital-approved termination of pregnancy—was being decided not by doctors but by legislators. In fact, as opinion surveys of the medical profession increasingly showed during the 1950s and 1960s (see Schur 1968, p. 144), large numbers of doctors—and especially obstetrician-gynecologists—by then believed that it would be broadly therapeutic to abort under a considerably wider range of conditions than those that constituted legal indications under existing statutes. It was in the matter of authority to determine general criteria for acceptable abortion, according to their best medical judgment, that doctors felt most threatened and limited by the restrictive legislation. If, instead, direct control over procedures for ruling on specific requests had been what was most crucially at stake, then the hospital abortion-board system might well have satisfied the profession. But even though physicians had themselves created this system, largely for protective reasons, they continued to view it with ambivalence. It seemed to institutionalize a harshly judgmental role for doctors, and many believed that the board approach was seriously deficient in meeting legitimate medical needs. For these reasons, prominent physicians came to be among those arguing most forcefully that the boards were impeding, rather than facilitating, good medical care.

During this period, as at other times, there was of course also an element of interreligious politics relating to abortion. The Roman Catholic Church continued to proclaim all intentional abortion — even when performed on allegedly therapeutic grounds, up to and including necessity to save the mother's life — murder and hence irrefutably immoral. (See various discussions in Noonan 1979.) While it would eventually be seen that substantial numbers of Catholics were coming to view the Church's doctrines in this area as overly restrictive (Rossi 1966), and although it was already known that a good many Catholic women did in fact obtain abortions, it seems likely the Church hierarchy did not at this point yet feel under great pressure to combat the evolving movement for legal change. Notwithstanding some membership defection on the abortion issue, the Church still had on its side an enormous potential constituency supportive of its position, direct and easy access to this constituency through the pulpit and other pastoral contacts and communications, and to top this off, powerful religious ideology and church sanctions buttressing its stand. Furthermore, the laws on the books at this time continued to come close to supporting the Church's position, thus in a way giving it a built-in advantage over the opposition, comparable to that usually held by an incumbent candidate in an election campaign.

The late 1950s and the 1960s saw a very much heightened drive for legal reform (Sarvis and Rodman 1974, chap. 1; Humphries 1977). In this period, numerous professional associations — concerned with law, medicine, public health, and even religion — commissioned reports, held conferences, and issued public statements, most of which advocated some change in the laws on abortion. A highly significant development came in 1962 when the prestigious American Law Institute, in its Model Penal Code, provided guidelines for broadening the legal indications for therapeutic abortion. According to the ALI proposal, abortion by a licensed physician would be deemed legal if there was "substantial risk that continuance of the pregnancy would gravely imperil the physical or mental health of the mother or that the child would be born with grave physical or mental defect." It also called for accepting abortion in cases of pregnancy resulting from rape, incest, or "other felonious assault," including illicit intercourse with a girl below the age of sixteen (American Law Institute 1962, pp. 189–190). Of great importance too was the formation during the 1960s of several organizations specifically concerned with the issue of abortion. Among the national organizations that would wield the most influence were the relatively moderate Association for the Study of Abortion, established in 1965, and the more activist National Association for the Repeal of Abortion Laws (NARAL), established in 1969. Numerous local groups aimed at overturning restrictive laws in particular jurisdictions also sprung up during this period. More and more books and articles on the abortion issue were appearing around this time, and results of numerous opinion polls on the matter were published. In general, for advocates of legal change, the 1960s marked a turning away from an emphasis on research and dissemination of information and a move toward more active development of policy recommendations and organization for collective political action (Sarvis and Rodman 1974, pp. 7–10).

These developments constituted a rapid and complex politicizing of the abortion issue — at least on the prochange side of the controversy — with a wide range of policy positions and recommendations that varied in degrees of militancy coming to the fore. Indeed, this evolving movement was sufficiently broad and diverse that one retrospective account has described it as having had discernible left-wing, center, and right-wing components. According to Humphries (1974, pp. 217–220), the left wing was represented by a radically feminist local group, New Yorkers for Abortion Law Repeal — which viewed abortion as an absolute right of women and hence argued for total repeal of all abortion laws. Humphries sees both of the major national organizations — the collective-action-oriented NARAL as well as the Association for the Study of Abortion — as representing the centrist position, apparently because they were more pragmatic than defiant in their approach, and because, at least in the case of the latter, the membership included reform as well as repeal advocates. On the right wing of the movement, Humphries suggests, were such organizations as the American Medical Association and its local affiliates, which supported moderate legal reform that fell short even of what the ALI had recommended.

While accounts of its role and influence in this area vary, the evolving movement for women's liberation should at least be credited with having served as one major catalyst of abortion-reform activity. The growing view that abortion constituted a major women's issue and the associated marshaling of support for change among women of diverse political perspectives may well have served to tip the balance of power in favor of the liberalization forces. Most of the organizing, canvassing, lobbying, and bringing of test cases into the courts that soon began to produce change occurred in the context of, and with strong support from, the now-active women's movement. Indeed, Lawrence Lader, one of the founders of NARAL has asserted:

> It was the surge and fervor of neofeminism that paved the way for the abortion movement. Each was essential to the other, and neither could have advanced without the other. Still, it was the voices of angry women, organizing across the country, that shook legislatures out of their complacency, and produced the first breakthrough for new abortion laws. [Lader 1973, p. 40]

By the end of the 1960s, twelve states had passed reform statutes, extending the legal grounds for abortion roughly along the lines suggested by the ALI (Sarvis and Rodman 1974, pp. 40–44). In 1970, three states, including New York, passed more-far-reaching repeal bills, which permitted abortion on the decision of the woman and her physician provided certain procedural requirements were met (Sarvis and Rodman 1974, pp. 44–46). The New York enactment followed a previous effort that failed, lengthy lobbying and harsh debate, dramatic speeches by individual lawmakers, and a crucial last-minute switch of position by one of the legislators (Lader 1973, chap. 10). Meanwhile, reform groups continued efforts in both state and federal courts to challenge the constitutionality of diverse legal restrictions on abortion. A variety of cases produced mixed rulings, leading finally to the landmark U.S. Supreme Court decision in *Roe* v. *Wade*.

As noted above, this ruling kindled yet a further intensification of the abortion controversy — in particular, producing heightened political activity on the part of those favoring restrictive laws. Antiabortionists marshaled broad support for a "right to life" movement and since then have scored a number of significant victories and become a noteworthy political force. In 1976 Congress passed an amendment to an appropriations bill (the so-called Hyde Amendment) prohibiting use of federal Medicaid funds for abortion unless a woman's life would be endangered if her pregnancy were not interrupted. As of this writing, the constitutionality of the Hyde Amendment is being challenged in the courts *(N.Y. Civil Liberties,* Jan.–Feb. 1979, p. 4; *NARAL Newsletter,* Jan.–Feb. 1979, p. 5). Two rulings of the U.S. Supreme Court in 1977 held that that states are not constitutionally required to fund nontherapeutic abortions, and most states now severely restrict the public funding of abortions. (Even before these recent restrictions were imposed there was considerable evidence that, without new hospital and funding policies, reform and even repeal laws were going to prove insufficient to guarantee needed abortion services for the poor.) (See Sarvis and Rodman 1974, pp. 46–53; also, Schultz 1977.)

In New York State a formal Right to Life Party has gained access to the ballot, having shown sufficient strength in the 1978 gubernatorial election "to make antiabortionists a new force in state politics," and to give them, "the highest visibility they have had in the state and also potential leverage with candidates for the legislature and local offices, particularly in marginal districts where Right to Life support could provide a margin of victory" (Lynn 1978). Nationally, the right to life forces have demonstrated considerable effectiveness in many state and local elections and referenda, sometimes managing to defeat candidates who previously had shown great strength. According to one recent account:

> Antiabortion leaders have mastered single-issue politics in a number of places so that they are able to defeat opponents or extract pledges of support from candidates even though the vast majority say in public opinion polls that their choice of a candidate does not depend on the abortion issue. They accomplish this by bringing out their supporters in full strength in elections in which overall voter participation is light. [Herbers 1978; see also DeWitt 1979, and Freeman 1979]

Whether or not these developments are taken to reflect or represent an antiabortion backlash, it is clear that there are now powerful forces arrayed on both sides of the controversy and that the contesting forces are prepared and able to employ all the standard political techniques in support of their goals. Advocates of both positions are making extensive use of propaganda, the manipulation of powerful symbols for partisan ends — even if each side sees itself instead as engaging in public education. Key features of this propaganda contest have been name calling — a speaker at a national right to life convention referred to abortion-performing physicians as "executioners" (Herbers 1979); shock tactics — such as displaying photographs of fetuses or actual fetuses *(New York Times*, Feb. 16, 1979, p. B7); and, particularly significant for both sides, various efforts to influence the ways in which the public views the disputants and the nature of the dispute itself. The terminology used to designate the parties to the controversy has thus become a hotly contested issue. Each side has its favored set of designations, the appropriateness of which the other disputes. The contesting forces repudiate descriptions of themselves as being "pro-abortion" or "anti-abortion," asking instead to be characterized as "pro-choice" or "pro-life," respectively. Some comments from a recent NARAL newsletter provide a further sense of this feature of the propaganda battle:

> *Who are the so-called "pro-life" people?* They are the COMPUL-SORY PREGNANCY people, and that's what they should be called. Whose life are they "pro"? Certainly not the life of the woman. Certainly not the life of a child born into poverty. Certainly not the life of a child certain to be born with severe defects. Do they show you women in the death throes of peritonitis? Do they show you the pain, the suicides, the wrecked lives? Do they show you the cost to the taxpayers for raising unwanted children. . . . Where is *their* responsibility after they compel a birth? Suddenly, "pro-life" doesn't sound so noble anymore [*NARAL Newsletter*, Jan.–Feb. 1979, p. 13]

Each side has sought to depict itself as favoring freedom and its opponents as favoring compulsion. Each has provided its version of the "horrible consequences" argument; the NARAL ad makes clear that conservatives have no monopoly on that standard technique. (See also Hardin 1964.) Each side has presented its own way of viewing the act of terminating a pregnancy — in one case, the killing of a "human being," in the other, the "removal of fetal protoplasm" — and of locating such acts on a continuum of interventions in reproduction and/or life, opponents of liberalization linking abortion with infanticide and other murder, proponents relating it to contraception or even family planning. The opposing forces also have offered alternative ways of conceptualizing the major moral issue with respect to abortion laws, even if right to life advocates sometimes have implied that it is only their side that is concerned with morals. Here, the clash actually has not been between those who adopt a moral position and those who do not, but rather between disputants with very different ideas about what the major moral issue is.

Right to life proponents have been almost totally preoccupied with the morality of abortion as an absolute and in the abstract, framing the dispute in the same general manner that even very sophisticated philosophers, on both sides of the policy issue, have tended to adopt. (See Cohen et al. 1974.) The primary concern of their opponents, however, has been to show not that abortion is moral but rather that particular abortion laws are immoral, in their operation and their consequences. Thus, they would insist, in an argument many find perplexing or difficult, that even if we were to conclude that the act of abortion is immoral, that would not settle the legal issue. Laws that make a bad situation worse are not socially desirable. This clash, between morality-of-the-act and morality-of-the-laws perspectives and arguments continues to compound a highly complex public controversy. The distinction seems also to have been glossed over in one analyst's contention that the recent critique of abortion laws has embodied a "technocratic" approach that "supersedes the discussion of moral order, because professionals in suspending such judgments emphasize the detrimental effects of moral prohibitions" (Humphries 1977, p. 220). Many of the reform advocates may oppose moral absolutism, but they do so in the very process of making their own kinds of moral assessments.

The conflict over abortion continues to erupt on a number of specific fronts, reflecting a range of general and subsidiary policy issues. In a review of these issues made at the beginning of 1979, the New York Civil Liberties Union cited the following areas of persisting dispute: the basic right to an abortion; public funding of abortion; abortions for minors; husband's consent or notification; requirements of pre-abortion counselling; the performing of abortion in public hospitals *(New York Civil Liberties,* Jan.–Feb. 1979, p. 5). With respect to most aspects of this continuing ferment there are, as we have seen, multiple interests at play, interests that at times elude neat classification. Though the argument has been forcefully made — and substantial documentation attempted — that poor people have a special stake in liberal abortion laws, at the same time there have been claims made that the entire liberalization effort represents some kind of conspiracy to impose restrictions on population increases among blacks. (See Sarvis and Rodman 1974, chap. 10, "Black Genocide.") While the medical profession has a presumed interest in maintaining its authority over the granting of abortions, the positions adopted by leading practitioners and medical organizations have varied greatly and have suggested considerable medical ambivalence on this topic. Notwithstanding the strong conviction on the part of feminists that "control over her own body" is a woman's basic right, women have emerged in the leadership of the opposing right to life movement. Given this kind of complexity, and the fact that as new social and legal developments occur attitudes, allegiances, and alliances are also likely to fluctuate, further shifts in the balance of power and influence regarding abortion can be expected — even if we cannot readily predict the timing, magnitude, or precise nature of such change.

References

Adam, Barry D. 1978. *The Survival of Domination*. New York: Elsevier North Holland.

Agel, Jerome et al. 1973. *Rough Times*. New York: Ballantine.

Allen, Francis A. 1964. *The Borderland of Criminal Justice*. Chicago: University of Chicago Press.

Altman, Dennis. 1973. *Homosexual: Oppression and Liberation*. New York: Avon.

American Law Institute. 1962. *Model Penal Code, Proposed Official Draft*. Philadelphia.

Armstrong, Gail, and Mary Wilson. 1973. "City Politics and Deviancy Amplification. In Ian Taylor and Laurie Taylor, eds., *Politics and Deviance*. Baltimore: Penguin.

Ball, Donald W. 1967. "An Abortion Clinic Ethnography." *Social Problems* 14 (winter): 293–301.

Becker, Howard S. 1963. *Outsiders.* New York: Free Press.

Bell, Daniel. 1961. "Crime as an American Way of Life," *The End of Ideology.* New York: Collier. Pp. 127–150.

Bloch, Sidney, and Peter Reddaway. 1977. *Psychiatric Terror.* New York: Basic Books.

Calderone, Mary Steichen, ed. 1958. *Abortion in the United States.* New York: Hoeber-Harper.

Chesler, Phyllis. 1972. *Women and Madness.* New York: Avon.

Cohen, Marshall et al., eds. 1974. *The Rights and Wrongs of Abortion.* Princeton: Princeton University Press.

Connor, Walter D. 1972. "The Manufacture of Deviance: The Case of the Soviet Purges, 1936–1938." *American Sociological Review* 37 (August): 403–413.

Conrad, Peter. 1975. "The Discovery of Hyperkinesis: Notes on the Medicalization of Deviant Behavior." *Social Problems* 23 (October): 12–21.

Coser, Lewis A. 1962. "Some Functions of Deviant Behavior and Normative Flexibility." *American Journal of Sociology* 68 (September): 171–181.

Currie, Elliott. 1968. "Crimes Without Criminals: Witchcraft and its Control in Renaissance Europe." *Law and Society Review* 3 (August): 7–32.

Dahrendorf, Ralf. 1959. *Class and Class Conflict in Industrial Society.* Stanford: Stanford University Press.

Davis, Fred. 1963. *Passage Through Crisis.* Indianapolis: Bobbs-Merrill.

Davis, Kingsley. 1937. "The Sociology of Prostitution." *American Sociological Review* 2 (October): 746–755.

Davis, Kingsley. 1938. "Mental Hygiene and the Class Structure." *Psychiatry* 1: 55–65.

de Beauvoir, Simone. 1953. *The Second Sex.* New York: Knopf.

De Witt, Karen. 1979. "Abortion Foes March in Capital on Anniversary of Legalization." *New York Times,* January 23, p. C10.

Dickson, Donald T. 1968. "Bureaucracy and Morality: An Organizational Perspective on a Moral Crusade." *Social Problems* 16 (fall): 143–156.

Douglas, Jack D. 1970. "Deviance and Respectability: The Social Construction of Moral Meanings." In Douglas, ed., *Deviance and Respectability.* New York: Basic Books. Pp. 3–30.

Durkheim, Emile. 1893, 1933. *The Division of Labor in Society.* Translated by George Simpson. New York: Free Press.

Edgerton, Robert B. 1976. *Deviance: A Cross-Cultural Perspective.* Menlo Park, Calif.: Cummings.

Ehrenreich, Barbara, and Deirdre English. 1973. *Complaints and Disorders: The Sexual Politics of Sickness.* Old Westbury, N.Y.: Feminist Press.

Emerson, Robert M. 1969. *Judging Delinquents.* Chicago: Aldine.

Emerson, Robert M. and Melvin Pollner. 1976. "Dirty Work Designations: Their Features and Consequences in a Psychiatric Setting." *Social Problems* 23 (February): 243–254.

Ennis, Bruce J., and Richard D. Emery. 1978. *The Rights of Mental Patients.* New York: Avon.

Erikson, Kai T. 1962. "Notes on the Sociology of Deviance." *Social Problems* 9 (spring): 307–314.

Erikson, Kai T. 1966. *Wayward Puritans.* New York: John Wiley.

Fishman, Mark. 1978. "Crime Waves as Ideology." *Social Problems* 25 (June): 531–543.

Foucault, Michel. 1977. *Discipline and Punish.* New York: Pantheon.

Freeman, Jo. 1979. "An Abortion Rights Group Adjusts its Strategy and Image." *In These Times,* May 9–15, p. 6.

Freidson, Eliot. 1965. "Disability as Social Deviance." In Marvin B. Sussman, ed., *Sociology and Rehabilitation.* Washington. D.C. American Sociological Association. Pp. 71–99.

Freidson, Eliot. 1971. *Profession of Medicine.* New York: Dodd, Mead.

Garfinkel, Harold. 1956. "Conditions of Successful Degradation Ceremonies." *American Journal of Sociology* 61 (March): 420–424.

Gaylin, Willard et al. 1978. *Doing Good: The Limits of Benevolence.* New York: Pantheon.

Gerth, H.H., and C. Wright Mills. 1958. *From Max Weber.* New York: Oxford University Press.

Goffman, Erving. 1961. *Asylums.* Garden City, N.Y.: Doubleday, Anchor Books.

Goffman, Erving. 1963. *Stigma: Notes on the Management of Spoiled Identity.* Englewood Cliffs, N.J.: Prentice-Hall.

Goffman, Erving. 1972. "The Insanity of Place," *Relations in Public.* New York: Harper, Colophon Books. Pp. 335–390.

Goode, Erich. 1978. *Deviant Behavior: An Interactionist Approach.* Englewood Cliffs, N.J.: Prentice-Hall.

Gove, Walter R. 1975. "Labelling and Mental Illness: A Critique." In Gove, ed., *The Labelling of Deviance.* New York: Sage/Wiley, pp. 35–81.

Gove, Walter, R., ed. 1975. *The Labelling of Deviance.* New York: Sage/Wiley.

Halleck, Seymour L. 1972. *The Politics of Therapy.* New York: Harper, Perennial Library.

Hardin, Garrett. 1964. "Abortion and Human Dignity." Public lecture, University of California, Berkeley, April 29.

Hawkins, Richard, and Gary Tiedeman. 1975. *The Creation of Deviance.* Columbus, Ohio: Chas. E. Merrill.

Herbers, John. 1978. "Anti-Abortionists' Impact is Felt in Elections Across the Nation." *New York Times,* June 20, pp. 1, B10.

Herbers, John. 1979. "Convention Speech Stirs Foes of Abortion." *New York Times,* June 24, p. 16.

Hoffman, Martin. 1969. *The Gay World.* New York: Bantam.

Hollingshead, August B., and Frederik C. Redlich. 1958. *Social Class and Mental Illness.* New York: John Wiley.

Hooker, Evelyn. 1963. "The Adjustment of the Male Overt Homosexual." In Hendrik M. Ruitenbeek, ed., *The Problem of Homosexuality in Modern Society.* New York: Dutton. Pp. 141–161.

Horowitz, Irving Louis, and Martin Liebowitz. 1968. "Social Deviance and Political Marginality: Toward a Redefinition of the Relation Between Sociology and Politics." *Social Problems* 15 (winter): 280–296.

Humphries, Drew. 1977. "The Movement to Legalize Abortion: A Historical Account." In David F. Greenberg, ed., *Corrections and Punishment.* Beverly Hills, Calif.: Sage Publications, Inc. Pp. 205–224.

Illich, Ivan. 1976. *Medical Nemesis.* New York: Pantheon.

Kameny, Franklin E. 1971. "Homosexuals as a Minority Group." In Edward Sagarin, ed., *The Other Minorities.* Lexington, Mass.: Ginn. Pp. 50–65.

Kitsuse, John I. 1962. "Societal Reactions to Deviant Behavior." *Social Problems* 9 (winter): 247–256.

Kitsuse, John I., and Aaron V. Cicourel. 1963. "A Note on the Use of Official Statistics." *Social Problems* 11 (fall): 131–139.

Kittrie, Nicholas N. 1971. *The Right to be Different*. Baltimore: The Johns Hopkins Press.

Lader, Lawrence. 1966. *Abortion*. Indianapolis: Bobbs-Merrill.

Lader, Lawrence. 1973. *Abortion II: Making the Revolution*. Boston: Beacon Press.

Laing R.D. 1965. *The Divided Self*. Baltimore: Penguin.

Lasswell, Harold D. 1936. *Politics: Who Gets What, When, How*. New York: McGraw-Hill.

Lasswell, Harold D., and Abraham Kaplan. 1950. *Power and Society*. New Haven: Yale University Press.

Lauderdale, Pat. 1976. "Deviance and Moral Boundaries." *American Sociological Review* 41 (August): 660–676.

Lee, Nancy Howell. 1969. *The Search for an Abortionist*. Chicago: University of Chicago Press.

Lehman, Edward W. 1977. *Political Society: A Macrosociology of Politics*. New York: Columbia University Press.

Leifer, Ronald. 1966. "Community Psychiatry and Social Power." *Social Problems* 14: (summer), 16–22.

Lemert, Edwin M. 1951. *Social Pathology*. New York: McGraw-Hill.

Lemert, Edwin M. 1962. "Paranoia and the Dynamics of Exclusion." *Sociometry* 25 (March): 2–25.

Lindesmith, Alfred R. 1940. "The Drug Addict as a Psychopath." *American Sociological Review* 5 (December): 914–920.

Lofland, John. 1969. *Deviance and Identity*. Englewood Cliffs, N.J.: Prentice-Hall.

Lynn, Frank. 1978. "Right to Life Party Shows its Strength." *New York Times*, November 10, pp. 1, B.

Marmor, Judd, ed. 1965. *Sexual Inversion*. New York: Basic Books.

Meislin, Richard J. 1976. "West Side Rehabilitation Center Proposed for Ex-Mental Patients." *New York Times*, December 20, p. B12.

Mercer, Jane R. 1973. *Labeling the Mentally Retarded*. Berkeley: University of California Press.

Merton, Robert K. 1976. "The Sociology of Social Problems." In Merton and Robert Nisbet, eds., *Contemporary Social Problems*. 4th ed. New York: Harcourt Brace Jovanovich, Inc. Pp. 5–43.

Newman, Graeme. 1976. *Comparative Deviance*. New York: Elsevier North Holland.

Noonan, John T., Jr., ed. 1970. *The Morality of Abortion*. Cambridge, Mass.: Harvard University Press.

O'Connor vs. *Donaldson.* 1975. 422 U.S. 563.

Packer, Herbert L. 1968. *The Limits of the Criminal Sanction.* Stanford: Stanford University Press.

Pfohl, Stephen J. 1977. "The 'Discovery' of Child Abuse." *Social Problems* 24 (February): 310–323.

Piliavin, Irving, and Scott Briar. 1964. "Police Encounters with Juveniles." *American Journal of Sociology* 69 (September): 206–214.

Piven, Frances Fox, and Richard A. Cloward. 1971. *Regulating the Poor.* New York: Pantheon.

Platt, Anthony M. 1969. *The Child Savers: The Invention of Delinquency.* Chicago: University of Chicago Press.

Roe v. Wade. 1973. 410 U.S. 113.

Rosen, Harold, ed. 1954. *Therapeutic Abortion.* New York: Julian Press.

Rosenhan, D.L. 1973. "On Being Sane in Insane Places." *Science* 179 (January 19): 250–258.

Rosenheim, Margaret. 1976. "Notes on Helping Juvenile Nuisances." In Rosenheim, ed., *Pursuing Justice for the Child.* Chicago: University of Chicago Press. Pp. 43–66.

Rossi, Alice S. 1966. "Abortion Laws and Their Victims." *Transaction,* September-October.

Rossi, Peter et al. 1974. "The Seriousness of Crimes." *American Sociological Review* 39 (April). 224–237.

Rubington, Earl, and Martin S. Weinberg, eds. 1978. *Deviance: The Interactionist Perspective.* 3rd ed., New York: Macmillan.

Sarvis, Betty, and Hyman Rodman. 1974. *The Abortion Controversy.* 2nd ed. New York: Columbia University Press.

Scheff, Thomas J. 1966. *Being Mentally Ill.* Chicago: Aldine.

Scheff, Thomas J. 1968. "Negotiating Reality: Notes on Power in the Assessment of Responsibility." *Social Problems* 16 (summer): 3–17.

Schrag, Peter, and Diane Divoky. 1976. *The Myth of the Hyperactive Child.* New York: Dell Pub. Co., Inc.

Schultz, Terri. 1977. "Though Legal, Abortions Are Not Always Available." *New York Times,* January 2, p. 8E.

Schur, Edwin M. 1955. "The Abortion Racket." *The Nation,* March 5.

Schur, Edwin M. 1965. *Crimes Without Victims.* Englewood Cliffs, N.J.: Prentice-Hall.

Schur, Edwin M. 1968. "Abortion." *The Annals of the American Academy of Political and Social Science* 376 (March): 136–147.

Schur, Edwin M. 1971. *Labeling Deviant Behavior.* New York: Harper & Row, Pub.

Schur, Edwin M. 1979. *Interpreting Deviance.* New York: Harper & Row, Pub.

Scott, Robert A. 1969. *The Making of Blind Men.* New York: Russell Sage Foundation.

Scull, Andrew T. 1977. *Decarceration.* Englewood Cliffs, N.J.: Prentice-Hall.

Severo, Richard. 1978. "Mental Patients Seeking a Voice in Determining Their Therapies." *New York Times,* December 11, pp. 1, D14.

Spector, Malcolm, and John I. Kitsuse. 1977. *Constructing Social Problems.* Menlo Park, Calif.: Cummings.

Suchar, Charles S. 1978. *Social Deviance: Perspectives and Prospects.* New York: Holt, Rinehart & Winston.

Sudnow, David. 1965. "Normal Crimes: Sociological Features of the Penal Code in a Public Defender Office." *Social Problems:* 12 (winter): 255–276.

Sullivan, Ronald. 1978. "Mental-Patient Releases Questioned." *New York Times,* March 13, p. B3.

Sutherland, Edwin H. 1950. "The Diffusion of Sexual Psychopath Laws." *American Journal of Sociology* 56 (September): 142–148.

Szasz, Thomas S. 1961. *The Myth of Mental Illness.* New York: Hoeber-Harper.

Szasz, Thomas S. 1963. *Law, Liberty and Psychiatry.* New York: Macmillan.

Szasz, Thomas S. 1965. *Psychiatric Justice.* New York: Macmillan.

Szasz, Thomas S. 1970. *Ideology and Insanity.* Garden City, N.Y.: Doubleday, Anchor Books.

Weinberg, George. 1972. *Society and the Healthy Homosexual.* Garden City, N.Y.: Doubleday, Anchor Books.

Weisstein, Naomi. 1972. "Psychology Constructs the Female." In Vivian Gornick and Barbara K. Moran, eds., *Woman in Sexist Society.* New York: Signet. Pp. 207–224.

Witten, Marsha et al. 1977. "State Abandons Mentally Ill to City Streets." *Village Voice,* October 31, pp. 1, 29.

Yarrow, Marian Radke et al. 1955. "The Psychological Meaning of Mental Illness in the Family." *Journal of Social Issues* 11: 12–24.

2
chapter

Containment and Control

". . . the agencies of control often seem to define their job as that of keeping deviance within bounds rather than of obliterating it altogether."

Kai Erikson,
Wayward Puritans *(1966)*

COMPLEXITIES OF CONTROL

Deviance-defining is not a static event but a continuous and changing process. This is so because, as we have seen, it is a way of characterizing and reacting, exhibited by individuals and groups whose interests and favored values, and their ability to impose them, vary greatly and in many instances change over time. Efforts to deviantize and success in this endeavor are two different things. Since the attempt to designate and treat behavior as deviant must be backed up by social power if it is to have any real effect, the distribution of power among persons and groups crucially shapes deviance outcomes. To study stigma contests or deviance struggles is, then, to study the sources and uses of power.

It is often said that contemporary deviance theory emphasizes social control. Usually this refers to the increased attention paid to social reactions in general and more specifically to the work and impact of designated "agents" and "agencies" of control. It also suggests the recent highlighting of interaction sequences in deviantizing, including those through which alleged control tends to contribute to and may even unintentionally amplify the "problem" toward which it is directed. Furthermore as we saw in chapter 1, in considering such possibilities the contemporary analyst of deviance will tend to give terms like *control agent* and *control agency* a broad interpretation. All those who regularly deal with deviance and the deviantized are seen as exerting control—the psychiatrist as well as the policeman, the agency for the blind along with the juvenile court.

In this sense "control" implies doing things *to* people, whatever the intention may be to do something *for* them. From a broader standpoint, the idea of control ought to be seen as roughly synonymous to that of power. To say that someone controls a situation, or exerts control "over" it, means that that person has some capacity to determine or (since control is rarely absolute) influence it, to bend events and participants to his or her will, to resist unwanted outcomes, to take advantage of what is for him or her a favorable balance of power. With respect to the politics of deviance, the concept of control raises many tricky questions. We need to ask ourselves whether control should be viewed primarily as a goal, as a technique, or as an observed outcome. Often it can usefully be thought of in all three of these ways. In addition, we should be careful not to use the concept in too abstract a way. Thus for any particular deviance situation we must try to specify *who* is attempting or exerting control, under what conditions, and in furtherance of what goals and interests. These strictures, though stated here in a slightly different form, are really the same ones we noted earlier with respect to interests, functions, and perceived threat. It is not always obvious whose interests are at stake, for which groups an arrangement or policy is most functional, or what kinds of perceived threats are being resisted or allayed. The full spectrum of political forces at work in any given deviance-problem area—especially the latent or covert forces—will elude us if we don't try to sort these matters out.

The need to sort them out becomes clear when we find writers on deviance suggesting that control, in one or another situation, is being exerted or attempted on behalf of such abstractions as *the system, the state,* or *the capitalist class.* While assertions of this sort frequently provide some general illumination, or suggest a valuable direction for further exploration, they can also be very misleading — when they are presented as, or taken to be, complete and definitive explanations. To assess such claims, or derive the most benefit from them, we must consider the precise nature of the tie-ins with system, state, or class, any additional interests that enter into the specific deviance-defining situation, and the necessary limits on the intentional control that any given unit or group can exert. It is little more than a truism that all patterns of social behavior, institutionalized social structures, and major public policies will in some degree and manner reflect the nature of the system in which they are found. Appreciating that such links exist is, of course, important; but we always need to go further — to explore more specifically what the links are and how they work.

As we noted in the last chapter, the very process of deviance-defining seems to serve some important overall functions for a social system. This thesis applies to any social system, rather than one particular sort, and regardless of the specific types of behavior or individuals that may acquire deviantness. Designating and reacting to perceived deviators is in effect one side of the process by which conformity is established and reinforced. It marks out boundaries or limits of acceptable variation and, among the reactors, "creates a sense of mutuality . . . by supplying a focus for group feeling" (Erikson 1966, p. 4). Perhaps partly because they failed to treat deviance as a product of definitions and reactions — taking it instead to be an absolute or given — early studies and theories tended to depict deviance as somehow being a departure from, rather than a part of, the ordinary workings of society. Recent theorizing reflects a *"decompartmentalizing of deviance"* (Schur 1979, pp. 66–73). Deviance-defining is now recognized to be central to the mainenance of social structures; as one writer puts it, it is "a property of social order" (Scott 1972). At the same time, from a microsociological standpoint it is seen to be a basic ingredient in the very process of social interaction — a process that is guided by the development of informal norms and sanctions, and even by unrecognized background expectancies (Garfinkel 1964). Thus, if I offend an acquaintance through rudeness, inattention, or apparent disloyalty, and he or she responds by ostracizing me or attempting to smear my reputation, such processes represent microcosmic conterparts of the deviance-control sequences we find in larger social contexts.

A major implication that flows from recognizing the centrality of deviance is that we are going to find it in any and all kinds of societies. This general defining-reacting process appears to be a cultural universal, though the specific forms it takes and the substantive content it exhibits will vary considerably. Some types of perceived deviance and deviants are virtually inevitable in any system — whether the offenders be labeled revolutionaries or counterrevolutionaries, common thieves or offenders against state property. The aforementioned mirror-image analyses, interpreting functional ties between the specific forms of perceived deviance and the other elements in a given system, can help us to understand the patterns deviance-defining takes in a particular society, at a particular time. But despite the fact that such specific linkages can be located and that more general functions are always served by (any form of) deviance-defining, attempts to attribute deviance in general and exclusively to any particular system (e.g., monopoly capitalism) are doomed to failure. This is borne out by the difficulty modern socialist societies have experienced in explaining how even "standard" forms of deviance — such as crime, delinquency, alcoholism, homosexuality — have persisted in their countries, notwithstanding an ideology that views these conditions as artifacts of capitalism. (See Connor 1972; also Jay and Young 1977, chap. 6, "Cuba: Gay as the Sun.") The centrality of deviance poses a similar problem for some radical sociologists who foresee its eventual demise (with the formation of a "true" socialist system)—as opposed to mere changes in the forms, rates, and treatment of deviance (e.g., Taylor, Walton, and Young 1974; Quinney 1974, 1977).

SPECIFYING INTERESTS

It follows, then, that when we consider deviance-defining and stigma contests in the United States today, we must be wary of purported explanations that attribute our society's entire deviance picture to control by "the state" or exploitation by "the ruling elite." Such assertions gloss over several important factors: the diversity of substantive areas in which deviance-defining occurs, which may vary greatly in the extent to which they pose issues for the state or ruling elite; the multiplicity of group interests and social forces that may come into play; the mixed or ambiguous interests that some groups may have; the inevitable limitations on absolute control that confront the state apparatus or ruling elite even in situations where they might seek to exert it.

That deviance issues are so heterogeneous—ranging from serious crimes to merely unsettling behavior or lifestyles— suggests at once the need in every situation to specify the interests at stake and even to identify which units and groups are most directly involved. Thinking in terms of the key element of perceived threat may help us to do this. Who is it that feels threatened and therefore seeks to impose deviance definitions and deviantizing reactions? Much of the sociological literature on collective social movements has focused on explicitly political protests and revolutionary movements and therefore has placed great emphasis on efforts by the state to maintain social control (Gamson 1968). From this standpoint, "social control" refers to the problem authorities have in managing discontent, fending off or "cooling out" direct challenges or overt disruptions, and in maintaining legitimacy and ultimately the capacity to govern. Such discussions, then, have to do with the efforts of specific political regimes to survive in the face of direct threats to their vital interests. If one thinks instead, however, of the broad spectrum of substantive areas in which deviance-defining occurs, it becomes clear that stigma contests only rarely involve such direct and severe threat to the state.

Role of the State

For that reason, it will often be a mistake to think of social control with respect to deviance issues simply as being imposed by, or in the interests of, the state. Indeed, in the broader sense, it seems that frequently such so-called control is not imposed at all. On the contrary, control — which is merely another way of referring to the deviantizing reaction present at any given time — is but a tenuous outcome that has "emerged" through the interplay of multiple forces, and which continues to be subject to such forces and to changes in them. How much interest the state or a particular regime has in the outcome of a given deviance struggle will vary considerably, depending in part on the nature and assumed ramifications of the substantive behavior that is at issue and also on perceptions of the extent of the threat and the potential social force lying behind it. In a very indirect sense, a governing regime always has some degree of interest in maintaining most aspects of the sociocultural status quo as well as the prevailing economic and political arrangements. But it is in the latter areas that its own interests are likely to be most pronounced. Insurrection, sabotage, espionage, the demand for a totally new kind of political system or economic order — perceived threats or potential "deviances" of this sort affect it most strongly and directly.

Although the substantive types of threat cannot be neatly or objectively ordered, there may be a rough continuum along which degrees of direct state involvement will be likely to range. Following the most overt and extreme political challenges in severity of perceived threat would usually be behaviors that in other ways carry a high potential to disrupt the social and economic order or to generate disloyalty and alienation. Presumably these behaviors would include major crimes against persons and property, significant modes of collective public disturbance (riots, looting, and the like), and perhaps some types of "seditious" speech and organizing. When one moves beyond these situations into areas of more vaguely troublesome or upsetting sociocultural variation, it becomes much less clear that the state has a strong and direct interest. For example, variations in sexual behavior would seem to be a direct concern of a governing regime only if, or to the extent that, they appear to strongly threaten major social institutions, such as the family. Bohemianism and recreational use of nonincapacitating drugs, religious heterodoxy, and minor political sectarianism likewise tend to pose rather indirect threats to the state. The same is true of personal handicaps that may give rise to stigma and to collective stigma contests.

As some of these examples may suggest, any generalizations of this sort must be accompanied by the standard caution, "all other things being equal." Concern and involvement of the state reflect the perceived extent and potential force of a threat, as well as its substantive nature. If the threat becomes widespread or produces dramatic adverse consequences, a behavior or condition that otherwise would elicit only mild state concern may be viewed by a particular regime as getting out of hand. U.S. governmental concern over cults, in the wake of the Jonestown People's Temple mass suicides in 1978, illustrates this point. Furthermore, what counts in these situations — as in deviantizing responses by individual moral entrepreneurs or moral crusade groups — is *perceived* threat. In reacting to any situation of potential "trouble," different regimes might well make different assessments or, we might also say, invoke different tolerance limits. These assessments will most likely be influenced by various factors not yet mentioned — including the regime's overall existing strength and degree of legitimacy, the other problems it simultaneously faces, its commitment to certain goals, its current reading of public opinion, and its perceptions of, and dealings with, diverse and possibly competing special interest groups.

Spector and Kitsuse (1977) have sensitively discussed deviance struggles, and indeed social problems more generally, in terms of "claims-making" activities. Adopting such a focus further helps us to appreciate the likelihood of variations in the extent to which the state apparatus becomes implicated in deviance-defining and the ways that it does. Since large-scale stigma contests center on questions of social power, the competing groups invariably would like to have the ultimate back-up force of official state power and legitimation used in support of their interests. But such groups vary considerably as to the more specific claims they advance. Sometimes they directly petition the state for redress of perceived wrongs. At other times, in a less direct approach, they seek to change public opinion and enhance their collective social and moral standing. In one sense the state can never remain totally aloof from major deviance struggles, since its inaction (on the legislative, judicial, or executive level) as well as its action is bound to have consequences that favor one side more than the other. At the same time the nature of the claims being advanced and the intended target of such claims affect the probability of the state's being actively drawn into any such struggle.

Clearly, this is but another aspect of, or way of talking about, the perceived-threat, perceived-interest issue. Some claims addressed to, or advanced against, the state apparatus are general ones; others are much more limited. The state's interest is bound to vary accordingly. Political revolutionaries assert a general claim of superior legitimacy, which if allowed, would mean the regime's demise. The claims asserted by other kinds of deviantized minorities, as well as those advanced by their explicit or implicit opponents, tend to be more limited and indirect ones, in which these groups seek not to undermine the state but rather to gain its support through specific legal sanctions and official legitimation. Theoretically, as the Horowitz-Liebowitz thesis on the fading distinction between deviance and political action (cited in the last chapter) suggests, a group with acceptable and rather benign goals or claims may behave in sufficiently troublesome ways that the governing regime might feel compelled, in its own interests, to oppose it. More typically, however, the state's role reflects complex influences—including evaluations of the validity of conflicting claims, the influence of competing groups, and the probable attitudes and interests of other, not directly involved, constituencies and segments of the population.

The part played by government in the treatment of homosexuals in our society and in the current collective struggle over such treatment illustrates some of these points. One can, to be sure, conceive of situations in which a governing regime might conclude that it had a strong direct interest in this matter. That could happen, for example, if homosexuality seemed to those in power to be alarmingly widespread and also sufficiently appealing to the masses that it threatened the continued dominance of the heterosexual family institution or the maintenance of adequate population strength. Indeed, increasingly open discussion of the topic and the willingness of individual homosexuals to come out of the closet have combined to reveal the existence in our society of considerable homosexuality. Yet there is no reason to believe that this has produced a strong direct governmental interest in repression. Although gay liberation groups are properly incensed about past injustices, many of which were administered by agents of the government (police, the courts, the military) and now seek from government the legal guarantee of basic rights and enhancement of sociopolitical legitimation, their core claims do not constitute a direct threat to the state itself.

If these limited claims were to remain officially unrecognized and unsatisfied for long, then mounting gay liberation discontent could become more directly focused on the government and, furthermore, could increasingly take disruptive forms that the state might find threatening. However, officialdom really has no special interest in denying all of these limited claims. For the most part, gay liberationists are not levelling a basic challenge against the ruling regime; they certainly have little desire to overturn it. Indeed, as we shall see below (example 7, p. 212), it has not been easy to organize and mobilize the gay community for political action — even on explicitly gay issues. Although gay political consciousness and militancy are increasing, the danger (from a ruling government's standpoint) of a more general radical protest evolving out of this movement is exceedingly slim. Homosexuals run the gamut of political viewpoints and degrees of interest in politics, and not even the undoubted sense of injustice at the hands of various state agents can be expected to create a serious revolutionary potential. And just as officialdom has no special stake in denying homosexual rights, it has no pronounced interest in placating the groups that actively oppose gay liberation. Rather than openly siding with either of these competing forces, government will probably continue to mediate the conflict, responding more or less ad hoc to overtures from the contestants and reflecting in its actions a range of influences such as those just noted above.

There is no question but that this mediating role is a crucial one, something that the participants in the dispute realize full well. Legislative, judicial, and administrative actions can produce desired outcomes they could not otherwise achieve. But the governmental role in this area is a responding and reflecting one, at least as much as, if not more than, an initiating and self-consciously determining one. These considerations apply to past official actions as well as to present and prospective measures. Thus, while it is quite true that homosexuals have long experienced and still experience routine harassment and a serious threat of more harsh treatment from law-enforcement authorities (see Schur 1965; Humphreys 1972; Altman 1973), it would be a gross oversimplification to describe such enforcement actions merely as indicating control by the state. Control *through* the agencies of the state — in furtherance of a variety of group, as well as governmental, interests — would be a more accurate description. Similar conclusions seem warranted with respect to the state's role in reference to a good many contested deviance issues — including at least prostitution (see example 4, later in this chapter), pornography, marihuana use, gambling, and abortion (the conflict over which was detailed above).

As one moves still further away from large-scale politicized situations posing serious threats to direct state interests — into such areas of deviantizing as nudism, the hippie counterculture, the mentally retarded, and sadomasochism, the state's participation in producing deviance outcomes becomes even less central. Some deviance issues — suicide, alcoholism, and heroin addiction might be examples — probably represent a middle ground. In these instances, although the most significant state interests are not threatened directly, at the same time a serious potential threat to major social institutions may well provoke strong governmental concern. And, as already noted, such threat may become overt in connection with certain behaviors other than political revolt — such as major crimes against property and persons. When a recognition develops that behavior in such categories is widespread — for example, as in the currently increased awareness of wife beating and child abuse — the government may well feel impelled to respond on its own initiative.

Advanced Capitalism

The key point we must keep in mind, then, is that whereas the state — in some degree, and indirectly if not directly — almost inevitably plays a role with respect to every deviance issue and is caught up in every deviance struggle, there is great variation as to the nature and degree of its participation and the centrality of its role. Much the same can be said of the role of "the capitalist class," and — by extension — the capitalist "system." No doubt all deviance situations and issues in contemporary American society exhibit certain features that in some manner reflect *advanced capitalism* (to use the term many Marxist theorists apply to our current economic system). To say this is merely to recognize that any socioeconomic order displays a widely ramifying set of dominant outlooks, priorities, and basic organizing principles. We need, without any question, to keep the influence of capitalism in mind and to explore its manifestations in specific situations, but to treat it as an exclusive and all-embracing explanation of deviantizing and deviance policies is to misread its relevance and to ignore other equally relevant considerations.

In his effort to frame a Marxian theory of deviance, Spitzer has written: "Problem populations tend to share a number of social characteristics, but most important among these is the fact that their behavior, personal qualities and/or position threaten the *social relations of production* in capitalist societies" (Spitzer 1975, p. 642). While it could be true that within a capitalist system populations posing such a threat may be especially likely to be viewed as problems, it may nonetheless be equally true that most of the populations that are at any given time being treated as problematic do not pose such a threat. If one looks far enough and is sufficiently willing to stretch a point, one can of course locate economic aspects and linkages in any deviance situation — for the simple reason that we all exist and interact within an economic framework as well as within other sociocultural frames. The more pertinent issue has to do with the relative importance of these economic aspects. Again, we can expect that to vary a great deal. It is much easier, for example, to construct an "economic theory" of corporate crime and responses to it (see example 6, p. 168) than to explain child abuse or adultery exclusively in economic terms. Furthermore, the frequent persistence of similar perceptions regarding deviance problems, and similar deviance policies, in non-capitalist countries raise serious questions about the supposed link to capitalism. Thus, the postrevolutionary regime in contemporary Cuba may have its special reasons for officially stigmatizing homosexuality — for example, on the grounds that it is tied to "counterrevolutionary sentiment" (Loney 1973). Nonetheless, and despite further assertions that homosexuality in such a context is a "survival" of prerevolutionary conditions, this situation indicates that there is certainly nothing distinctive about capitalism or about the interests of the capitalist class that dictates a policy of this sort.

Of course, there are quite legitimate theories about the economic conditions and pressures that drive people to one or another kind of deviating act, but the same types of acts seem to occur in diverse kinds of economic systems. Nor do such theories usually seek to explain the relevant social definitions and reactions. However, a considerable amount of Marxist-oriented theorizing has recently focused on reactions, suggesting that certain types of deviance policy are profitable to the capitalist class. Thus a well-known radical criminologist asserts:

> The new technocratic approach to crime and social control has developed rapidly in the last decade. Especially under the direction of LEAA [Law Enforcement Assistance Administration], a multimillion-dollar market in domestic control has been established for hundreds of industries and research institutes. . . . to develop and manufacture a wide range of weapons and technical devices for use in the criminal justice system . . . a field of research and development in criminal justice has emerged, putting control on a scientific basis as well as making a profitable industry. Under the sponsorship of LEAA, with lucrative contracts, private corporations, research institutes, and universities are gaining profits from the new system of criminal justice. [Quinney 1977, pp. 120–121]

Quinney's depiction of a "criminal justice-industrial complex" is useful (see also Quinney 1974; Silver 1974), although a policy critique along those lines does not require that we adopt a broad

Marxist theory. As mentioned earlier, an important contribution of the recent definitions-reactions approach to deviance has been to point up the possibility that deviance-processing agencies (including governmental units) can develop vested interests in particular problem designations and in general deviance policies. Similarly, many "labeling" studies, along with Marxist critiques, have documented the frequency with which socioeconomic-class factors come into play in the selection and processing of individual "offenders."

All of these analyses direct our attention to certain aspects of the politics of deviance in particular situations that must be included in any efforts at comprehensive interpretation. For the most part, however, they have been concerned with major street crime, the bulk of which consists of property offenses — and for which the elements of economic causation, the state's control interest, and the linkages between control efforts and the economic system are fairly apparent. The applicability of these ideas to deviantizing responses and policies in other substantive areas is, as already noted, much less evident. There is little doubt that socioeconomic status represents one crucial resource for "managing" life situations of particular individuals subject to stigma in these areas — alcoholism, physical disability, homosexuality, or whatever. To that extent, at least, the class system is implicated even in situations of this sort. But it seems unlikely that the very existence of stigma in these areas — as reflected in either dominant public conceptions and responses or official policies and practices — can be attributed entirely to the interests or efforts of the "capitalist class" or the capitalist system. In fact, these responses seem to cut across the various classes, much as do the social distributions of the stigmatized conditions themselves. As a consequence, the class bases for alignment in collective deviance struggles — a topic to which we shall return in chapter 4 — are usually unclear. References to the inherent "contradictions" of capitalism, to the currently much-vaunted "fiscal crisis of the state" (O'Connor 1973), and to "hegemonic domination by the privileged class" (Krisberg 1975, p. 54) have but limited use in illuminating complex situations of this sort.

RECOGNIZING LIMITS

Power and domination are not absolutes. In our society, the centralized state apparatus and also the ruling elite — very roughly, the "capitalist class" — are without question extremely powerful entities. Government, in American society as in other societies, controls the ultimate sanction of socially approved force. Within our capitalist system, financial-corporate-military interests clearly exert an influence that is way out of proportion to their representation in the total population and that ramifies throughout different spheres of American life (Mills 1957; Domhoff 1971). However, to see the social control of deviance in reductionist conspiratorial terms — with the state and/or ruling class playing the villain's role — is as deceptively easy, and just as misleading, as is the opposite extreme of seeing deviance-defining as simply reflecting the will of the people or the common value system.

More accurately, deviance definitions and policies must be seen as reflecting the will of some of the people and the ascendancy of certain values, emerging through complicated intergroup processes in which the ruling circles and the state apparatus — while not sole instigators of action or absolute controllers of outcomes — represent at the very least major sources of potential support that will be actively sought by the contesting forces. That the role of the society's major power holders is not more central, let alone fully determinative on deviance issues is partly due to the fact, already emphasized, that often they do not have a clearly defined direct interest in the outcomes that are being contested. Or, in a given situation, either the governing regime or the socioeconomic power holders may have

multiple interests. Thus, in his Marxist-oriented study of the
1960s urban racial disorders, Balbus noted:

> . . . the response of American legal authorities to the black
> ghetto revolts was a function of a delicate balance that these
> authorities were compelled to strike among three essential, yet
> contradictory authority interests: the interest in *order* (in ending
> the revolts), the interest in *formal rationality* (in adhering to
> normal legal procedures), and the interest in *organizational
> maintenance* (in preventing the court organization from being
> overwhelmed by the inflow of cases). [Balbus 1977, p. xviii]

In deviance areas where the sense of threat to government itself
is not so clear, the state's or ruling elite's interests may be
equally complex and probably will be even more diffuse and
elusive.

Even if those with access to state power had a clear interest in
each and every deviance outcome, there would remain several
reasons why they could not exert or maintain absolute control.
At least in formal terms, American society is after all a political
democracy, albeit a most imperfect one. From that standpoint,
although there is indeed enormous concentration and consolidation of various kinds of power in the society, there are still some
limits on these tendencies and on the uses to which such power
can be put — even by the legitimate state authorities. Post-
Watergate revelations have brought to public attention the frequent and extensive involvement of the government itself in
corruption, deceptive practices, illegal surveillance, and the
like. Yet it is also true that once revealed, such behaviors, if
extensive enough, render even public authorities susceptible to
deviantizing (see Douglas and Johnson 1977; also Wise 1973;
Halperin et al. 1976) — despite the fact that some of these very
practices were being used to combat what those authorities perceived to be deviance (for example, domestic radicalism and
international spying).

Not only does the formal commitment to democracy imply
eventual limits on the use of power but the structures of demo-

cratic government also complicate the social-control picture. Both horizontal and vertical differentiation of governmental authority in the United States contribute to this complexity. Even at the federal level, to objectify "the state," as though it were a single fully coordinated, smooth-working, and single-mindedly staffed machine, is to gloss over these important structural features which influence official activity on deviance issues. Whatever major deviance controversy we choose to examine — the abortion conflict discussed above, the struggle over gay liberation, and the debate over national drug policies would be but three obvious examples — we find at any time that actions of the major branches of government (legislative, judicial, and executive) indicate a far from unified "state" position. In fact, it is understandably characteristic of conflict groups in the deviance areas, as in others, to turn to one branch for help (sometimes with success) after being rebuffed by another, or to play off the branches against each other — as when the courts are asked to rule unconstitutional legislation that a protest group considers limiting and improper. While the operation of these checks and balances does not totally preclude at least short-term trends in the overall role of the state on a given deviance issue, when we note as well the inevitable fluctuations over time in the actions taken even by one of the major branches of government, the notion of a cohesive state role in furtherance of precise interests becomes highly questionable.

Vertical differentiation of government must also be taken into account. That includes subordinate organizations within each major branch at the federal level and, even more significant, the federal system through which separate state governments — each with its own horizontal differentiation into three branches — maintain significant jurisdiction over many questions relating to deviance-defining. Indeed, as the reference in chapter 1 to the situated politics of deviance began to suggest, much of the direct deviantizing of individuals through the actions of formal deviance-processing organizations occurs under the auspices of the several states and, of course, within even more specific local contexts. Actions taken at these levels will reflect the interplay of various localized units and forces, not all of which are subject to centralized authority and control. Appeal to the federal courts, however, for limits on state and local action, as in the major abortion cases cited above, represents one way in which contesting groups seek to invoke such control.

For all of these reasons, the steps taken by specific agents and agencies of control in particular deviance situations can only in the most indirect sense be said to further an identifiable state interest. When police in a given locality harass streetwalkers, when courts in a particular state commit persons to mental hospitals on grounds of social dangerous, or when authorities in one state jurisdiction investigate graft, they can no doubt be described as employing or applying the official sanctions of state power. But to refer to them simply as agents of control may sometimes beg the hidden question — agents for whom? Frequently, they are in a way both less and more than "agents of the establishment" — as they are often described. Their ties to the centralized state apparatus and to a national ruling class are extremely limited. At the same time, these agents and agencies have interests of their own. As Balbus's reference to the need for organizational maintenance, cited above, suggests, and as the recent outlooks on deviance discussed in the last chapter emphasize, deviance processing typically reflects emerging organizational needs and also the specific situations and work problems of personnel in those organizations. In addition, there may be multiple control agencies that deal with a given problem, competing for support and in considerable and often active conflict over the general policies and practices that ought to prevail. The continuous and vituperative disputes, at local and federal levels, over approaches and between agencies dealing with heroin addiction (law enforcement versus medical, methadone maintenance treatment programs versus drug-free therapeutic communities, and so on) illustrates this possibility. (See for example, Lindesmith 1965; also Wald et al. 1972.)

Democratic government in a federal system, then, imposes various structural constraints that would limit state power wielding even if the state had a clear and precise interest in all deviance outcomes. In fact, it often does not have any such interest. Furthermore, commitment to democracy, even if largely formal, implies that the government's role will in large measure be a responding one, in the sense that attention must be paid to the competing claims, interests, and attitudes of diverse constituencies. Particularly since the membership of many of the directly interested constituencies (e.g., homosexuals, the mentally ill, alcoholics, abortion seekers, and their most vocal opponents as well) cuts across or transcends the standard categories of socioeconomic class and political allegiance, government often can no better afford to neglect the claims on one side than those on the other. And those constituencies that are not so directly involved — throughout which outlooks on deviance issues vary greatly but nonetheless certainly are present — cannot be ignored either.

None of this is to suggest that such a system tends to produce just outcomes, or that all groups are on an equal footing in seeking government and other support. We know that this is far from being the case, that the already powerful invariably have the greatest prospects of advancing their interests. Furthermore, as we have seen, the very process of being defined and treated as deviant has the continuing effect of lowering such prospects; this is one of the important aspects of their situations that groups protesting deviantizing seek to alter. But the socioeconomically mixed nature of many of the groups competing on deviance issues and the very fact that such groups and issues are numerous as well as diverse mean that the government is less likely in some of these areas than in others to lean toward or defer to class-based power. Deviance-protest groups sometimes try to demonstrate their economic power, but often they hope to rely on manifested power of other sorts in order to gain access and legitimation.

As we are going to see in chapter 4, from the standpoint of attempts to mobilize protest, this multiplicity of issues, groups, and interests — and particularly the intersecting or overlapping memberships between specific protest groups and the various political and socioeconomic groups and categories among which they might hope to recruit support — represents a considerable problem. From the standpoint of a governing regime's general interest in maintaining order and managing discontent, it is sometimes suggested, this same multiplicity may prove beneficial (Gamson 1968, pp. 13–14; Lehman 1977, pp. 148–149). These overlapping interests and memberships help to keep specific conflicts from becoming too intense and encourage compromise among the competing groups. With that in mind, one might even conclude that if the state has any overall interest with respect to deviance issues, it could be to ensure the persistence of many overlapping groups and a multiplicity of contested issues. Encouraging a broad range of discrete stigma contests might serve to discourage any tendencies for directly anti-governmental interests to coalesce. This approach would make sense with respect to deviance contests in which few demands on the government itself were being advanced and few governmental interests seriously threatened. One student of specifically political protests has noted that even in some of those situations, there may be "a triadic relationship between protest group, target group and social control agents" (Wilson 1977, p. 471). In conflicts where overtly political goals are limited and where the state is not itself the major target of the protest, a relatively aloof third-party role may be in the government's interest.

When those who rule do conclude that their major interests are threatened, they are of course in a good position to do something about it. This is but the other side of the point made earlier that state power is a valuable resource sought after by contesting groups. As the literature on political protest movements elaborates, a governing regime can take measures to insulate a group, impose sanctions on it, try to use persuasion rather than force, or try to co-opt it by allowing minor concessions or limited participation in decision making (Gamson 1968, chap. 6). For our purposes, co-optation may be especially interesting. One writer, in a usage rather different from that adopted in this book, even refers to it as politicization. That is, by allowing protestors apparent but minor political concessions, the state apparatus or ruling elite, "minimizes their power, substituting ritualistic participation or representation. . . . Politicization can be taken as a signal that nonelites have renounced resort to disorder and that substantial concessions are not necessary" (Edelman 1977, p. 125). This process of drawing into the formal political mechanisms that which seems to threaten them is also, according to some radical critics, frequently at work when social researchers are funded by the government, hired as consultants to governmental agencies, or enlisted to work on or with official commissions of inquiry. Government-funded research on numerous types of perceived deviance is currently widespread, and special commissions have investigated a great many deviance issues, ranging from mental illness to prison riots, from juvenile justice to pornography, from violence to drinking problems.

According to the conventional wisdom, when a government favors taking no policy action, it appoints a commission. In a sense this device may combine the advantages of broad co-optation — since it may draw in academic specialists and critics, representatives of actual or potential protest groups, and influential public figures — with those of an aloof stance, in which officialdom waits out a given deviance struggle in the hope that its own political strength will not be affected. Before concluding that co-optation had been successful, however, we would need to examine the nature and implications of the work turned out in such instances (e.g., by funded researchers, government commissions, and the like). Considering the broad range of deviance issues involved, it is not surprising that the results are mixed. Some findings, reports, and recommendations seem in varying degrees to support the status quo, many others do not. We need to keep in mind, furthermore, that claims of co-optation always imply that those using the device definitely favor a specific outcome. As we have already seen, that is not always so — as regards either the centralized state apparatus or the ruling economic classes. State and ruling class do most assuredly always have a general interest in maintaining overall dominance, but in many deviance-related matters it is far from clear which outcome will better further that goal.

ACCOMMODATION AND CONTAINMENT

Even if the more specific interests of state and ruling class were clear-cut and their power overwhelming, the magnitude and heterogeniety of perceived deviance problems would alone ensure that the "solutions" adopted would usually be incomplete and unstable. Since in fact such interests are often obscure or mixed and such power is limited, it is even more likely that such a state of affairs will prevail. For all the reasons indicated, including its centrality to the processes of social life, it would be impossible to totally eradicate "deviance" even if one wanted to. There is simply too much potentially perceived deviance around at any one time — varying in nature, depending on whose assessments are adopted — for that to be a feasible policymaking goal. Moreover, and as earlier discussion has suggested, deviance outcomes do not result from single, consciously arrived-at, policy decisions and actions. They are not simply made, but, instead they emerge.

Actually, ruling regimes and classes — and indeed societies generally — can, must, and do live with a great deal of uncontrolled deviance. Since the line between deviance and acceptable diversity often is hazy, and in many problematic areas differentially assessed by various groups and population segments, deviance policies are invariably tentative and shifting. Even in those areas where the greatest consensus exists (for example, violent crimes against persons and major personal property crimes), the applications of policy remain incomplete simply because there are limits on the exercise of power by those who hold it. Differentials in socioeconomic power do count enormously in determining which types of persons in our society are most likely to be defined and treated as the most serious offenders and also what happens to them. Thus a social-class model of deviance-defining finds considerable support in the facts that poor people, including blacks, are disproportionately involved in, and imprisoned for, street crime (Schur 1969, chap. 4), and conversely that corporate and other white-collar offenders (see example 6, p. 168) successfully shield themselves from stigma and negative sanctions.

Even these situations are subject to at least a degree of change, partly through conscious political efforts — as we shall see below. In the areas of deviance-defining that are less directly related to the economic system, the socioeconomic postions of particular individuals subject to stigma may indeed affect their options — and hence become a central ingredient in the *mi-cro*politics of deviance (intrinsic, situated, and so on). But the *macro*politics in such areas are another matter, since they have so much to do with the collective definitions of types of behavior and thus the creation of deviance categories as such. The connection between many of these broad-based stigma judgments and economic factors is indirect or unclear. Such judgments are best viewed as an emerging product of explicit or implicit collective deviance contests, reflecting multiple group and value influences and likely to fluctuate along with changes in the overall balance of power.

Since problematic behaviors and conditions cannot simply be obliterated through applications of absolute power that are also based on conscious and widely agreed-upon decisions, we frequently encounter the paradoxical situation noted in this chapter's epigraph. Given ambivalent and mixed attitudes and reactions in many areas of deviance-defining, situations evolve in which public policy (the purported solution) seems almost to support the problem rather than to significantly curb it. Indeed, in a sense, "problem" and "solution" appear to be little more than two ways of describing a single interwoven set of facts. Several aspects of the deviance-control relation that were cited earlier imply this possibility — that a society has the types of deviance with which it is preoccupied; that the amount of deviance is partly a function of the nature and extent of the control apparatus and control activity; that the process of deviance-defining serves important functions for the society at large; and that deviantizing, in general, can have unintended deviance-amplifying consequences.

So it isn't too surprising that prisons and mental hospitals do not eliminate crime and mental illness; that official responses to various kinds of perceived deviation (such as public drunkenness, streetwalking, vagrancy) amount to no more than a revolving-door (in-and-out-of jail) process; that restrictive legal policies on heroin are self-defeating to the extent that they support the black market and drive addicts to habit-supporting crimes; that the physically handicapped do not, overall, become well integrated into the mainstream of American society. We cannot do without deviance because most of the stigmatized behaviors or conditions are ones that many people want to engage in, or need to engage in, or cannot help exhibiting, while at the same time the stigmatizing responses also appear to be deeply rooted at both social and psychological levels. What tends to emerge is a kind of implicit accommodation between these opposing desires or forces. In some respects, such accommodations represent society-level counterparts of the bargains struck or negotiated by individuals who face stigma — as when the homosexual compartmentalizes his work and leisure lives, as the price paid for being left alone; or when the blind person acts out a stereotypical blindness role in order to gain a degree of interpersonal acceptance. At the collective level, we find generalized arrangements through which deviantizing persists, yet that which is deviantized also persists — albeit only in prescribed forms and within accepted bounds. Deviance problems and deviating individuals thus are held in check, placed within limits, regulated. They are, in various ways, contained.

Modes of Containment

In discussing techniques a society or elite can use to cope with problematic populations, Spitzer (1975 p. 649) mentions, as one method, containment, by which he appears to have in mind primarily geographical segregation. As just suggested, however, when a broader notion of containment is adopted, it can be applied to virtually all deviance situations. To begin with, the very process of deviantizing, as described in chapter 1, represents and produces *social-psychological and moral containment*. Individuals are defined and treated in terms of the stigmatized category and are, as it were, contained within it. In the eyes of others, and sometimes even in their own eyes, they become primarily (or at an extreme, nothing but) prostitutes, drug addicts, thieves, or cripples. Since they are viewed as cases or instances of the disvalued category, rather than full human beings, numerous unwarranted assumptions are made about "the kinds of people" they are. These categorical responses by others leave them little room to step back from the discredited role and identity, and because stigma once imposed becomes extremely difficult to disavow the likelihood is stong that their "containment" will persist. "Once a thief, always a thief" and "I should have realized a queer would act like that" exemplify this encapsulation of the perceived deviant. As we noted, lowered self-esteem can easily result and, when it does, can in turn make breaking out of the containment all that much harder.

Most often, this kind of containment is accompanied by other kinds as well. *Interpersonal containment* occurs to the extent the offending person is shunned by "respectables" or "normals," declines in perceived value as a potential partner in everyday social interaction, and encounters imposed obstacles to participating in various social situations. In some respects, containment that involves only the moral, social-psychological, and interpersonal dimensions might seem less oppressive than other varieties (to be discussed in a moment). Yet the experience of persons who were born with or have acquired stigmatized physical or mental handicaps — who face none of the harsh legal reactions that confront more consciously condemned deviators — suggests that even these forms of containment will have a strong impact on the individual. From the standpoint of "normal" society, a major technique for containing the "problem" that the handicapped represent is avoidance. (See Scott 1969, pp. 26–38; also Edgerton 1967; and Goffman 1963.) This avoidance tendency dramatically affects the social contacts and activities of disabled persons. Limits on participation as well as strains on interaction are common. Thus one researcher reports: "Paraplegics and pre-trauma friends alike find it difficult to maintain their pre-trauma relationships" (Cogswell 1967, p. 21), and similarly Fred Davis's study of childhood polio victims revealed "a gradual, socially coerced process of downward mobility in the 'normal' peer group," with the child, following initial exclusion from peer activities, forming "a close friendship with another child whose status and acceptance in the group was also marginal" (F. Davis 1963, pp. 147, 148).

Typically, perceived deviants also experience some degree of *economic containment*. Certain instances of this are striking and widely recognized: for example, the difficulty exconvicts and former addicts face in obtaining legitimate employment and the more general tendency for criminal sanctions to simply reinforce, in the cases of many offenders, an already-existing situation of being locked into a poverty-and-crime cycle. But it is important to realize that the economic-life chances of other types of deviantized persons are also frequently impaired and restricted. While job discrimination against those with stigmatized handicaps can sometimes be rationalized in terms of literal disability, in other areas no such evasion is possible. For example, Humphreys reports:

> My research indicates that a disproportionately high number of male homosexuals find employment as hospital orderlies and technicians, travelling salesmen, retail sales clerks, short order cooks, and waiters. I doubt that gay men gravitate to these jobs because they enjoy changing bed linen, washing dishes, waiting tables, or stocking merchandise. The greater probability is that these are the only positions open to discreditable individuals. [Humphreys 1972, p. 34]

Acceptance of male homosexuals in stereotypically "gay" occupations (e.g., dancer, interior decorator, hairdresser) — to the extent it has permitted "straights" to maintain some avoidance in other realms of work — has served similar insulation and restriction functions. Early studies showed that covert homosexuals were more likely to hold high-status jobs than those who openly disclosed their sexual orientation (Leznoff and Westley 1956). As that may suggest, an important consequence of containment often is that it contains the deviation visually. *Visual containment*, obviously, abets the general avoidance tendency that permeates deviance-defining and permits supposed conformists to look the other way and sweep the problem under the rug. (Of course, in the case of homosexuality several of these tendencies are currently undergoing rapid change — partly through the impact of the gay liberation movement.)

Serving somewhat similar insulation-avoidance functions is the *geographical containment* of certain classes of deviantized individuals. In a sense, the placing of offending persons in prisons and mental hospitals can be seen to promote this out-of-sight, out-of-mind tendency. Furthermore, both the characteristic effort to locate such institutions in out-of-the-way settings and the resistance to release of former inmates into residential communities heighten the containment. Red-light districts in which prostitution is openly practiced, or X-rated zones set aside for the location and practice of various sexually oriented businesses (pornographic movies and bookstores, massage parlors, and the like) represent another type of geographical containment. Residential concentrations of deviators — much akin to the internal "colonization" (Blauner 1969) of blacks under racial segregation — can also occur. The main example would be the "gay ghetto" (Levine 1979) — the substantial concentration of homosexuals' residences and homosexually oriented businesses and services in particular neighborhoods in large American cities. While congregating of this sort no doubt serves to promote both convenience and congeniality within the gay community, it can hardly be treated as entirely a consequence of voluntary self-segregation. Whatever the degree to which exclusion elsewhere produces such a result, the containment effect — from the standpoint of the surrounding straight community — is obvious.

Beyond these modes of containment lie others that involve the imposition of even more-direct control on individual offenders. Various techniques *for pharmacological and electronic containment* are now being widely used to keep the behavior of many kinds of presumed deviators in check and within bounds. Those subjected to these unusual containment methods range all the way from "dangerous radicals" to "troublesome" schoolchildren, from "incorrigible" prisoners to alleged sexual deviators and the mentally ill. (See Schrag 1978; also Geiser 1976.) These mind-control techniques include administration of mood-altering drugs, electronic surveillance devices and schemes, different sorts of behavior-modification "therapy," and in extreme instances, psychosurgery.

Also very extreme, but more conventionally containing, is the *physical containment* produced by incarceration in prisons, mental hospitals, and other "total institutions." We touched earlier on some of the features of such treatment in connection with mental hospitalization, and we shall explore further some aspects of imprisonment in example 3, later in this chapter. At this point it should suffice to recall the themes of identity stripping and reconstituting and of depersonalization emphasized in the aforementioned writings of Goffman and Rosenhan. The all-enveloping round of life in total institutions makes for an almost-complete engulfment (one could also say, containment) in the inmate role. Severe depersonalization and objectification — classification even to the extent of becoming "a number" — makes for a potent form of social-psychological containment. This greatly heightens the direct impact of incarceration. For society at large, this mixture of physical and social-psychological aspects means that prisoners are kept out of the way, in strict confinement, under official authority, and with an imputed identity that is discredited and very difficult to disown. Collectively, one could even say, it amounts to construction of, and containment within, a prisoner class.

Before we look at a couple of specific examples in more detail, a few general comments about these several broad modes of containment may be in order. We can see that they vary considerably — in degrees of severity, and also in terms of physicality and completeness. Whereas all deviance-defining implies some moral, social-psychological, and interpersonal differentiation and containment, the other dimensions of containment arise, or are made use of, only in certain kinds of deviance situations. Both the nature and extent of the perceived threat and the corresponding groundings and intensity of the deviantizing reactions will contribute to these diverse containment pictures. We know, furthermore, that the most severe forms of containment usually appear, indeed are intentionally employed, in connection with what are in the dominant view the most serious deviance problems — although incarceration of nondangerous mental patients and even of the elderly and the drugging of schoolchildren show how specific instances tend to confound this apparent relation. Spitzer develops an interesting distinction between "social junk" — perceived deviance that a system or dominant class can treat as "a costly yet relatively harmless burden to society," and "social dynamite" — problematic conditions that are more acute, more volatile, and more directly threatening to the ruling elements (Spitzer 1975, pp. 645–646). He properly notes that the categories are not clear-cut and fixed. Shifting priorities of those in power, but also the extent of political activity on the part of the oppressed (whatever their substantive "deviance" is), may affect how a given "problem population" (to use Spitzer's pertinent term) will be treated. This suggests another point, to which much of the discussion throughout the rest of this book will be relevant. The general modes and numerous specific applications of containment will probably vary in the extent to which, and the ways that, they can be affected by intentional political efforts. Since each deviance situation will exhibit its distinctive mix of containment functions and will reveal as well a specific configuration of power elements and political forces, it's difficult to generalize about such outcomes. Most likely, however, no pattern of containment is totally or permanently immune to challenge or alteration through organized politicization.

EXAMPLE 3. *The Uneasy Containment of Prisoners*

The armed guard, the locked cell, the routine search for contraband, the fortresslike surroundings, constant surveillance and consistent depersonalization, a monotonous daily routine, an almost complete deprivation of freedom — for the individual prisoner, these are continuous reminders of his or her degraded status, imposed and sustained through the state's monopoly on the legitimate use of force. Although, theoretically, execution would be the ultimate in this use of force and the most total containment, moral and constitutional considerations are likely to keep the use of capital punishment in our society to a minimum (Bedau 1967; Black 1974), notwithstanding recent efforts to justify it by intellectual rationalizers of a punitive law-and-order backlash (van den Haag 1975, pp. 207–228; Berns 1979). Despite the regular insistence of specialists that a large proportion of those imprisoned need not be — from the standpoint of society's protection — and even in the face of considerable evidence that prisoners are not being rehabilitated (see below), such incarceration remains our society's ultimate response to what Spitzer calls social dynamite. While the recent policy trend has been to impose prison sentences in a smaller proportion of criminal convictions than in earlier years, rising crime rates during the same period have produced overall increases in the absolute numbers (and rates computed by proportion to the general population) of persons imprisoned (Scull 1977, chap. 3; Gottfredson et al 1978, pp. 628–631).

Imprisonment represents containment not merely in the sense that processed offenders are rigorously controlled and kept "out of circulation" — whatever that implies for public safety — but also in the sense that those on the outside are largely shielded from the very fact that control is being imposed and from direct awareness of the ways in which control is being administered. It is only through occasional public disclosures of prison conditions and through sporadic reporting of prison uprisings and incidents of violence that the general citizenry is exposed to direct knowledge of the harsh punishment being imposed in its name. An exceptional exposure of this sort came about through the 1971 rebellion at Attica prison — which, above all, highlighted the ultimate power wielding that supports imprisonment.

Forty-three citizens of New York State died at Attica Correctional Facility between September 9 and 13, 1971. Thirty-nine of that number were killed and more than 80 others were wounded by gunfire during the 15 minutes it took the State Police to retake the prison on September 13. With the exception of Indian massacres in the late 19th century, the State Police assault which ended the four-day prison uprising was the bloodiest one-day encounter between Americans since the Civil War. [New York State Special Commission on Attica 1972, p. xi]

That such incidents, however much temporary public furor they may provoke, do not lead to basic alterations in the system was illustrated by an official investigating team's finding that in 1976 conditions at Attica were then "just as bad, perhaps worse" than at the time of the rebellion. Describing a "combat situation," the investigators stated: "The environment is so physical, so potentially dangerous, the power of both the inmates and the guards is so awesome, that it can go off at any time. Both sides have the power of death in their hands" (quoted by Ferretti 1976, p. 1).

As this account suggests, the prison system is in large measure built around the structuring and manipulation of power, under conditions that always carry a substantial potential for the overt eruption of violence. Despite the awesome force at the disposal of corrections officials, the unwillingness of most persons to submit docilely and unequivocally to authoritarian control implies — along with several other basic and emerging obstacles to absolute control — that even in its most severe forms imprisonment remains a volatile, uneasy mode of containment. Sociologists have long recognized that the prison system, while placing a premium on power, at the same time implies limits on its use. As one classic study of a maximum-security prison noted:

The custodians of the New Jersey State Prison, far from being converted into brutal tyrants, are under strong pressure to compromise with their captives, for it is a paradox that they can insure their dominance only by allowing it to be corrupted. Only by tolerating violations of "minor" rules and regulations can the guard secure compliance in the "major" areas of the custodial

regime. . . . the custodians are led into a modus vivendi with
their captives which bears little resemblance to the stereotypical
picture of guards and their prisoners. [Sykes 1958, p. 58]

Such tendencies toward "corruption of authority" no doubt persist today, but they are often greatly restricted through official
scrutiny of internal power wielding in the prison. Studies emphasizing the "indigenous" social system within the prison have
somewhat given way to more complex analysis that takes account of outside influences and forces that affect prison life (Irwin 1977). Major currents of change in American society have
encouraged a much heightened political consciousness among
prisoners, and, increasingly, inmates have had contact with
specific outside groups working to politicize prison issues.
Under these circumstances, earlier views of the prison system
require modification:

> . . . the mutual accommodation between prisoners and guards is
> unstable because many prisoners know it is a sham. It is "mutual"
> only in a very limited sense . . . prisoners are still prisoners, and
> the "freedom" created by the modus vivendi in the prison is, to
> most prisoners, totally empty. An increasing number of prisoners
> see the "mutual" accommodation as another technique of pacify-
> ing the prison population, of manipulating the prisoner's condi-
> tion so that he accepts it and won't fight back. They see the
> modus vivdendi . . . as a device to keep prisoners from resisting
> their own oppression. With that realization, the modus vivendi
> within the prison becomes increasingly precarious. [Wright 1973,
> p. 145]

These developing perceptions reflect such influences as the
antiwar movement and student rebellions of the 1960s and particularly the growth of a militant black-power movement in the
wake of disenchantment regarding moderate civil rights efforts.
As noted earlier, such movements have provided general models
encouraging the politicization of a broad range of deviance issues. With respect to prisons, this indirect influence certainly
was present — raising questions about governmental legitimacy

and suggesting the value of civil disobedience and organized resistance. The relation between prisons and these outside movements, however, was a direct one as well. With the incarceration of large numbers of politicized persons, and as it became increasingly difficult for penal authorities to limit and censor outside contacts and communications, the ideological containment of prisoners (in an apolitical vacuum, as it were) was greatly weakened. As Jessica Mitford wrote in the early 1970s:

> A new and more sophisticated type of prisoner is entering the system: the civil disobedient, the collegiate narcotics user, the black and brown militant. These maintain links with radical organizations in their respective communities via smuggled letters, the good offices of sympathetic "free-world" prison employees (teachers, chaplains, etc.), illicit radical publications. [Mitford 1973, p. 233]

Political discussion and even political organizing increased — within as well as outside the prison walls; predictably, this increase led to countermeasures by correctional administrators, as seen in the common efforts to depict militant inmates as troublemakers, to isolate them in "administrative segregation" units, or to transfer them frequently from institution to institution.

According to many observers, the resulting polarization between prisoners and the prison authorities has been accompanied by a considerable decline in the internal interracial antagonisms and group cleavages that earlier had impeded prisoner solidarity (Pallas and Barber 1973; Mitford 1973, chap. 131; also Atkins and Glick 1972.) As a result of the influx of new political thinking, several major prison rebellions that occurred during the 1960s and early 1970s, and the growth of major efforts to organize prisoner unions — both locally and nationally — a radical prisoner movement of considerable dimensions has emerged. This movement has adopted goals, techniques, and rhetoric that differ sharply from the ones involved in the prison protests of the early 1950s. Those protests tended to center on the traditional demands for reform of specific prison conditions. The more recent militants have adopted a broader and more blatantly politicized stance — asserting that they have been collectively oppressed, treating the prison system as but part of a broader system of social, economic, and legal oppression, demanding their basic human rights, and in general challenging the legitimacy of imprisonment (Pallas and Barber 1973). As one observer states, furthermore: "With the legacy of the '50s fresh in their minds, today's prison organizers don't speak the same language as the prison reformists. The reason is simple. The reformers went to graduate school, and make a living at reform. The organizers went to prison, and learned to build strikes" (Browning 1972, p. 134).

This difference in thinking and rhetoric has been evident in the typical wording of demands and manifestoes issued during recent prison uprisings. Thus the "manifesto of demands and anti-oppression platform" disseminated during the 1970 Folsom, California, prison strike sought "an end to the injustice suffered by all prisoners, regardless of race, creed, or color," noted that the document had been prepared through "the unified efforts of all races and social segments of this prison," and proclaimed that "institutions which were designed to socially correct men" had been turned into "the facist [sic] concentration camps of modern America" (quoted in Pell 1973, pp. 177–178). Similarly, when inmates in New York City's Tombs prison rioted, their list of specific grievances (as in the Folsom strike) was accompanied by militant and far-reaching proclamations. For example: "We are firm in our resolve and we demand, as human beings, the dignity and justice that is due to us by right of our birth. We do not know how the present system of brutality and dehumanization has been allowed to be perpetuated in this day of enlightenment, but we are the living proof of its existence and we cannot allow it to continue [quoted by American Friends Service Committee 1971, pp. 5–6].

Also feeding into these changes in the nature of prison protest have been major social-scientific and legal developments, notably, recent reevaluations of correctional efforts and recent civil liberties activity in the area of prisoner rights. The general "unmasking of euphemism" mentioned in example 1 has not gone unnoticed or unused by prisoners and prison reform organizations. If most inmates already knew full well that rehabilitation was a sham, major research findings that documented the ineffectiveness of treatment programs (Lipton, Martinson, and Wilks 1975; Greenberg 1977) now serve as an authoritative resource for prisoner and, particularly, public education. Evidence of this kind supports the claim that even at its best the prison system represents "liberal totalitarianism" (Wright 1973, chap. 7)—that is, an evasive focus on "treating" individuals instead of on solving underlying social and economic problems and, basically, a demand for obedience to control and respect for public authority.

The fading reverence for—or lip service to—rehabilitation has led, however, in a number of different directions, the full political implications of which remain unclear. One somewhat hidden trend (masked, as we saw, by the rising rates of crime to which it applies) is deinstitutionalization or "decarceration"— the search for alternatives to imprisonment. "Diversion" schemes, and community-treatment programs have become the vogue, even if they do not yet threaten to replace the prison entirely. (Scull 1977; Lerman 1975; also Nejelski 1976) Critics see these approaches as but another mode of social control imposed by the state, one that is neither any more likely to rehabilitate nor any less likely to stigmatize and oppress. According to Scull, intensified fiscal pressures on the state during the 1960s and 1970s are largely responsible for the appeal of decarceration—in this area, as in that of mental illness. But as the same writer goes on to note, that appeal is bound to be a limited one: "Noninstitutional approaches are less immediately palatable when, instead of "sick" people, their object is criminals and delinquents. Incarceration, after all, has come to be virtually synonymous with punishment over the past century and a half; and the notion that lawbreakers deserve to suffer (i.e., be imprisoned) for their offenses is a belief not easily abandoned" (Scull 1977, p. 135). Because of such sentiment and other factors as well, the situated politics surrounding specific decarceration efforts and proposals — again, as in the case of diversion or release from mental hospitals — are bound to be complex. As we saw in example 1, the web of interests at stake in such matters is likely to be extensive. Those of local community residents, state and other funding units, and administrators of correctional institutions and alternative programs, as well as those of prisoners themselves and their legal and social science "allies," can all be involved.

Another development of recent import has been the attempt by neoconservative writers on crime (van den Haag 1975; Wilson 1975) to turn the social science disenchantment regarding rehabilitation into a call for sternly punitive policies explicitly based on retribution. (See discussion in Schur 1974; Curtis 1976; Silver 1976). Indeed, according to van den Haag, retributive punishment is "the payment of a debt to, at least as much as by, the offender," it is something society owes to the criminal and to itself and represents also "fairness to the law-abiding" (van den Haag 1975, pp. 15–17, 21). Furthermore, he asserts: "A criminal becomes unsuccessful inasmuch as he is punished. Rehabilitative efforts make sense only if offenses are made unrewarding, self-defeating, irrational, and ultimately painful. Only punishment can achieve this. Hence rehabilitation can follow, but it cannot take the place of punishment" (ibid. p. 191). And Wilson asserts, "Whatever they may do when they are released, they cannot harm society while confined or closely supervised" (Wilson 1975 p. 173). The widely read books of van den Haag and Wilson have been taken by many to reflect a new hard-headed realism about crime and punishment, despite the fact that both men almost totally ignore the role of poverty and racial oppression in shaping our society's crime problems. Their general message, that punishment is necessary and desirable even if it neither helps nor deters specific individuals, has an obvious appeal for law-and-order advocates and for politicians whose crime-fearing constituencies place them under pressure to advocate stringent policies.

Falling somewhere in between the liberal impulse toward decarceration and the blatant urge to retaliate that encourages a war-against-crime outlook, is the recently proclaimed "justice model" (von Hirsch 1976; also Morris 1974, chap. 3). Directly based on critiques of the total institution and on evidence indicating the failure to rehabilitate, this view particularly opposes the indeterminate sentence. The latter is a central element in the rehabilitative approach and also a key target of attack by prisoner and prison-reform organizations. The core of the justice-model proposals is the limiting of judicial-sentencing discretion by the establishment of fixed or "presumptive" sentences. Such sentences would be geared to a principle of "just desert": offenses would be ranked according to perceived seriousness, and punishments would vary in severity correspondingly. In some versions, the proposals also include complete abolition of parole. As can be seen, this approach rests too on the aforementioned findings indicating considerable public consensus on rankings of this sort. The political implications of this approach remain murky. Although part of the motivation behind it was to prevent excessive as well as arbitrary or discriminatory sentences, the organizing principle of fixed or limited-discretion sentencing has also found favor with those who advocate long sentences for the most serious offenses. It is not clear whether this result is primarily a co-optation of the justice model by conservative forces (Greenberg and Humphries, forthcoming) or whether instead it is mainly due to the approach's inherently apolitical or even conservative leanings. At any rate, early and recent statements of the justice concept differ greatly. Thus, the American Friends Service Committee's early critique of rehabilitation-based discretion insisted that "the construction of a just system of criminal justice in an unjust society is a contradiction in terms" (American Friends Service Committee 1971, p. 16). By contrast, the author of the final report of the Committee for the Study of Incarceration — a major justice-model statement — writes:

> That social injustice exists in America seems difficult to dispute; but how profoundly does it distort the essentials of the criminal law? Our earlier defense of the existence of punishment necessarily presupposes at least a partial acceptance of this society's laws: one that permits us to consider violators as, by and large, deserving of punishment. A radical social critic might well dispute our assumption and condemn this society and its criminal prohibitions as fundamentally and irretrievably unjust. But the logic of that position leads to opposing the existing institutions of punishment entirely — not to their defense on grounds other than desert. [von Hirsch 1976, p. 145]

The role of the prison and the merits of different modes of treatment continue to be debated by specialists. In particular, disputes concerning the place of psychiatry in correctional institutions bring an element of professional politics into the prison issue. The psychiatric view, as well as interest, in these matters is not all of one piece. Thus, while we do find considerable discussion and practice of diverse behavior-modification techniques in the prison system (Geiser 1976, chap. 3; also Speiglman 1977), socially conscious psychiatrists will oppose such methods and may even reject efforts at enforced value indoctrination of prisoners. One has gone so far as to suggest that a correctional system might even seek to help violent offenders "consider the extent to which they have been victimized. . . . learn about the social and political as well as the psychological causes of their violence" (Halleck 1975, p. 46).

Another development affecting the status and consequences of imprisonment has been the effort by civil liberties organizations to advance recognition of the constitutional rights of prisoners and exoffenders. A recent ACLU handbook notes:

The "hands-off policy" is now slowly being replaced by a judicial attitude that seeks to eliminate the major abuses suffered by prisoners. But despite substantial legal victories over the last decade, the prisoners' lot has improved, practically speaking, only with respect to major abuses and severe physical punishment. The erosion of the hands-off doctrine has hardly resulted in judicial activism. [Rudovsky et al. 1977, p. 12]

Another legal expert comments, "Time is short and growing shorter. Inmate expectations for some kind of reasonableness and fairness within prison are mounting, and these expectations simply cannot be met by federal judicial process" (Orland 1975, p. 151). That writer looks to the legislatures for an answer, but as yet another observer points out, "The legislature, like most political bodies, is skillful at appearing concerned and dedicated to resolving the problem, while at the same time endlessly delaying any meaningful change that might be controversial" (Smith 1973, p. 276).

The ACLU analysis makes clear that while there have been some real advances through court decisions regarding cruel and inhuman punishment, failure to provide adequate medical care, and infringements of procedural due process, in other matters — the right to privacy, free communication, and particularly the right to free political expression and association — inmates remain largely under the discretionary authority of prison officials. With respect to political freedom, "The courts have generally subordinated first amendment rights to the prison's determination that the speech or political activity threatened prison discipline or security" (Rudovsky et al. 1977, p. 70). A major setback came in a 1977 U.S. Supreme Court decision upholding a state regulation that prohibited prisoners from soliciting others to join a union and banned union meetings and bulk union mailings from outside sources. In that ruling, the Court held that "the state need only show a rational basis for interfering with the First Amendment rights of prisoners rather than the traditional compelling state interest" (ibid., p. 72). Decisions such as this one, together with the "widespread inmate fear of reprisals" (Huff 1977, p. 260) that understandably inhibits organizing and participation, make it unlikely that prisoner unionization will achieve significant force and legitimacy in the near future. Efforts to protect the rights of exprisoners — impaired by such legislated "civil disabilities" as restrictions on the right to vote, to hold political office, and to obtain an occupational or professional license, and by widespread employment discrimination — are summarized in a separate ACLU report as follows:

> The trend is the right way. States are reducing the number of disabilities applicable to ex-convicts and improving restoration devices; a few have adopted anti-discrimination statutes. But change has been difficult and slow and may continue to be so, even though current disabilities lack a defender and are criticized by scholars, study commissions, and anyone else who has taken an interest in the field. [Rudenstine 1979, pp. 154–155]

Although the legal advances of prisoners have not, then, been dramatic overall, each increment of favorable change sustains prisoner reform efforts in general, just as each major prison protest helps to publicize the need to further prisoner rights.

In the wake of all these diverse trends, the politics of imprisonment continues to reflect a multitude of forces and interests. This situation also reflects the complexity of our federal legal system (noted earlier), as the ACLU handbook on prisoner rights emphasizes:

> Each level of government operates independently of the others in administering its prisons and correctional apparatus. Thus, the Federal Government has no control over state corrections; the states have responsibility for prisons but usually no control over county or city jails; and the rules and regulations vary substantially from penal institution to penal institution. [Rudovsky et al. 1977, p. 15]

One study of the role of local political elites in connection with changes in their states' prison systems, revealed, furthermore, that "each state showed clusters of active groups peculiar to that state," and that "states differ in the coalitions dominating corrections issues" (Rossi and Berk 1977, p. 87). Apart from the crucial role of such elites as "gatekeepers" of change, a variety of socioeconomic interests may operate, generally or in local situations.

Theories asserting that overall trends in imprisonment reflect variations in the general state of the labor market (Rusche and Kirchheimer 1939; see also Krisberg 1975, chap. 4) are provocative but uncertainly applicable to all time periods and places. Some specific short-term economic interests can, however, be pinpointed. Thus, one recent news account referred to prison construction as "a growth industry" and stated:

> About 860 prison facilities are either under construction or in planning stages, reports *Corrections*, a trade magazine. Prison experts estimate that the new projects will cost some $5 billion — a sum that means business for contractors, architects, and equipment producers, who have been hard hit by the decline in school and public housing projects in recent years." [Luxenberg 1977]

At the same time, financially based resistance to liberalizing change is not restricted to capitalists. As Rudenstine (1979, p. 79) mentions, for example, "A comprehensive 1969 report prepared for the Manpower Administration of the U.S. Department of Labor reported that discrimination by labor unions seriously hindered the employment of ex-convicts." He cites as well a 1973 study, which revealed that whereas New York labor laws declare that apprentices in approved programs should be chosen on the basis of qualifications alone, they also require approved programs to obtain proof that applicants have no police records and to reject those who have been arrested (ibid., p. 80).

This raises the more general question of working-class interests in relation to prison issues. Since prisoners are drawn heavily from the ranks of the poor and of racial minorities, we might expect members of these constituencies on the outside to display solidarity with them and to advocate radical change. There is little evidence that this is happening. Low levels of sociopolitical awareness and the persistence outside the prison of interracial and interethnic cleavages combine with our society's individualist ethos (which prizes upward mobility above class consciousness) to militate against such cohesion. Furthermore, as numerous studies have revealed, these same segments of the population are among those most heavily and directly victimized by crime — especially crimes of interpersonal violence — and most fearful of it. Though it might be argued that ultimately even this victimization is at the hands of the ruling capitalists, who have driven working-class citizens to these acts of desperation, no widespread consciousness of this sort of relationship seems imminent in the United States. Mathiesen, in his discussion of prison organizing in Scandinavia, notes that one way in which protest groups can become a serious counterforce to official coercion is through coalition with outside political elements. Though several outside groups represent potential allies, he argues that "in the *last* analysis, the outside force must be the radical part of the working class — the class to which the prisoners belong, and with which the prisoners have concrete interests in common" (Mathiesen 1974, p. 177). In this country and at this stage, however, it would require an enormous collective leap toward heightened politicization for such a coalition to appear on any sizeable scale.

The problem of class solidarity is dramatically pointed up by the ambiguous situation of prison guards. Heavily drawn from the working and lower-middle classes (but predominantly white — in contrast to the inmate population, which in most large prisons is now heavily black), the guards might feel some overall identity of interests with the prisoners; yet their job situation dictates that they serve as "agents of the establishment." That phrase, however, oversimplifies their position, for the considerable recent growth of unions among the guards and their various strikes and job actions indicate that their position is not identical with that of higher officialdom, that the guards have interests of their own. Referring to his study of Stateville Penitentiary in Illinois, a leading student of guard unions notes, "By 1975 the prison had been transformed from a bipolar to a tripolar world, where prisoners, administration, and [guard] union competed for power" (Jacobs and Crotty 1978, p. vii; also see Jacobs 1977). Not surprisingly, some of the same factors that have encouraged prisoner militancy have also led guards to organize to advance their special interests. The influx of politicized inmates posed a direct threat to their authority and security. The long-term trend toward humanizing the prison as a "treatment" institution (even if recently challenged as euphemistic window-dressing) cast them into unaccustomed roles and subordinated them to a new class of professionally trained prison administrators and staff (Jacobs and Crotty 1978, pp. 6–8). Fiscal pressures on the state meant low pay in persistently dangerous and depressing work conditions.

A recent study compared the attitudes of black and white prison guards working in the Stateville and Joliet maximum-security prisons in Illinois (Jacobs and Kraft 1978). Blacks more than whites (67 percent versus 60) said they identified with the working class; blacks were also more likely (57 percent versus 25 percent of whites) to describe themselves as either "very" or "somewhat" liberal. Sixteen percent of blacks and 31 percent of white, however, said they were either "very" or "somewhat" conservative. Yet despite such differences, when the guards were questioned regarding their attitudes toward prisoners (75 percent of the combined inmate population in the two prisons was black, another 10 percent Latin) and the running of prisons, the responses of black and white guards did not differ greatly. If these findings are widely representative (and if working practices mirror reported attitudes), it seems unlikely that racial and ethnic democratization of the guard force will significantly alter the guard-inmate relation. The guard remains a classic example of the caught-in-the-middle "marginal man." At least as regards situated prison struggles or issues, the guards represent a third collective force that inevitably complicates the political picture.

We can expect that the continuing politics of imprisonment will be played out within a context that not only exhibits the many specific aspects mentioned so far but also reflects broad trends in American society at large. In an influential recent book, the French writer Foucault (1977) has argued that the secure total-surveillance and discipline-maintaining prison is in many respects a metaphor for the technological, bureaucratic, and depersonalizing kind of society we live in. (See also Schrag 1978.) It is characteristic of such a society that those who cause trouble are dealt with through isolation, classification (converted into "cases"), and all-enveloping control, and that specialized institutions and professions develop to serve these functions. Foucault also sees a close relation between these developments and the stratification and political structure of society, though his discussion of this point is rather murky. At any rate, whether there is something distinctive about modern capitalism that especially encourages this "carceral" system (as Foucault calls it) or whether instead it is likely to play a key role in all postindustrial societies, socialist as well as capitalist, the prison seems destined to be with us for some time to come. Those who seek to undermine its control will need to attain great strength if the social forces sustaining it are to be overcome.

EXAMPLE 4. *Prostitution: Social Ambivalence and the Facade of Control*

The prison is, of course, a general mode of containment. It is, literally a catch-all type, through which control is exerted over diverse kinds of troublemakers. Turning to the control of prostitution and prostitutes, we confront a different sort of example

—primarily, one of containing a specific deviance "problem," of controlling a particular category of perceived offenders. It is an example, furthermore, that points up the fact that containment need not be literal or physical. It can be "ambulatory" as well. As in the case of abortion (and, indeed, virtually all female "deviances"), prostitution is inextricably tied to—and, at a variety of levels and in numerous ways, reflects—the institutionalized sexism of our society. Both the prevalence of prostitution and the nature of public response to it reflect not only contemporary America's ambivalent evaluations of sexual behavior but also persisting uncertainty regarding the status of women. Dramatizing, in addition, an uneasy coexistence of America's commercial ethos and the recent trend toward being sexually "free," the prostitution issue presents a complex example of the politics of deviance—one in which all of the major dimensions of politicality (cited in chapter 1) are important.

From the standpoint of regulating prostitution overall, as a deplored, yet-ineradicable problem, the primary modes of containment—of which, more below—are geographical and visual. Public display and disturbance are to be kept to a minimum, so that avoidance possibilities can be maintained. As for the containment experienced by individual prostitutes, the major elements appear to be economic, social-psychological, and above all, "moral." These factors combine to produce the containment of prostitutes as a virtually distinctive class of women, social and morally debased, insulated from the world of "respectables," and with limited prospects for breaking out of the containment.

Prostitution illustrates the inevitable shortcomings of deviance research that assumes "deviants" to be basically different from "normals," and that focuses exclusively on supposed individual causes of deviance. Such an approach tends to neglect basics: "The primary cause of women becoming prostitutes is that there has existed a demand by men for sexual services which men pay well for and which, overwhelmingly, they have required be filled by women" (James et al. 1975, p. 43). We shall return shortly to some of the social groundings of this demand. But it is important to recognize that in one way or another, economic factors bring women into prostitution and keep them there. Current research does not consistently uphold the traditional stereotype of prostitutes "as wretched creatures forced into their profession by extreme economic deprivation"; at the same time, however, it seems clear that "most of the women choose prostitution as the occupational alternative that affords them the highest attainable standard of living" (James 1977, p. 389). Thus the social distribution of alternative job opportunities greatly affects entry into this type of work. Though the range of kinds of prostitutes is such that different situations reveal differing degrees of relative economic deprivation or financial disadvantage, it is nonetheless still true, as one exprostitute asserts, that "all prostitutes are in it for the money" (Millett et al. 1973, p. 55). For poor and minority women who participate in "the life" primarily at the streetwalker level and especially those who become indebted to, or even dependent on, pimps, the prospects for moving from prostitution to an equally lucrative "respectable" job are exceedingly slim. Even at the more affluent call-girl level, legitimate earning power does not usually keep pace with illegitimate. As one feminist commentary suggests, "When a woman decides, 'If you've ever been a clerk-typist, you'd rather be a prostitute,' we cannot annul her choice" (James et al. 1975, p. 4).

What may often represent a rational job choice in the face of limited options, produces however a work and life situation that relatively few women can accept with complete equanimity. At best, a "business, just like any other business" attitude and a compartmentalizing of work and leisure activities may help some of the better-situated prostitutes shield themselves from encapsulation in the debased role. Call girls studied by Bryan (1966) had been socialized into an ideology that may have served to lessen the stigma — one that emphasized the "service" they provide and their "useful social functions." By and large, though, the intrinsic nature of prostituting must almost invariably convey a pervading consciousness of social shame and personal powerlessness. It is true that for some prostitutes there may be a degree of positive reinforcement of self-esteem and independence provided by "making the man pay for it." But, as de Beauvoir (1953, chap. 19) has properly emphasized, this element of self-assertion is overwhelmed by the context of dependency and exploitation within which it occurs.

Because the woman is depersonalized and converted into a commercial object, the worst part of prostitution, according to one former practitioner, is selling "your human dignity . . . in accepting the agreement — in becoming a bought person." Furthermore, she goes on, "There's a special indignity in prostitution, as if sex were dirty and men can only enjoy it with someone *low*" (Millett et al. 1973, pp. 57, 58). Although one study of call girls failed to produce evidence in support of "the assumption that 'all whores hate men' " (Bryan 1965, p. 292), and relations with pimps (see Hall 1972; Milner 1973) must presumably be distinguished from those with customers ("johns"), relations with customers, at least, are unlikely to encourage a positive attitude toward males. One researcher, whose studies have revealed that a high proportion of prostitutes had engaged in homosexual activity, insists that the idea that latent homosexuality is a causal factor in becoming a prostitute is unwarranted: "Rather than motivating women to become prostitutes, homosexuality may be a result of being a prostitute" (James 1977, p. 400). Along with those intrinsic factors that breed low self-esteem and hostile outlooks, the prostitute finds herself scorned by "respectables," male and female, and assigned a stigma that seems ineradicable. On the difficulty of removing this stigma, the exprostitute quoted above comments: "It makes a kind of total state out of prostitution so that the whore is always a whore. It's as if — you did it once, you become it" (Millett et al. 1973, p. 65). More generally, these aspects combine to produce an overall containment in which "the sharing of a special alienation and distance from the conventional society forces the prostitute back to other prostitutes for her social life" (Gagnon and Simon 1973, p. 229).

If the intrinsic politics of prostitution center on the very act of submitting to the purchaser's buying power and being degraded through being bought, the everyday situated politics of prostitution tend to be dominated by police harassment — at least this is so for the streetwalker. Containment of prostitutes through imposed legal control is, of course, even more imperfect than containment of prisoners, though by the same token such efforts produce a much less incendiary situation. Because prostitution, like abortion, consists of a widely sought-after consensual transaction, laws seeking to curb it are in very large measure unenforceable (Schur 1965; Schur and Bedau 1974). The consequence, as one observer of the New York courts has noted, is that "prostitution is accepted by everyone — police, judges, clerks, and lawyers. Arrest and prosecution are purely gestures that have to be made to keep up the facade of public morality" (Millett et al. 1973, p. 143; see also Winick and Kinsie 1972, chap. 8). Routine street harassment, repeated revolving-door arrests followed by fines or brief jail sentences, and occasional crackdowns in particular areas, are the dominant law-enforcement responses to prostitution. Obviously, the brunt of this activity falls on the ordinary streetwalker much more than on the less visible, and probably already more-advantaged, call girl. Such efforts represent a substantial drain on limited criminal-justice resources.

> There are about 100,000 arrests a year for prostitution and related crimes. [There are estimates that] at least 30 percent of the population of most women's jails are convicted prostitutes; in New York they exceed 50 percent. A San Francisco study commission found that it cost San Francisco $375,000 to arrest 2,000 prostitutes and transport the women to the stationhouse. It also found that most were back working the streets soon after they were released. [Vorenberg 1977, p. 32]

Hardly any law-enforcement specialist asserts that efforts of this sort can significantly reduce prostitution. Thus, the police chief of one major American city has been quoted as admitting, "We can move it around, make it uncomfortable for the girls. My undercover officers make themselves available for solicitation, but this is not very effective. My uniformed officers make it uncomfortable for the customers. We have to react to complaints, but it's only street cosmetics" (quoted ibid.). It is widely recognized that police practices with respect to prostitution tend to be ethically and constitutionally questionable. Such a result follows directly from the difficulty of obtaining needed evidence in situations in which directly victimized citizen-complainants rarely come forth. One major study of the police (in a West Coast community) disclosed three major techniques used in antiprostitution enforcement: "the field-glass technique" — police surveillance aimed at detecting acts of intercourse in customers' parked cars; information from informers; and the decoy method — in which a "special employee," or sometimes a policeman, placed himself in a position to be solicited (Skolnick 1966, pp. 100–103). Quite apart from the risk that the use of decoys will go beyond acceptable constitutional limits and be ruled to have constituted "entrapment," this approach takes a heavy toll on police morale. Skolnick found that

> the police recognize the element of bad faith and trickery involved in such deceptive interactions. . . . in describing their enforcement activities regarding prostitution, they emphasize the less successful enforcement technique of surveillance. Thus, although all of the policemen interviewed maintained that surveillance accounted for by far the highest proportion of arrests, in fact, solicitations accounted for 56 percent. . . . In addition, policemen in conversation indicated a certain uneasiness regarding solicitation arrests, varying of course from individual to individual. [ibid., p. 102]

The unsavory nature of antiprostitution tactics was underlined in a 1976 New York City incident in which the Manhattan district attorney's office refused to make use of evidence obtained by private investigators hired by a "midtown cleanup" task force. These investigators had been hired by the task force to circumvent the difficulty presented by a police department regulation prohibiting officers from disrobing while on duty — prostitutes were unwilling to say or do anything incriminating until the patron had undressed. In declining to follow through on cases initiated by the private investigators, an assistant district attorney said, "The practice of using private investigators to perform sexual acts as a way to get evidence [was] 'offensive to high standards of law enforcement,' and he stated, 'I would not present a case to a grand jury based on that type of evidence' " (Meislin 1976). Presumably because of such obstacles to prosecuting directly for prostitution, statutes imposing a less rigid standard of proof — such as New York State's controversial "loitering" law — receive some support from police and prosecutors.

The New York statute was passed in July 1976 just before the Democratic National Convention began in New York City. It rather loosely defined as an offense certain types of loitering "for the purpose of prostitution, or of patronizing a prostitute." Although challenged as unconstitutionally vague, a challenge that was upheld in one lower-court ruling, in June 1978 it was finally ruled constitutional by the state's highest court (Goldstein 1978). The expanded civil liberties danger posed by such vague measures was pointed up by at least two subsequent incidents: one in which a church worker who often counselled prostitutes was mistakenly arrested for prostitution, arraigned, and held overnight; another in which a twenty-five-year-old woman employed by a New York publishing firm asserted that while walking home from a late movie she had been arrested for prostitution by police, who allegedly dragged her through the street by her hair. Both incidents produced considerable publicity and led to sizeable damage suits against officials *(New York Times,* July 27, 1978, p. 32). Suggesting that "Americans pay a heavy price for pitting the police against the prostitutes," two observers note additional ways in which antiprostitution laws add to the supposed problem rather than control it:

Many women, needing protection against the law enforcement system and illegal violence, turn to pimps. The police can permit prostitutes to do business in return for bribes of money or sexual services. Since the sexual transaction is outlawed, the customer is also without police protection and rarely will report theft or extortion. The police are given an assignment at which they must fail; thus they become the objects of contempt and hostility from the community that are matched only by what the prostitutes themselves feel. [Vorenberg 1977, p. 37]

A final significant point regarding laws against prostitution should be noted: the grossly unequal enforcement of the laws directed at prostitutes and those directed at their customers. One report notes:

Unequal enforcement is prevalent throughout the country. For instance, although patronizing a prostitute is a crime in New York City, 1972 arrests for prostitution were more than one hundred times greater than were arrests for patronizing a prostitute. . . . During the same year in Seattle, Washington, where the law is facially neutral, 620 women — and only 41 men — were arrested on prostitution charges." (James et al. 1975, p. 29)

Liz Schneider, an observer of New York antiprostitution policies, even concluded from this singling-out of the female participant for sanctioning that "there's no clearer indication than prostitution that all women are a potential species of social or political prisoner" (Millett et al. 1973, p. 146). In 1978 the New York legislature passed a special provision (the "john law") increasing the minimum charge for patronizing a prostitute from a violation to a misdemeanor, subjecting patrons to the same penalties as prostitutes, and requiring also that customers be fingerprinted, photographed, and booked upon arrest (Meislin 1978). Around the same time, the police in New York City assigned decoy plainclothes policewomen to patrol midtown Manhattan streets on the lookout for men seeking prostitutes (Raab 1978). What the primary result of such efforts will be — a reduction of sexism in law enforcement, or simply an expansion of questionable entrapment techniques — remains unclear. The practice of having New York's municipal radio station broadcast the names of convicted customers of prostitutes—suggested by Mayor Edward Koch, and begun in October of 1979 — generated considerable controversy. *(New York Times,* Oct. 26, 1979, p. A30) Notwithstanding these recent developments, at the time of this writing the prospects for a significant change in the overall pattern of discriminatory enforcement do not seem great.

These enforcement differentials suggest a broader social dimension of the prostitution issue, one, however, that the general public is considerablely less aware of. It consists of prostitution's "institutional politics," or what in this instance might be referred to as its gender politics. As stated above, in the case of prostitution both the perceived deviance and our reactions to it are deeply grounded in social and moral ambivalence regarding sexuality and the roles of women. At virtually all levels, prostitution and antiprostitution attitudes and policies display outlooks and male-female differentials of the sort that are so common generally in a sexist society. In considering the intrinsic nature of prostitution, we saw that the relative power positions of men and women are central to it. If we look more specifically at the arrangements through which prostitution as a business is conducted in American society, we find that on this basis too it constitutes "an extreme case of sex stratification" (Heyl 1979).

Thus Heyl notes various aspects of the "dominance of prostitution by males," basically through their control over the conditions under which women will work in this occupation. She points out that this control includes "men's ability to arrest the prostitute, to take a systematic 'cut' (or even all) of her earnings, or to provide her with a necessary set of business arrangements (a setting, a 'front,' or a steady well-paying clientele)" (ibid., p. 200). Police, pimps, businessmen who employ prostitutes, and clients are all almost exclusively male; the control they exert involves, respectively, political power, physical and psychological power, economic power, and consumer power. As Heyl goes on to show, the types of power wielding and power wielders to which a prostitute is most likely to be subjected vary according to her position in the stratified prostitution system. Streetwalkers have to deal primarily with police and pimps; middle-range prostitutes (in houses, massage parlors, hotels and so forth) are subject to the power of "fringe" businessmen as well as pimps; independent call girls and "party girls" are largely dependent on legitimate, even top level businessmen, who arrange contacts (with their out-of-town buyers, for example) and ensure a steady clientele. Of this highest level in the prostitute ranking, Heyl comments:

> In one sense, the call girl with strong business ties has traded her pimp for the businessman. It is an improvement. Her money is her own. But he provides the clients and is thus a pimp in the older, "procurer" meaning of the term. He can cut her off when she no longer pleases him; and for each client she sees for him, he gains, perhaps in vast sums of money for his business, while she earns her salary or is simply paid for seeing the one man. The legitimate businessman benefits from prostitution but avoids its stigma, while the prostitute is vulnerable to the penalties — socially and legally — for what she does. [Heyl 1979, p. 208]

At all levels of prostitution, Heyl concludes, "all the males win, and only the women pay the costs."

Even further removed from the general public consciousness, although it is basic to the sexism surrounding prostitution, is the relation of prostitution to other socially institutionalized arrangements and outlooks regarding sexuality and marriage. Here we see a dramatic illustration of the "mirror image" aspect of deviance noted in the opening chapter. Influential writers representing such diverse viewpoints as those of Marxian socialism (Engels 1884, 1942), sociological "functionalism" (K. Davis 1937), existential philosophy (de Beauvoir 1953), and contemporary feminism (Millett et al. 1973) have argued that an essential and similar element of economic exchange characterizes both prostitution and modern marriage, that the difference between the two is largely one of degree. This widespread recognition and the fact that prostitutes themselves emphasize the same point (Strong 1970; Millett et al. 1973; also Bryan 1966), suggest that the analogy does not rest solely on a particular political ideology. Perhaps the classic statement, however, is that of Engels, who asserted that bourgeois marriage "turns often enough into crassest prostitution — sometimes of both partners, but far more commonly of the woman, who only differs from the ordinary courtesan in that she does not let out her body on piece-work as a wage-worker, but sells it once and for all into slavery" (Engels 1884, 1942, p. 63). Expanding on this general theme, the authors of a recent feminist-oriented essay on prostitution state:

> This demand which fosters prostitution occurs because of the way in which men and women have been taught to view themselves and members of the opposite sex. Men have been socialized to view sex as a commodity that can be purchased for a twenty-dollar bill and quantity of sexual partners has been more highly valued in the male culture than has been the quality of each experience. Women's training has socialized them to supply the other half of this sexual equation. They have been conditioned to view themselves as sexual objects long before junior high school and encouraged to exchange attractiveness (or sexuality) for things like engagement rings or popularity. While the message is that "good girls" subtly exchange sex, women nevertheless view their bodies as salable. [James et al. 1975, p. 43]

Or, as another writer has remarked, "From the time a girl is old enough to go to school, she begins her education in the basic principles of hustling." (Strong 1970, p. 290)

A subtle indicator of the extent to which the cash nexus colors male-female relationships and the dominant ways of evaluating women in our society is the use of the designation "cheap." Presumably, reference to a woman as being cheap refers to a flashy display of overt sexuality—in clothing, makeup, demeanor, and to (inferred) sexual "promiscuity." Yet the direct opposite of cheap would seem to be "expensive." The implication, therefore, is that the offense of the so-called cheap woman is primarily an economic one—she doesn't prize her sexual favors *highly enough.* Our ambivalence about the meaning of woman's sexuality is clear from the fact that sexual display, at least up to a point, is actively promoted by movie stars and models and in the advertising of cosmetics and clothes that permeates our society. That there is a limit beyond which this sexual display should not go or will no longer be viewed as respectable is perhaps signified by the stereotypical attire, speech usage, and body language of prostitutes and other nonrespectables, such as strippers, go-go dancers, and (on the sociomoral borderline) cocktail waitresses. And the fact that "cheap" or "promiscuous" are not applied in the same way to men (if men are called cheap, this usually, in fact, refers to the purchasing role in economic exchange) shows, furthermore, how the meaning of prostitution is crucially tied up with the waning yet still strong double standard regarding sexual behavior. As numerous sociologists have noted, the double standard is really a "double-double" standard—since for men to be allowed greater (premarital or extramarital) sexual freedom than women requires that there be a category of "bad women" with whom they can exercise this freedom. While this good-bad dichotomy is no doubt becoming increasingly blurred over along with a general lessening of sexual restriction and suppression, it is far from being eliminated completely. The prostitute remains a hostage to such ambivalence, a scapegoat for our uneasiness about sex and our dominant sexual arrangements.

Recent feminist efforts to come to grips with such complexities have helped to produce a (limited) politicizing of prostitution. At the same time, however, as one account notes, "The way in which prostitutes perceive their profession and the way they are treated under the law, compounded by how 'straight' people (including feminists) see prostitutes, has presented the women's movement with a complicated and controversial issue" (James et al. 1975, p. 74). Kate Millett describes a 1971 feminist conference on prostitution in which latent hostility between prostitutes (who felt they were being condescendingly treated as a problem to be analyzed and dealt with) and straight women was continuously brewing and eventually erupted into an open clash: "The accusation, so long buried in liberal rhetoric — 'you're selling it, I could too but I won't' — was finally heard" (Millett et al. 1973, p. 25). Quite apart from the fact that even feminists have long been exposed to traditional attitudes and ambivalences, prostitution continues to pose a distinct dilemma for the women's movement. On the one hand, the prostitutes are seen as women deserving of support — sisters who are being maligned, harassed, and generally ill-treated; on the other hand, prostitution is in a sense the epitome of the system that makes objects and commodities of women, a system that feminists totally oppose as constituting the core of sexism. Since the 1971 conference, groups and organizations within the women's movement appear to have worked out a way of confronting the dilemma — namely, by favoring decriminalization of prostitution in the short run (instead of legal regulation, a complete removal of the practice from legal control); and in the long run, looking to a major reduction in prostitution, once institutionalized sexism has been overcome. This dual position is seen in a resolution passed by the International Tribunal on Crimes Against Women:

> Be it resolved that sexual acts in private between consenting adults shall be outside the purview of the criminal laws, that commercial sexual activities be recognized as a service business, not as a criminal act, and that it be treated as such, that women

be as free to walk and converse on the streets of the world as men. All laws that discriminate against such activity by statute or by enforcement shall be eliminated, that women who choose to be prostitutes do so of their own free will after the age of consent and that no coercion by anyone be tolerated. That prostitution be recognized as dependent on a repressive sexist socialization that can eventually be changed. Women and men who are free from sexual stereotypes and economic discrimination will be free from commercial sexual exchange. [Russell and Van de Ven 1976, p. 196]

In recent years several organizations of prostitutes and those favoring changes in prostitution law have been formed. (See James et al. 1973, chap. 5). The best known is a national organization, COYOTE (Call Off Your Old Tired Ethics); local groups include ASP (Association of Seattle Prostitutes), PONY (Prostitutes of New York), CAT (California Association of Trollops), and PUMA (Prostitute Union of Massachusetts Association). The droll guerilla-theatre style of these groups (as per the acronyms, the sponsoring of an annual Hookers Convention and Hookers Ball, presentation of Trick of the Year, and Vice Cop of the Year awards, and so on) may have limited the extent to which they have been taken seriously as a political force. They have served useful morale-enhancing and practical-assistance functions for prostitutes and have done quite a bit of educational and lobbying work. Efforts to strengthen and build upon this preliminary network face some serious obstacles. The ambivalence within even the women's movement suggests this problem, and there is likewise little reason to assume that working-class solidarity (even among females, let alone more generally) could readily be mobilized in behalf of the predominantly poor streetwalkers. In fact, surveys often show that working-class respondents are considerably more conservative on issues of this sort than their middle-class counterparts. Finally, it has to be noted that prostitutes as a group are not notable for political activism nor even for displaying much social solidarity among themselves. One feminist sociologist has criticized certain male researchers for commenting on this lack of solidarity, arguing that such comments reflect male stereotyping of women (Millman 1975, pp. 260–261), but the fact that female researchers also regularly find prostitute solidarity to be low (Heyl 1979; Milner 1973; also Millett et al. 1973) seems to belie this interpretation.

At any rate, there is at present no powerful and cohesive large-scale coalition challenging the sociomoral and legal treatment of prostitution, although feminist groups, civil liberties organizations, and prostitutes' organizations all contribute to efforts for change. In specific controversies, for instance a proposal for a legislative change in a particular jurisdiction (Roby 1969), or the long-term and fluctuating campaign to clean up a specific neighborhood—as in the case of New York City's Times Square area (see Carroll 1976), localized influences come into play. Spokespersons for various kinds of local organizations and localized interests (including law-enforcement interests, social welfare interests, realty and other local business interests, and general community interests) will seek and sometimes wield decisive power. There is, in other words, a highly "situated" politics of prostitution which proceeds apace, in numerous local settings—at the same time that broader efforts to reshape the society's dominant outlooks and social patterns are occurring.

Overall, the major sociolegal trend toward decriminalization of borderline offenses (see Schur and Bedau 1974), and perhaps as well the more general trend often labeled the "sexual revolution," seem to promise some degree of eventual success for the advocates of new approaches to prostitution. In the meantime, however, it is hardly open to dispute that prostitutes remain a morally and socially contained class.

References

Altman, Dennis. 1973. *Homosexual: Oppression and Liberation.* New York: Avon.

American Friends Service Committee, 1971. *Struggle for Justice.* New York: Hill and Wang.

Atkins, Burton M., and Henry R. Glick, eds. 1972. *Prisons, Protest, and Politics.* Englewood Cliffs, N.J.: Prentice-Hall.

Balbus, Issac D. 1977. *The Dialectics of Legal Repression.* New Brunswick, N.J.: Transaction Books.

Bedau, Hugo Adam, ed. 1967. *The Death Penalty in America.* Garden City, N.Y.: Doubleday, Anchor Books.

Berns, Walter. 1979. *For Capital Punishment.* New York: Basic Books.

Black, Charles L., Jr. 1974. *Capital Punishment.* New York: W.W. Norton & Co., Inc.

Blauner, Robert. 1969. "Internal Colonialism and Ghetto Revolt." *Social Problems* 16 (spring): 393–408.

Browning, Frank. 1972. "Organizing Behind Bars." In Atkins and Glick, eds., *Prisons, Protest, and Politics.* Englewood Cliffs, N.J.: Prentice-Hall. Pp. 132–139.

Bryan, James H. 1965. "Apprenticeships in Prostitution." *Social Problems* 12 (winter): 287–297.

Bryan, James H. 1966. "Occupational Ideologies and Individual Attitudes of Call Girls." *Social Problems* 13 (spring): 441–450.

Carroll, Maurice. 1976. "Times Square Cleanup: Breach of Civil Liberties?" *New York Times*, November 15, p. 35.

Cogswell, Betty E. 1967. "Rehabilitation of the Paraplegic: Processes of Socialization." *Sociological Inquiry* 37 (winter): 11–26.

Connor, Walter D. 1972. *Deviance in Soviet Society.* New York: Columbia University Press.

Curtis, Lynn A. 1976. "The Conservative New Criminology." *Society* 14 (March-April): 8, 14–15.

Davis, Fred. 1963. *Passage Through Crisis.* Indianapolis: Bobbs-Merrill.

Davis, Kingsley. 1937. "The Sociology of Prostitution." *American Sociological Review* 2 (October): 746–755.

de Beauvoir, Simone. 1953. *The Second Sex.* New York: Knopf.

Domhoff, G. William. 1971. *The Higher Circles.* New York: Vintage.

Douglas, Jack D., and John M. Johnson, eds. 1977. *Official Deviance.* Philadelphia: J.B. Lippincott.

Edelman, Murray. 1977. *Political Language.* New York: Academic Press.

Edgerton, Robert B. 1967. *The Cloak of Competence.* Berkeley: University of California Press.

Engels, Friedrich. 1884, 1942. *The Origin of the Family, Private Property, and the State.* New York: International Publishers.

Erikson, Kai T. 1966. *Wayward Puritans.* New York: John Wiley.

Ferreti, Fred. 1976. "Attica Is Termed as Bad as Before 1971 Rebellion." *New York Times*, July 21, pp. 1, 53.

Foucault, Michel. 1977. *Discipline and Punish.* New York: Pantheon.

Gagnon, John H., and William Simon. 1973. *Sexual Conduct.* Chicago: Aldine.

Gamson, William A. 1968. *Power and Discontent.* Homewood, Ill.: Dorsey Press.

Garfinkel, Harold. 1964. "Studies of the Routine Grounds of Everyday Activities." *Social Problems* 11 (winter): 225–250.

Geiser, Robert L. 1976. *Behavior Mod and the Managed Society.* Boston: Beacon Press.

Goffman, Erving. 1963. *Stigma.* Englewood Cliffs, N.J.: Prentice-Hall.

Goldstein, Tom. 1978. "New York Appeals Court Upholds Law to Reduce Street Prostitution." *New York Times*, June 16, pp. 1, 19.

Gottfredson, Michael et al., eds. 1978. *Sourcebook of Criminal Justice Statistics — 1977.* Washington, D.C.: Government Printing Office.

Greenberg, David F. 1977. "The Correctional Effects of Corrections: A Survey of Evaluations." In Greenberg, ed., *Corrections and Punishment.* Beverly Hills, Calif.: Sage Publications, Inc. Pp. 111–145.

Greenberg, David F., and Drew Humphries. "The Cooptation of Fixed Sentencing Reform," *Crime and Delinquency*, forthcoming.

Hall, Susan. 1972. *Gentlemen of Leisure.* New York: Signet.

Halleck, Seymour L. 1975. "A Multi-Dimensional Approach to Violence." In Duncan Chappel and John Monahan, eds., *Violence and Criminal Justice.* Lexington, Mass.: Heath. Pp. 33–47.

Halperin, Morton H. et al. 1976. *The Lawless State*. New York: Penguin.

Heyl, Barbara. 1979. "Prostitution: An Extreme Case of Sex Stratification." In Freda Adler and Rita James Simon, eds., *The Criminology of Deviant Women*. Boston: Houghton Mifflin Co. Pp. 196–212.

Huff. C. Ronald. 1977. "Prisoner Militancy and Politicization." In Greenberg, ed., *Corrections and Punishment*. Beverly Hills, Calif.: Sage Publications, Inc. Pp. 247–264.

Humphreys, Laud. 1972. *Out of the Closets: The Sociology of Homosexual Liberation*. Englewood Cliffs, N.J.: Prentice-Hall.

Irwin, John. 1977. "The Changing Social Structure of the Men's Prison." In Greenberg, ed., *Corrections and Punishment*. Beverly Hills, Calif.: Sage Publications, Inc. Pp. 21–40.

Jacobs, James B. 1977. *Stateville*. Chicago: University of Chicago Press.

Jacobs, James B., and Norma Meacham Crotty. 1978. *Guard Unions and the Future of the Prisons*. Ithaca, N.Y.: New York State School of Industrial and Labor Relations.

Jacobs, James B., and Lawrence J. Kraft. 1978. "Integrating the Keepers: A Comparison of Black and White Prison Guards in Illinois." *Social Problems* 25 (February): 304–318.

James, Jennifer. 1977. "Prostitutes and Prostitution." In Edward Sagarin and Fred Montranino, eds., *Deviants: Voluntary Actors in a Hostile World*. Morristown, N.J.: General Learning Press. Pp. 368–428.

James, Jennifer et al. 1975. *The Politics of Prostitution*. Seattle: Social Research Associates.

Jay, Karla, and Allen Young, eds. *Out of the Closets: Voices of Gay Liberation*. New York: Harcourt Brace Jovanovich.

Krisberg, Barry. 1975. *Crime and Privilege*. Englewood Cliffs, N.J.: Prentice-Hall.

Lehman, Edward W. 1977. *Political Society: A Macrosociology of Politics*. New York: Columbia University Press.

Lerman, Paul. 1975. *Community Treatment and Social Control*. Chicago: University of Chicago Press.

Levine, Martin P. 1979. "Gay Ghetto." In Levine, ed., *Gay Men*. New York: Harper & Row, Pub. Pp. 182–204.

Leznoff, Maurice, and William A. Westley. 1956. "The Homosexual Community." *Social Problems* 3 (April): 257–263.

Lindesmith, Alfred R. 1965. *The Addict and the Law*. Bloomington: Indiana University Press.

Lipton, Douglas; Robert Martinson; and Judith Wilks. 1975. *The Effectiveness of Correctional Treatment*. New York: Praeger.

Loney, Martin. 1973. "Social Control in Cuba." In Ian Taylor and Laurie Taylor, eds., *Politics and Deviance*. Baltimore: Penguin. Pp. 42–60.

Luxenberg, Stan. 1977. "Crime Pays—A Prison Boom." *New York Times*, July 17, p. C1.

Mathiesen, Thomas. 1974. *The Politics of Abolition*. New York: John Wiley.

Meislin, Richard J. 1976. "Prostitution Inquiry Tactics Scored as Too Disgusting for Grand Jury." *New York Times*, December 2, p. 47.

Meislin, Richard J. 1978. "Carey Signs Bill Raising Sentences for Pimps and Prostitute's Patrons." *New York Times*, July 29, pp. 1, 22.

Millett, Kate et al. 1973. *The Prostitution Papers*. New York: Avon.

Millman, Marcia. 1975. "She Did it All for Love: A Feminist View of the Sociology of Deviance." In Millman and Rosabeth Moss Kanter, eds., *Another Voice*. Garden City, N.Y.: Doubleday, Anchor Books. Pp. 251–279.

Mills, C. Wright. 1957. *The Power Elite*. New York: Oxford University Press.

Milner, Christina, and Richard. 1973. *Black Players*. New York: Bantam.

Mitford, Jessica. 1973. *Kind and Usual Punishment*. New York: Knopf.

Morris, Norval. 1974. *The Future of Imprisonment*. Chicago: University of Chicago Press.

Nejelski, Paul. 1976. "Diversion: Unleashing the Hound of Heaven?" In M. Rosenheim, ed., *Pursuing Justice for the Child*. Chicago: University of Chicago Press. Pp. 94–118.

New York State Special Commission on Attica. 1972. *Attica: The Official Report*. New York: Bantam.

O'Connor, James. 1973. *The Fiscal Crisis of the State*. New York: St. Martin's Press.

Orland, Leonard. 1975. *Prisons: Houses of Darkness.* New York: Free Press.

Pallas, John, and Robert Barber. 1973. "From Riot to Revolution." In Erik Olin Wright, *The Politics of Punishment.* New York: Harper, Colophon Books. Pp. 237–261.

Pell, Eve. ed. 1973. *Maximum Security: Letters from Prison.* New York: Bantam.

Quinney, Richard. 1974. *Critique of Legal Order.* Boston: Little, Brown.

Quinney, Richard. 1977. *Class, State and Crime.* New York: D. McKay.

Raab, Selwyn. 1978. "Women Officers Arresting Men Seeking Prostitutes." *New York Times,* July 4, p. 8.

Reiwald, Paul. 1949. *Society and its Criminals.* Translated by T. James. London: William Heinemann.

Roby, Pamela A. 1969. "Politics and Criminal Law: Revision of the New York Penal Law on Prostitution." *Social Problems* 17 (summer): 83–109.

Rossi, Peter H., and Richard A. Berk. 1977. "The Politics of State Corrections." In Greenberg, ed., *Corrections and Punishment.* Beverly Hills, Calif.; Sage Publications, Inc. Pp. 69–88.

Rudenstine, David. 1979. *The Right of Ex-Offenders.* New York: Avon.

Rudovsky, David et al. 1977. *The Right of Prisoners.* New York: Avon.

Rusche, Georg, and Otto Kirchheimer. 1939. *Punishment and Social Structure.* New York: Columbia University Press.

Russell, Diana E.H., and Nicole Van de Ven, eds. 1976. *Crimes Against Women: Proceedings of the International Tribunal.* Millbrae, Calif.: Less Femmes.

Schrag, Peter. 1978. *Mind Control.* New York· Pantheon.

Schur, Edwin M. 1965. *Crimes Without Victims.* Englewood Cliffs, N.J.: Prentice-Hall.

Schur, Edwin M. 1969. *Our Criminal Society.* Englewood Cliffs, N.J.: Prentice-Hall.

Schur, Edwin M. 1974. "Crime and the New Conservatives." In Irving Howe, ed., *The New Conservatives.* New York: Quadrangle/The N.Y. Times. Pp. 228–242.

Schur, Edwin M. 1979. *Interpreting Deviance*. New York: Harper & Row, Pub.

Schur, Edwin, M., and Hugo Adam Bedau. 1974. *Victimless Crimes*. Englewood Cliffs, N.J.: Prentice-Hall.

Scott, Robert A. 1969. *The Making of Blind Men*. New York: Russell Sage Foundation.

Scott, Robert A. 1972. "A Proposed Framework for Analyzing Deviance as a Property of Social Order." In Scott and Jack D. Douglas, eds., *Theoretical Perspectives on Deviance*. New York: Basic Books. Pp. 9–35.

Scull, Andrew T. 1977. *Decarceration*. Englewood Cliffs, N.J.: Prentice-Hall.

Silver, Isidore. 1976. "Crime and Conventional Wisdom." *Society* 14 (March-April): 9, 15–19.

Silver, Isidore, ed. 1974. *The Crime-Control Establishment*. Englewood Cliffs, N.J.: Prentice-Hall.

Skolnick, Jerome H. 1966. *Justice Without Trial*. New York: John Wiley.

Smith, James F. 1973. "Prison Reform Through the Legislature." In Erik Olin Wright, *The Politics of Punishment*. New York: Harper, Colophon Books. Pp. 262–280.

Spector, Malcolm, and John I. Kitsuse. 1977. *Constructing Social Problems*. Menlo Park, Calif.: Cummings.

Speiglman, Richard. 1977. "Prison Drugs, Psychiatry, and the State." In Greenberg, ed., *Corrections and Punishment*. Beverly Hills, Calif.: Sage Publications, Inc. Pp. 149–167.

Spitzer, Steven. 1975. "Toward a Marxian Theory of Deviance." *Social Problems* 22 (June): 638–651.

Strong, Ellen. 1970. "The Hooker." In Robin Morgan, ed., *Sisterhood is Powerful*. New York: Vintage. Pp. 289–297.

Sykes, Gresham M. 1958. *Society of Captives*. Princeton: Princeton University Press.

Taylor, Ian; Paul Walton; and Jock Young. 1974. *The New Criminology*. New York: Harper, Torchbooks.

van den Haag, Ernest. 1975. *Punishing Criminals*. New York: Harper, Colophon Books.

von Hirsch, Andrew. 1976. *Doing Justice*. New York: Hill and Wang.

Vorenberg, Elizabeth, and James. 1977. " 'The Biggest Pimp of All': Prostitution and Some Facts of Life." *The Atlantic*, January, 27–38.

Wald, Patricia M. et al. 1972. *Dealing with Drug Abuse.* New York: Praeger.

Wilson James, Q. 1975. *Thinking about Crime.* New York: Basic Books.

Wilson, John. 1977. "Social Protest and Social Control." *Social Problems* 24 (April): 469–481.

Winick, Charles, and Paul M. Kinsie. 1972. *The Lively Commerce.* New York: Signet.

Wise, David. 1973. *The Politics of Lying.* New York: Vintage.

Wright, Erik Olin. 1973. *The Politics of Punishment.* New York: Harper, Colophon Books.

3
chapter

The Struggle to Define

" . . . we do not first see, then define, we define first and then see. . . ."

Walter Lippmann,
Public Opinion *(1922)*

MANIPULATING MEANING

Deviance, we have noted, is essentially a matter of definition. For the most part, stigma is not inherent in or automatically attached to the behaviors and conditions that come to be treated as socially problematic. Rather, these behaviors and conditions acquire their deviantness — which is usually a matter of degree — through a defining-responding process in which aspects of discreditability are assigned, ascribed, imputed to them and to individuals who exhibit them. Social and moral meanings are, therefore, central elements in all deviance situations and issues. It is what people make of a condition they deem problematic — whether it be ill treatment of children, cheating in college, group sex, commercial bribery, or mugging — and what they do about it, that counts most socially. And, as this statements implies, what they do invariably depends on initial and gradually built up responses — how they "feel about" whatever it is that unsettles them, what they know or think they know about it, how they assess its meaning for themselves and for their society. What they do, in other words, hinges on their overall "definition of the situation."

As we have also seen, in a good many potential deviance situations the definitions people would choose to apply vary considerably. At a given time and in a given place certain definitions gain a position of dominance. This prevailing definition of the situation is then — much like "power" and "control" — a manifested and observable outcome of earlier developments. Yet, with respect to the dominance of definitions just as with respect to power and control, what has emerged is itself always subject to further elaboration and change. Precisely because of the lack of complete consensus in so many areas of possible deviance defining, we often encounter running struggles over competing definitions of the situation.

In these struggles, partisans typically seek to achieve various concrete goals — the passage or removal of a law; new policies on the part of law enforcers, of helping agencies, or of schools; change in mass-media content; and so on. But at the heart of all this is the effort to affect basic social and moral meanings. Among the most central techniques of politics are persuasion and pressure; nor are the two mutually exclusive. People are frequently "persuaded" through the exercise of pressure and may also sometimes be "pressured" through continuous exposure to persuasion techniques. The uses of collective social power to influence deviance outcomes usually reflect a mixture of the two approaches. It is true that when crusaders on either side of a deviance issue manage to win the support of those in power or to obtain authoritative backing through decisions of state agencies, they hope, for one thing, to thereby pressure their opponents to act in ways they otherwise might not. It is also true that the manifestation of sheer political clout may sometimes induce political figures to take action on deviance issues that their personal beliefs and responses might not otherwise dictate. Yet, by and large, promoting change involves convincing people — at the very least in the sense that they conclude or simply feel that such change is in their interest or that they should, on other grounds, support it.

Especially pivotal, of course, are key gatekeepers to change, such as legislators and judges, those who control the mass media, influential public figures, and members of any specifically relevant sociopolitical elites. They represent particularly important targets for persuasion efforts as well as for pressure tactics. It is also worth keeping in mind, however, that large numbers of citizens will be — with respect to any given deviance issue — neither in positions of major influence nor likely to consider themselves direct partisans on either side of the contest. Within a democratic political system, their roles as voters as well as participants in everyday situations that may be pertinent to the issue make them another target of considerable importance — albeit a widely dispersed and socially heterogeneous one. Efforts to shape the social and moral meanings they will apply in responding to specific substantive issues and situations represent an important aspect of the politics of deviance. These efforts may involve broadly based attempts to mold public attitudes directly or to affect them indirectly — through key opinion leaders via the so-called two-step flow of communication (Lazarsfeld, Berelson, and Gaudet 1948; also E. Katz 1960).

Linking these two broad groups of targets is the characteristic effort to convince those in positions of power that public opinion requires or even demands that they should take particular kinds of actions. Here again it is the perception — this time that of key influentials and decision makers — that counts most. The "objective" state of public opinion, including the likelihood that there really are numerous relevant public opinions, is not as important. As Edelman (1977, p. 9) succinctly notes, "Public policies rest on the beliefs and perceptions of those who help make them, whether or not those cognitions are accurate." The dissemination by partisan groups of the results of opinion surveys purporting to favor their positions — a tactic that, as we saw, has been widely used in the abortion controversy — thus becomes an important technique for influencing policymakers as well as an invitation to undecided laypersons to jump on the bandwagon. As the frequent appearance of conflicting poll results suggests, this technique is in itself morally and politically neutral. In the case of abortion, it has been most forcefully used by advocates of change, who early on used poll findings to show that legal rules had not kept up with changes in lay and professional attitudes. Equally often, opinion research and also unsupported claims regarding the general climate or state of public opinion have been used by those who insist that the public "could never accept," "would not countenance," "would be outraged by" various proposed changes — such as decriminalization of consensual homosexual acts, abolition of capital punishment for violent crimes, and provision of low-cost legal heroin for addicts.

It is clear, then, that partisans in collective stigma contests are widely engaged in the use of propaganda: the manipulation of political symbols for the control of public opinion (Lasswell and Kaplan 1951, p. 111). Some of the types of symbols that are manipulated and some of the specific purposes of this manipulation are discussed in the next section. Any or all of the standard propaganda techniques — name calling, glittering generality, transfer (linking to authoritative or prestigious symbols), testimonial, the "plain folks" device, "card stacking," and the bandwagon theme (Lee and Lee, 1939) — can be, and often are, used in the course of deviance struggles. How much propaganda any particular partisan group uses, what kinds, and at which stages in a dispute will probably depend upon a number of considerations, including degree of already existing success in achieving its goals, nature of the relevant target groups, appropriateness, access to the mass media, and so on. In short, both the need and the ability to use propaganda will tend to vary. Those who support the status quo on a specific deviance issue may at times feel that the carry-over effect of legitimacy and the tendency toward public inertia make a heavy propaganda campaign unnecessary. Those who seek to bring about dramatic changes, on the other hand, will be likely to have a greater need of such efforts. Yet at the same time, they will often not be in as good a position to make them — because of limited organization, inadequate financial support, and limited access to media.

On most deviance issues, however, we will find some recourse to propaganda by each contesting force. As Lasswell and Kaplan suggest, "More propaganda is needed the more heterogeneous is the public whose opinion is to be controlled, and the more the desired opinion deviates from the established perspectives. . . . In general, any large and rapid social change will be accompanied by considerable propaganda; hence its extensiveness in modern society" (Lasswell and Kaplan 1950, p. 115). For propaganda to exist or have an impact it is not, of course, necessary that partisans acknowledge that they are using it. In fact, as we well know, such acknowledgement is infrequent. What the opponent calls propaganda, the user typically labels education. For our purposes, there is little need to judge these competing claims. The important points are simply the pervasive effort to influence beliefs, attitudes, and gut reactions, and the common manipulation of key symbols in furtherance of such goals.

REALMS OF SYMBOLISM

Symbolic Threats and Interests

Symbolic factors enter into the politics of deviance in a number of different ways. In a study of the Women's Christian Temperance Union and its antidrinking campaigns from the 1820s into the present century, Gusfield concluded that the perceived threat to which it was responding was primarily a symbolic one involving "status politics."

> What Prohibition symbolized was the superior power and prestige of the old middle class in American society. The threat of decline in that position had made explicit actions of government necessary to defend it. Legislation did this in two ways. It dem-

onstrated the power of the old middle class by showing that they could mobilize sufficient political strength to bring it about and it gave dominance to the character and style of old middle-class life in contrast to that of the urban lower and middle classes. [Gusfield 1966, p. 122]

Similarly, the subsequent repeal of the Eighteenth Amendment was significant primarily on a symbolic level: "It meant the repudiation of old middle-class virtues and end of rural, Protestant dominance" (ibid., p. 126).

A recent study of two antipornography campaigns (one in the Midwest, another in the Southwest) likewise reported them to have been "symbolic more than utilitarian" — support of a general lifestyle and set of values was more important to the crusaders than were the specific steps they advocated to eliminate pornography (Zurcher et al. 1971). Gusfield himself once again returned to his symbolic-crusade theme in commenting on the 1978 defeat of the Briggs Initiative in California (an electoral initiative proposition, which if passed, would have permitted the firing of schoolteachers who were homosexual or who advocated or encouraged private or public homosexuality). Commenting that the dispute over this initiative was "a way whereby the meaning and place of homosexuality in American society could be defined and evaluated," he went on to argue that the proposal as an instrument to achieve a specific goal was "less significant than the fact of its acceptance or rejection by the voters. Whether it would have or could have been implemented is less vital than the fact that it was rejected. That intrinsic character is what I have in mind in labeling the Briggs initiative a symbolic and ceremonial political act." Increasingly in contemporary American society, according to Gusfield, "ceremonial and symbolic issues begin to pre-empt space customarily reserved for a more instrumental politics" (Gusfield 1978, pp. 633–634, 635).

Gusfield cites such issues as abortion, pornography, drugs, and criminal punishment. Clearly he has in mind precisely the broadening of the meanings and uses of "politics" noted in chapter 1. Whether "symbolic" crusades and issues in such areas can be sharply distinguished from the more instrumental variety is uncertain, since some people's direct interests are always at stake, even as the more general symbolic meaning of the outcomes has importance for them as well as for others. As Gusfield properly notes, however, the interests involved in these areas do not fall neatly into the standard social-class and ethnic patterns; again, that is a central theme in this book. At any rate, symbolic threats and symbolic interests are important ingredients in deviance situations. Indeed, if we recall the idea that deviance defining reflects and establishes a kind of moral stratification, we can see that in a way collective deviance struggles are always partly symbolic in character. The relative moral standings of groups, population segments, or categories of actors are always at stake, as are the degrees of social legitimacy that will attach to the values they hold and the general behavior patterns they display and "represent." Invariably, stigma contests at the societal level center on issues of "collectivity identity" (Cohen 1974, pp. 14–15), just as deviantizing efforts at the interpersonal level pose crucial questions about individual identity.

In attempts to maintain a favorable collective identity for themselves or to impose unfavorable identities on other groups, partisans seek influence and control over important moral and social meanings. Each specific victory scored in such efforts is likely to have immediate and direct consequences and also broader long-term ramifications. Legal victories are likely to be especially consequential, not only because of the additional specific goals that can be achieved with the back-up power of state force but also because of the great symbolic significance that attaches to such "authoritative or semiauthoritative" symbols (Lasswell and Kaplan 1950, p. 103). Such victories are desirable in the first instance because they get things done — for example, by prohibiting job discrimination against former mental patients or by imposing restrictions on pornographic bookstores. At the same time, however, they exert symbolic influence on nonpartisans, create or reinforce a climate favorable to further victories, and encourage and assist the victorious groups' efforts at mobilization. Each positive effect for the victors tends to be accompanied, of course, by negative impacts on the opposing forces. Perhaps the extreme point in such negative ramifications occurs when a contesting group is treated en masse as criminal and subjected to what Balbus calls repression by formal rationality. When racial protesters are subjected to criminal processing routinely and on a large scale, it "tends to depoliticize the consciousness of the participants, deligitimate their claims and grievances, and militate against alliances between participants and other nonelites or elite moderates, [and thus] it is likely effectively to minimize revolutionary potential and maximize long-run [state] legitimacy" (Balbus 1977, p. 13).

Victories and defeats in deviance struggles are also likely to carry symbolic as well as tangible implications for various potentially interested groups of nonpartisans. As we have already seen, there are at least two ways that groups not directly involved in a given deviance conflict will nonetheless be likely to acquire an interest in the outcome. One has to do with the fact that perceived deviance can become a big business (Hawkins and Tiedeman 1975, chap. 6), opening up an array of specialized job opportunities. Some (illegitimate ones) facilitate the "deviance"; others are provided through efforts to curb or contain it; yet additional ones are developed in connection with attempts to punish, correct, treat, or otherwise help individual "offenders." At the same time, deviance outcomes will often carry a broader symbolic or "jurisdictional" significance in that they serve to mark out domains in which particular types of specialized expertise are deemed appropriate.

Edelman states, "The policeman, and the psychiatrist, like everyone else, are likely to focus on definitions of people and situations that call for the skills and authority they have, rather than those others have; for in defining controversial political phenomena they define their own roles as well" (Edelman 1977, p. 11). The specific examples we have touched on above make clear two additional points. First, the symbolic and tangible benefits and interests in these situations tend to be intermixed. Psychiatrists, law enforcers, social workers, corrections officials, and other specialists who may be affected by deviance contests are affected materially as well as symbolically by policy outcomes. Their jobs as well as their distinctive authority may be at stake. In addition, these existing and potential interests are likely to affect the stance that such not-necessarily-partisan groups will adopt in specific disputes. Depending on their stake in the matter and the apparent prospects for (what to them would be) favorable or unfavorable outcomes, they may choose to remain aloof from the struggle and hope to gain from the active contest among others; or, as we have seen, they may themselves become directly engaged in overt politicizing. Let us now take a look at some of the major kinds of definitions that activists typically seek to influence and that will also tend to affect nonpartisans.

Depicting the Problem

In an important early essay, sociologist Willard Waller asserted: "The term *social problem* indicates not merely an observed phenomenon but the state of mind of the observer as well. Value judgments define certain conditions of human life and certain kinds of behavior as social problems; there can be no social problem without a value judgment" (Waller 1936, p. 922). Clearly, this idea lies at the core of the recent definitional or social-reactions interpretation of deviance developed in chapter 1. In particular, Waller's statement underscores the importance of the distinction emphasized there — between the mere presence of a behavior or condition and how that behavior or condition is characterized and responded to. Deviance outcomes, at the societal level as well as at the level of individual deviantizing, reflect whatever moral assessments are currently dominant. By the same token, each side in a stigma contest tries to get other people to share and apply *its* value judgments, to make and impose *its* favored moral assessments.

As a result, propaganda and virtually all political effort on deviance issues revolve around shaping collective perceptions of purported problems. Characteristically, the perceptions and corresponding actions that partisans seek to influence concern the following more specific matters: *Is there a problem? If so, exactly what constitutes the problem? What are the likely ramifications of this problem? What kinds of people are they, who pose this problem? What should be done about it, and about them?* It should be evident from our earlier discussion that these perceptions are not mutually exclusive or even easily separable from one another. People commonly characterize and respond to *pot smoking, child abuse, gambling, robbery, male prostitution, alcoholism,* and *race riots,* without consciously thinking through each of those questions separately or carefully "tabulating" an overall assessment. Their reactions will often be more in the nature of a gestalt — an all-at-once, composite or total cognitive response. But even as they invariably meld into one another, these several questions indicate the key ingredients that make up such overall cognitions and, hence, key focal points for those who wish to shape them.

The answers to the questions listed above are never self-evident. Indeed, the very existence of a problem is always highly problematic. As two observers note, "The career of a social problem begins with its being *privately* recognized as a problem. Some individual or group comes to believe that a certain social problem exists because what their ideology designates as an ideal state of affairs diverges significantly from what they perceive the real situation to be" (Ross and Staines 1972, p. 19). A sense of trouble (Emerson and Messinger 1977) must exist, and those who experience it must convey it to others. Unless the trouble is highly circumscribed, other people must help do something about it. In fact, "An understanding of the problem's dimensions may only begin to emerge as the troubled person thinks about them, discusses the matter with others, and begins to implement remedial strategies. The effort *to find and implement a remedy* is critical to the processes of organizing, identifying and consolidating the trouble" (ibid., p. 122). If this is true in small-scale interpersonal situations, it is certainly also true at the broader societal level. Actually, it is characteristic for social problems to "move outwards" from smaller-scale, more-private responses to larger-scale and more-public recognitions and actions (Ross and Staines, 1972). As noted in chapter 1, some sociologists have concluded — through tracing out this progressive development — that all social problems may go through a typical sequence of stages, in a way that allows us to speak of their having a common natural history (Spector and Kitsuse 1977, esp. chap. 7). Be that as it may, the fact remains that unless those who are initially troubled can push the perceived problem into the public arena by convincing others it exists, it will remain theirs alone and will "go" nowhere.

Even if the existence of *some* problem is conveyed and acknowledged, precisely what it is and why it's a problem may remain open to conflicting interpretations and political dispute. Frequently people will disagree as to which condition is threatening or disturbing, and also as to the source of this threat or disturbance. Their different versions of what the problem is may then become a central point at issue in a collective deviance struggle. By definition, all such struggles at least imply such different interpretations — often one group specifying a problem and the opposing one asserting that the situation isn't really a problem at all. Sometimes, however, alternative ways of depicting some generally acknowledged trouble will vie with one another. In this connection, what Edelman astutely terms "the linguistic structuring of social problems" (Edelman 1977, p. 26) becomes extremely important.

Public perceptions are influenced by the way in which a given problem is named, and contesting forces will attempt to disseminate their favored terminology. Thus, "draft-dodging" is one way of describing a certain situation, while "forcing people to fight unjust wars" is another. The alternative "right to life" and "compulsory pregnancy" depictions offered by opposing forces on abortion (and noted in the last chapter) illustrate the same point. Very often, policy recommendations reflect and reinforce one such version of a trouble at the expense of another:

> Campaigns urging car owners to drive safely, whether sponsored by a government agency or a trade association, focus attention on the driver as the cause of accidents. . . . Whether or not a "drive safely" campaign makes drivers more careful, it creates an assumption about what the problem is and who is responsible for it . . . [which] is helpful to car manufacturers and to the highway lobby, while encouraging public criticism of the driver involved in an accident and creating self-doubt and guilt in drivers. [Edelman 1977, p. 36]

Since deviance-defining consists largely of the construction of stigmatizing classifications, the broad problem categories under which given situations might be subsumed have great significance and therefore may become objects of dispute. The alternative designations of "crime" and "mental illness" (to which we will return shortly) have been applied to a great many kinds of perceived trouble and therefore have become central in a range of definitional struggles. Literal classification — as seen in the aforementioned dispute regarding inclusion of homosexuality in the American Psychiatric Association's list of mental disorders — can also be very consequential. Similar kinds of listings, even in more ordinary, everyday contexts, can also have importance through their possible impact on public perceptions. Thus, one recent discussion (Spector and Kitsuse 1977, pp. 13–16) noted the implications of the Library of Congress's card catalog classification of books on homosexuality. Under this cataloging scheme — used by most libraries in North

America — homosexuality had been a subcategory of "abnormal sex relations," and another listing was provided for books on "sexual perversion in women." Protests by a concerned librarian led to an eventual reclassification. The "abnormal sex relations" heading was removed, "lesbianism" replaced "sexual perversion in women," and a new category for "gay liberation movement" was added.

Perhaps especially interesting is a naming tactic widely adopted by stigmatized groups and their allies, which designates the stigmatizers as constituting, or being the source of, the alleged social problem. A major example of this renaming of the problem would be the insistence by gay liberation supporters that it is not homosexuality that is a problem but rather "homophobia" — fear or dread of homosexuality. Equivalents in other, analogous areas of social stigmatization include the assertions that blacks, women, and the elderly do not pose special problems. According to such portrayals, *white racism, institutional sexism*, and *ageism*, represent the real problems. Even where specific redesignating terms of this sort do not emerge, branding the opposition as constituting the problem is almost always an implicit feature of stigma contests. If one side asserts that "something must be done about" the mentally ill, or drug addicts, or the handicapped, the other side insists to the contrary that a large part of the problem consists precisely of the treatment — stereotyping, debasement, harassment, discrimination — presently accorded such persons. Public policy should first be directed, therefore, toward reducing the bigotry and oppression in these areas, rather than simply focusing on efforts to "deal with" the troublesome individuals.

As to the ramifications of perceived problems, contesting forces in deviance struggles, again, favor and promote alternative definitions of the situation — centering, for these purposes, on the alleged existence or nonexistence of threat to prized values and major social interests, along with claims regarding the probable consequences of alternative actions and policies. A

major technique in this regard is the "doctrine of horrible consequences," something akin to the domino theory in foreign relations — with assertions being made that if this or that one step
is taken, it will open the floodgates to all kinds of undesirable
conditions. This device is, of course, especially popular with
opponents of so-called permissiveness, who see various "deviances" singly or in combination as "undermining the moral
fiber" of our society, threatening the very survival of "civiliza-
tion as we know it," and so on. However, as we saw above,
certain depictions favored by those who support liberalized
abortion laws — conjuring up visions of oppressive overpopula-
tion, hoards of unwanted children, myriad victims of back-street
abortionists or self-induced "butchery," — make clear that the
technique is politically neutral, available to both sides in almost
any deviance contest. To be sure, disinterested persons
may — with respect to any of these aspects of competing
depictions — conclude that one side in a given contest is on
firmer ground than the other, and then that side's version will
probably not be seen as constituting mere propaganda. The
central point for us, however, is that the appeal of such techniques makes it likely that such depictions will continue to be
offered in one form or another.

Another facet of depicting a problem's ramifications has to do
with whose interests are likely to be affected under a particular
state of affairs. Each contesting group, obviously, insists that
the interests of its own members are vitally at stake, but beyond
that, the opposing forces often will try to persuade other powerful constituencies that they too have an interest in the struggle's
outcome. We can see here something similar to what happens in
international politics — as when nations seek to define broadly
their own spheres of legitimate interest and to develop strong
alliances in furtherance of their goals. As we have seen, in many
areas of deviance-defining, success in depicting a matter in dispute as a women's issue, or a working-class issue could have
very significant consequences. By the same token, framing an

issue in terms of morality, decency, or patriotism also represents an appeal to broad constituencies. Much of the problem that activist groups face in developing strong coalitions (discussed in the next chapter) has to do with the difficulties encountered in effectuating such interconstituency appeals.

"Kinds of People" Depictions

Deviantizing, we saw early in this book, entails categorical typing of individuals — the imputation to them of standardized forms of debased identity. Deviance situations reveal, at all levels — interpersonal, organizational, societal — the pervasive role played by stereotypes in determining outcomes (Schur 1971, pp. 38–52). We have noted that because the supposedly deviant status takes on a special saliency, people (and perceived problems) are "reread" in terms of a host of ancillary qualities believed to be characteristic of a given type of presumed deviator. In a recent study comparing the stigma problems faced by Jews, blacks, and gay people, Adam presents a "composite portrait of the inferiorized person" (1978, pp. 42–51). According to him, such persons are commonly depicted as animals, as being hypersexual, and as being overvisible. While these particular sub-themes may not hold up across-the-board with respect to every area of deviance-defining, the formulation is at the very least highly suggestive. If not every type of perceived deviator is described literally in animalistic terms, nonetheless the tendency to view and the attempt to depict those who offend as being basically different — perhaps biologically so — is remarkably persistent (Schur 1979, chap. 2). The third element in Adam's scheme, the charge of overvisibility, certainly is a part of all deviance-defining. "Contamination" of alleged conformists or normals seems to be a central theme, giving rise to characteristic avoidance tendencies and containment practices. While Adam's second point, about hypersexuality, may apply only to certain types of perceived deviators, it does suggest the more general inclination to respond to those seen as deviating as stepping beyond the bounds of decency, as constituting some kind of direct affront to the ordinary ways.

Above all, we know that deviance-defining depersonalizes, implies that the individual is nothing but an instance of the discredited category, and, correspondingly, that all members of the category are basically alike. This supposed alikeness, as well as the particular characteristics that are imputed to the type, will often become a focal point for dispute in deviance conflicts. For those seeking to impose stigma, the composite *type-of-person* depiction may have special value in providing a "personified" source of threat. As Edelman points out, "Personified threats are politically potent regardless of the seriousness or triviality of their impact upon people's lives. The personified threat, no matter how atypical, marshals public support for controls over a much larger number of ambiguous cases symbolically condensed into the threatening stereotype" (Edelman 1977, p. 14). For those subject to stigma, it becomes important not merely to refute the specific substantive misconceptions but also to document the diversity of persons in any stigmatized category — the fact that not all homosexuals (Bell and Weinberg 1978) or all mentally retarded persons (Edgerton 1967) or all heroin users (Gould et al. 1974) are alike.

Definitional struggles, furthermore, will often involve competing versions of "what it is about" the kinds of persons fitting into the stigmatized categories that put them there in the first place. Different versions of the "causes" of individual deviation may carry varying moral and political implications. To that extent, kinds-of-people depictions and prescriptions regarding what should be done will be interrelated. The distinction is often drawn between "crime" and "illness" definitions of problematic behaviors, with special attention focused on the supposed difference in general attitude toward the two: "Hostile sentiments toward sick people are not legitimate. The sick person is not responsible for his acts" (Gusfield 1967, p. 180). Yet, as our earlier discussion made clear, in terms of actual stigmatizing and restricting response, the distinction between the two categories will often be far from clear-cut. In many instances, medical and criminal definitions of a given situation may simply represent alternative rationales for containment and control. From the standpoint of officially processed deviators, for example, treatment in a state mental hospital and correction in a penal institution may not appear as strikingly different outcomes. What the crime-illness dichotomy typically does offer is an arena for potential struggle over the question of who will administer containment and control, and in what specific forms.

The medical profession and law-enforcement authorities, in particular, often seem pitted against each other in efforts to establish substantive areas within which their respective types of expertise will be seen as most appropriate to dealing with a supposed problem. The "medicalization of deviance" (Conrad and Schneider, forthcoming; also Freidson 1971 pp. 247–255) is frequently attributed to active efforts by the medical profession to expand its sphere of jurisdiction or legitimated authority. In some areas of deviance-defining, that is no doubt an apt description of what has happened. Yet the profession has in addition been the beneficiary of the general deference our society accords to science and medicine and also of medical definitions promoted in some instances by nonmedical groups — through deviance struggles in which the profession itself did not play a major role. There have also been situations in which the medical profession has appeared content to sacrifice major jurisdiction over a significant area of deviance-defining. For example, the question of American policy regarding the treatment of heroin addicts prior to around 1955 (see Schur 1962; Lindesmith 1965) posed a largely intractable problem that the doctors preferred to leave to the law enforcers.

For moral crusaders intent on imposing control over troublesome behavior, it may not always matter much whether the problem is dealt with on medical or law-enforcement terms, so long as it is dealt with — in one way or another, contained. For groups seeking to wipe out categorical stigma, neither a crime nor an illness definition of their situation will, ultimately, prove satisfactory. In the short run, the medical approach may sometimes seem the lesser evil and may be endorsed by the deviantized on tactical grounds as a rationale for relatively nonpunitive policy measures. At both the individual and collective levels, the illness definition does have the advantage of relieving perceived deviators of full responsibility for their offending behavior. Some of the stigmatizing pressure is reduced because, as Gusfield notes, "Acts which we can perceive as those of sick and diseased people are irrelevant to the norm; they neither attack nor defend it" (Gusfield 1967, p. 180). By the same token, however, the illness definition precludes according these individuals full status as untarnished human beings who can freely and competently participate in everyday life. Both stigma and restriction, therefore, are likely to persist under such a definition. Such conditions, and particularly the implication that the "problem" lies within them and hence something must be done to help or change them, will eventually cause the stigmatized to find medicalization unacceptable.

Under a criminal definition, the problem again lies within them, except now they are typically seen as unwilling, rather than unable, to meet everyday social obligations and expectations. At least this depiction — given our legal system's grounding in the notion of the individual's responsibility for the predictable consequences of his or her behavior — seems to accord the deviator some status as a freely choosing social actor. In the legal model, Aubert and Messinger have pointed out, "To become a criminal it is necessary to have appeared to be striving for a value. This is not necessary in order to become ill. In order to become ill it is necessary to undergo an apparent change for the worse" (Aubert and Messinger 1958, p. 139). But such a conception merely implies having chosen not to observe the norm; it in no way accords legitimacy to this kind of value choice.

On the contrary, whatever values the perceived criminal is seen as pursuing are at the very least widely held to have been sought through improper means. This reaction is so strong that even where it is apparent that the offender's goals were common and legitimate ones, repudiation of the means overwhelms any public acknowledgment of that aspect. Furthermore, the corollary of recognizing free choice is the admitting of no excuses. Considering that society reserves its harshest negative sanctions for those deemed criminal, the crime definition cannot finally be desired by stigmatized groups — even if in some ways it affords some potential for preserving self-respect and a domain of free assertion.

CONTEXT AND CREDIBILITY

In the last analysis, what stigma-protest groups aim for is such a politicization or "normalization" of the perceived deviation that it will gain full acceptance as falling within a range of acceptable variation. Defining the situation as involving a "variation" presumably carries no connotation of disvalue or discredit, even if it continues to imply something slightly out of the ordinary. At a theoretical extreme, the latter implication might also be removed, so that the behavior or condition could be treated as but one of many, equally ordinary patterns. Opposing groups, seeking to invoke or perpetuate stigma, obviously aim to accentuate the unacceptable differentness of that which they deplore or fear; they want to make sure it is responded to as extraordinary.

As they strive to reduce the stigma and oppression they experience, stigma-protest groups may find a number of intermediate definitions of their situation that are advantageous. One such definition is that of the oppressed minority (Sagarin 1971). Discussion throughout this book has suggested the close similarities between deviantizing and the treatment accorded members of racial, ethnic, gender-based, and age-based minorities. Indeed, these groups may be only diverse substantive examples of victims of a common "inferiorization" process (Adam 1978). Stereotyping, "master status" tendencies toward perceiving in categorical terms, general social disvaluation, avoidance tendencies and restriction of opportunities, the possibility of "role engulfment" and low self-esteem, and the need to engage in various defensive adaptation efforts are all present in each of these substantive cases (Schur 1979, pp. 430–431). At the same time, collective efforts at political action to overcome stigmatization develop along the same general lines and incorporate much the same specific techniques, whether the stigmatized condition be race, sex, or what is perceived as deviance.

An assertion of minority status may help a group in pressing claims for the systematic undoing of past and present injustices, in generating public support and some degree of legitimacy, and it may also encourage the protest group's own mobilization efforts and enhance its internal cohesion and morale. On the other hand, it may have some disadvantages as well. It tends to produce a continuous focus of public attention on the stigmatized status. And public attention is already a problem. It may also at times present a risk of declining militancy, if and when it encourages an overly supplicatory stance. One usual accompaniment of growing acceptance of a movement's minority status has a definite substantive payoff, at least in the short run. That is the organizing of legal efforts, by other groups, to protect and advance the civil liberties of persons in the stigmatized category. We have seen this development recently in many substantive areas of deviance-defining.

The claim to minority-group status will not always be credited, of course. One line of objection may come from the already-acknowledged more "conventional" minorities — racial, ethnic, and so on — whose response may be, "Why link 'us' (the good guys) with 'them' (the bad guys)?" (Sagarin 1971, p. 10). In addition, and depending upon the specific situation, there may well be many people who conclude that a protest group is improperly seeking to "use the 'minority group' umbrella in order to receive the fallout of respectability and in order to be seen as victims of injustice" (ibid., p. 12). Needless to say, such a conclusion is an important part of what stigma-supporting groups will seek to encourage in their opposing efforts to control definitions of the situation.

Another approach stigmatized groups may adopt, one that also faces inevitable problems regarding public acceptance, is to try to depict themselves as "nonconformists." As Robert Merton noted in a classic essay, the nonconformist (he apparently had in mind particularly political dissidents) is viewed as being sincere and largely disinterested, as appealing to some higher morality, as advocating some change for the better. But, in order for this nonconformist image to be acknowledged, it will be necessary to convince people that one is advocating strongly believed-in ideals and goals and not simply trying to get around the prevailing norm (Merton 1957, pp. 360–361). In a sense, that is the impression that deviance protest groups want to advance through their politicization efforts. When Horowitz and Liebowitz (cited earlier) wrote of the blurred distinction between deviance and political marginality, they approached the matter largely as analytic observers noting new modes of behavior that didn't fit neatly into one or another of these categories. But if such a distinction is fading, when viewed objectively, that does not mean it is irrelevant to deviance struggles. On the contrary, it probably has considerable viability in determining public perceptions. The public in fact is continuously engaged in making evaluative distinctions of just this sort. So while groups protesting stigma seek to convince the public that they act in ways and out of motives that are politically acceptable, the forces opposing these groups seek to depict them as falling clearly into the deviance (politically unacceptable) category.

Efforts of the sort we have just been considering — to manipulate key meanings, to define the situation and the contesting parties — are central to virtually all aspects of the politics of deviance. In the next chapter we will be noting some of the more tangible aspects of deviance-protest movements — size of the potential constituency, mobilization of protesting forces, development of coalitions, and the like. Without any question, size and organization (Lofland 1969, p. 15) are two key elements in exercising power on deviance issues. Yet, as the above comments concerning public acceptability of various claims should begin to suggest, power and organization are certainly not the only factors involved. We need to keep in mind that specific deviance struggles always take place within a broader sociocultural context.

Major social trends and currently dominant general value systems and cultural priorities can indirectly but significantly influence particular deviance outcomes. Groups and movements whose goals are congruent with existing trends and dominant values start with an edge, whereas those whose goals diverge from such trends and values cannot avoid being at a disadvantage. We should realize, in addition, that the substantive nature of particular types of perceived deviance does make a difference. We cannot pretend that all alleged deviations are on equal footing, with their moral status being determined solely through power manipulations. What it is that unsettles or threatens people helps to determine the course politicization efforts will take and, indeed, whether even initial politicizing efforts are likely to occur. Certain deviance-related "causes" have very little appeal. Thus, we are not about to see a Society for the Protection of Professional Killers or a Wife-Beaters' Liberation Movement.

Even if the sociocultural context of trends and values does provide some basis for a movement's legitimacy, the manner in which it undertakes collective action can influence public response. A group or movement must not only have reasonable or justifiable goals, it must also convey an acceptable image of itself. Thus, a study of public perceptions of urban racial disorders has noted:

To be credible as protestors, troublemakers must seem to constitute a major part of a group whose grievances are already well
documented, who are believed to be individually or collectively
powerless to correct their grievances, and who show signs of
moral virtue that render them "deserving." Any indication that
only few participated or felt sympathy with the disturbances
predisposes observers to see the activities as deviance or as revolutionary activity by a small cadre of agitators. [Turner 1969, p.
818]

Although Turner is describing a rather special, highly dramatic
type of situation, it is likely that some similar considerations will
affect the ways in which most groups organized to contest deviance issues will be defined by nonpartisans. A stable and
committed constituency, indigenous leadership, and politically
"proper" demeanor will tend to evoke a positive image. Fluctuating commitment, the apparent involvement of professional
agitators or organizers and "improper" demeanor will be likely
to generate unfavorable response. In difficult struggles to define
problematic situations, these are not just public relations issues.
The already stigmatized, in particular, need all the public support they can get. This is not to imply that they should acquiesce
in their own degradation — which would undermine the very
cause to which they are dedicated — or play the game scrupu-
lously according to rules endorsed by the dominant majority.
Ignoring these issues entirely, however, may reinforce an initially weak power position, whereas some attention to them may
help maximize whatever potential for success may exist.

EXAMPLE 5. *Rape: Redefining*
The Situation

Since lack of consensus sets the stage for overt politicization,
it is not surprising that many of the recent large-scale stigma
contests involving conflict over the criminal law have centered
on borderline offenses — illegal transactions or other behaviors

about which there is strong moral ambivalence. The recent public controversy regarding forcible (heterosexual) rape is helping us to realize, however, that even the most violent and widely condemned crimes also have political dimensions and can pose pressing political issues.

To the extent that we treat all power relations as inherently political in nature, the intrinsic and situated politics of rape — from the standpoint of the individuals directly involved in specific rape incidents — are quite apparent. At this immediate level of micropolitics, it is precisely because of differential power, primarily sheer physical power, that forcible rape can occur at all. It is also likely that what is done about an actual or alleged rape, how the specific participants are treated, will be influcnced by their preexisting relative power positions — including especially socioeconomic status. But we are now beginning to see that the situation of heterosexual rape, viewed more generally, exhibits other kinds and dimensions of politicality as well. The very fact that we have legally defined the offense as one committed by men against women dramatically brings its gender politics to the fore. Perhaps even more starkly than in the cases of abortion and prostitution, the relation between this act and situation and our society's approved values and arrangements regarding heterosexual relations and the status of women seems to require exploration.

Rape, as we know, has become a major issue pressed by the women's liberation movement. As a consequence, there has emerged an open and organized collective politics of rape in which its latent institutional or gender politics are being publicly aired and debated. It is an especially interesting example of the collective politics of deviance, for several reasons. First of all, as just noted, a political struggle has developed in this area despite the fact that — with undoubted variations in response, depending on the circumstances of the offense — there is a high degree of public consensus (at least as revealed by survey responses) regarding the seriousness of this crime (Rossi et al. 1974) and the desirability of severe criminal sanctions against it (see Gottfredson et al. 1978, p. 275). Given these professed attitudes, the polarization of forces on the rape issue differs somewhat from the pattern found in certain other deviance-related struggles. No organized group, composed either of "rapists" or other concerned citizens, is going to argue that rape is an acceptable "variation," a freely-chosen "occupation" or an "alternative lifestyle." Groups — primarily, women's groups — actively seeking change in our social and legal approaches to rape, are for the most part merely arrayed against the general forces of inertia and conservatism. Their clearest "opponents" are entrenched laws and legal procedures, and even more, the deep-seated sexist outlooks and patterns that permeate our social system.

At the same time, of course, their intent is not to overturn the broad surface consensus condemning rape but rather to bring actual perceptions and practices more into line with that condemnation, and to encourage new ways of thinking and acting that will make rape less prevalent. The political struggle that has emerged has produced two interrelated focal points: the meanings men and women actually apply, in thinking about rape; and (a reflection of those meanings) the rationale, substance, and administration of the criminal law relating to rape. The composite target of reformist zeal, in other words, is the prevailing sociolegal definition of the situation. That under this dominant but not-always-acknowledged definition the direct *victims* of violent sexual assault were themselves typically deviantized — discredited, abused, treated as shameful, and made to feel ashamed — has dual significance. It points up nicely the enormous power of imputed meanings and definitional processes in determining deviance outcomes — thus documenting a general theme developed throughout this book. With respect to rape more specifically, it indicates the gross distortions of substantive meaning that have come to dominate our perceptions and responses.

The recent campaign to redefine rape has developed along a number of complementary lines. One key theme emphasized by feminist reformers is that rape should not be viewed as being merely, or even primarily, a sexual offense. It should be recognized instead as constituting an offense of aggression and domination, a violent attack on the victim's total personhood and human dignity. The author of a pioneering feminist essay on rape asserts, "It is an act of aggression in which the victim is denied her self-determination. It is an act of violence which, if not actually followed by beatings or murder, nevertheless always carries with it the threat of death" (Griffin 1971, in Chappell, Geis and Geis 1977, p. 64). According to Kate Millett (1971 p. 44), "In rape, the emotions of aggression, hatred, contempt, and the desire to break or violate personality, take a form consummately appropriate to sexual politics" (Millett 1971, p. 44). These qualities make the rape much more than a highly unpleasant and frightening sexual act. Recent work with rape victims has shown that they characteristically experience a severe and comprehensive *rape trauma syndrome* (Burgess and Holmstrom 1974, in Chappell, Geis, and Geis 1977). Immediate and short-term reactions are, understandably, for the most part emotional and physical and involve strong feelings of personal disorientation. Beyond that, however, there remains a longer-term phase of the traumatic reaction in which the woman typically finds it necessary to undertake various life "reorganization" efforts. Changing residence, shifting jobs, altering one's network of everyday interpersonal contacts are all common occurrences. Often the victims nonetheless experience long-term fear and anxiety, shame (see discussion below), have continuous nightmares, or succumb to various phobias — which might include fear of indoors, fear of outdoors, fear of being alone, fear of crowds, fear of people behind them, and sexual fears (ibid, pp. 323–325). A close study of five women who had been raped at work found that "one year after the rape, four of the five victims were still not working full time" (Brodsky 1976, p. 44). Adolescent victims may drop out of school; housewives and mothers frequently find themselves unable to perform routine domestic tasks. Women who have been raped experience difficulty in telling those around them about the event and often find when they do that the reactions of these significant others are negative ones (Burgess and Holmstrom 1976).

In addition to documenting the violently aggressive and pervasively traumatic nature of rape, recent analyses have also suggested the extent to which — though we are loathe to admit it — our outlooks and laws on this offense are actually grounded in a conception of rape as a property violation. Under a system in which sexual relationship is a commodity (recall the discussion of prostitution, in example 4), a "respectable" woman is, or will eventually be, one man's exclusive sexual property. From this standpoint, "Rape is simply theft of sexual property under the ownership of someone other than the rapist" (Clark and Lewis 1977, p. 116). As various writers have noted, this kind of interpretation enables us to understand the traditional legal provisions under which a husband could not be convicted of raping his wife. This rule — a major target of feminist wrath, and now undergoing some change — can mean only one thing: taking your own property is not theft. If the underlying gist of the rape offense were either violence or coerced intercourse, there would be no rationale for automatically exempting marital situations.

This latent rationale explains why the reaction to rape has always been strongest when the victim has been an unmarried virgin, or a chaste married woman. Since the system requires, furthermore, that women make certain they protect that which makes them a valuable acquisition, we can understand why certain women are viewed as improbable rape victims:

> Why is it that certain types of rape victims are popularly viewed as women who "got what they deserved," "were asking for it," or, simply, as women who are not credible because of their

"promiscuity" or "lewd and unchaste" behaviour? The simple explanation is that women who voluntarily give up that which makes them desirable as objects of an exclusive sexual relationship are seen as "common property," to be appropriated without penalty for the use, however temporary, of any man who desires their services. [Clark and Lewis 1977, p. 121]

As we are going to see further, the dominant perceptions of rape in our society — everyday social responses, as well as reactions of the legal system — invariably have incorporated the implicit theme that there are, in effect, social circumstances under which men are somehow entitled to rape women. The husband-wife example is but one instance of this idea, notable because it has been formally acknowledged in the law.

As well as throwing new light on its specific nature and real meaning, feminists have asserted that rape is an offense not just against the individual victims of direct attack but against womanhood in general. The most famous statement of this point was made in Susan Brownmiller's best-selling book, *Against Our Will:* "It is nothing more or less than a conscious process of intimidation by which *all men* keep *all women* in a state of fear" (Brownmiller 1976, p. 5; italics in original). While this depiction, in terms of a conscious conspiracy, will continue to be debated and indeed strongly disputed by some, Brownmiller's claim highlights one undeniable consequence of rape and our responses to it. In her widely disseminated and highly personal essay, Griffin began by stating: "I have never been free of the fear of rape" (Griffin 1971, in Chappell, Geis, and Geis 1977, p. 47). As Brownmiller went on to remark, the continuous fear of rape, and the need both to guard against it and to adopt behavior patterns that will not be deemed to encourage it, crucially impairs woman's autonomy: "The ultimate effect of rape upon the woman's mental and emotional health has been accomplished *even without the act.* For to accept a special burden of self-protection is to reinforce the concept that women must live and move about in fear and can never expect to achieve the personal freedom, independence, and self-assurance of men" (Brownmiller 1976, p. 449; italics in original).

Another key theme being emphasized in the emerging effort to redefine rape is that the offense is not really aberrational or idiosyncratic. The rapist and the victim, it is argued, play out in extreme form a scenario that in some ways is deeply rooted in our socially approved norms and everyday behavior patterns. Thus, two contributors to a radical feminist sourcebook on rape ask, "How different is predatory criminal rape from normal sexual behavior?" and proceed to answer the question: "We suggest that the difference is essentially one of degree, that we live in a culture that, at best, condones and, at worst, encourages women to be perennial victims, men to be continual predators, and sexual relations to be fundamentally aggressive" (Melani and Fodaski 1974, p. 84). Rape, then, is simply at the extreme end (along with other direct violent assaults) of a continuum of sexually tinged acts of aggression against women, which vary in the degrees of indignity and harm that they present. Along this line, one essay (Medea and Thompson 1974, chap. 5) refers to "the little rapes" that women endure daily—routine sexual commentary and harassment in public places as well as at work. (See also MacKinnon 1979.)

These unwanted "attentions" are not, however, the only indicators of the similarity between rape and other sexual activity in our society. Indeed, according to Griffin, "The basic elements of rape are involved in all heterosexual relationships" (Griffin 1971, in Chappell, Geis, and Geis 1977, p. 52), and this she suggests may be the reason that men often identify with the offender in a rape situation. Central to this "similarity" argument is the overall pattern of socialization in which both men and women in our society are taught from an early age that men are to be strong, aggressive, and insistent while women are to be weak, dependent, and submissive. It is this pattern that feminists have in mind when they assert that men learn to be rapists and women are taught to be victims. These roles in the rape situation are, in other words, symbolic manifestations of the logical extremes toward which our dominant notions about "masculine" and "feminine" behavior point.

This argument draws some additional strength from evidence that the average rape offender does not conform to widely held stereotypes. Brownmiller notes, "The typical American rapist is no weirdo, psycho schizophrenic beset by timidity, sexual deprivation, and a domineering wife or mother" (Brownmiller 1976, p. 191). While it may seem a bit extreme to insist as a general matter that "the rapist is the man next door" (Medea and Thompson 1974, p. 36), as a metaphorical comment indicating that rapes are committed by all sorts of men the statement cannot be faulted. Even psychological studies of imprisoned rape offenders disclose that "not all individuals who commit rape fit neatly into the same personality or behavioral classifications" (Pacht 1976, p. 92). And it should be noted that these offenders comprise a highly limited sample of actual rape-committers, one from which many of the most "normal" and "conventional" rapists and those who commit rape in nonalarming everyday contexts, already will have been eliminated (see below).

A picture of the average rapist's motivation that is much more plausible than the "crazed sex-offender" version is Clark and Lewis's depiction of variations in male use of coercion to obtain desirable "female sexual property." Noting that there are many types and degrees of enticement, persuasion, and force that men can use to gain sexual access to women, they suggest that "The tactics of coercion which a man uses will depend on the personal assets which he has at hand." And they comment further:

> Many men lack the purchasing power to buy the sexual property they want, at least at some point in their lives, and some men will take what they want. . . . will use physical force to take the sexuality they desire. It is not surprising, therefore, that most of what is labelled "rape" is committed by working-class men who do not have the ability to use middle-class strategies of persua-

sion and economic inducement. [Clark and Lewis 1977, pp. 129,
130]

While this explanation is not likely to cover all rapes — and it
certainly does not tell us why some men with few personal assets refrain from rape, whereas others do not — it may apply to
a great many. Ironically, as the same authors note, stressing the
normality of most rapists may backfire — as a tactical matter —
in one respect. If offenders do not conform to the "real rapist"
mythology, reactions to them may be less stringent; for it may
be their supposed derangement rather than the mere fact of
committing rape that is seen to threaten society (ibid. pp. 133–
134).

A final cornerstone of this redefinition campaign, one that is
implicit in all of the points mentioned so far, is the need to alter
dominant conceptions of the victim's role in the rape situation.
The tendency to be suspicious of rape claims and to impute
impropriety to the victim is pervasive. As already noted, it colors other people's responses to the assaulted woman in ways
that can be very consequential. The socially defined shamefulness of being raped is illustrated by the statement of one adolescent victim: "I can't play with my old friends because they all
know. It's embarrassing that they know. I can't trust anyone
and I liked them. I'd have to make new friends" (Burgess and
Holmstrom 1976, p. 26). Women are often implicitly blamed for
the offense, as in the recent case of a twenty-two-year-old rookie
cab driver in San Francisco who was raped at gunpoint in her
cab and then "dismissed by her supervisor for not screening her
customers carefully enough" (*New York Times*, June 24, 1979,
p. 34). The experience of rape victims with the criminal justice
system — at all levels, from the police who investigate to the
judge who presides in court — regularly conveys the same impu-
tations of shamefulness and victim guilt. This tendency is not
restricted to the United States, but is generally characteristic of
the approach to rape in virtually all contemporary Western legal

systems. Thus, a French witness before the International Tribunal on Crimes Against Women asserted: "And after the rape, the rape goes on. One is raped morally in the name of justice. The interrogation, the repeating of the minutest details, is very upsetting. The raped woman is forced to prove that she has been raped, and these proofs are then turned back against her" (Russell and Van de Ven 1976, pp. 112–113).

Social stigma and the hope of returning to a normal existence and state of mind make women very reluctant, in the first place, to initiate rape complaints. When they are aware of the likelihood of being further humiliated by the police and in court proceedings, or of the low probability that the offender will ever be convicted, the tendency not to report rapes is reinforced. National surveys in which samples of the general population are questioned regarding incidents in which they have been crime victims indicate that from one-fourth to one-half of all rapes are unreported to the police (Hindelang and Davis 1977). Given the powerful stigma surrounding rape—which could inhibit respondents from reporting it even in these later surveys—and the variable definitions of what constitutes the offense, the underreporting of sexual assault may be even greater than these findings suggest.

Even when an incident is reported, police and prosecution may not define it as constituting rape, or they may otherwise classify the complaint as *unfounded*. One comparative analysis of police practices revealed, for example, that a considerably broader definition of what constituted forcible rape prevailed in Los Angeles than in Boston and saw this as part of the reason that Boston's rape rate was only half as high as the national average, whereas Los Angeles had the highest rate in the country (Chappell et al. 1977, p. 235). Such variations clearly affect rape statistics in general and also influence decisions to proceed in specific instances. The *unfounding* of rape complaints (as it is officially termed) represents the police and prosecution's version of the denial of respect and credibility to the rape victim, an attitude toward rape that runs through the entire criminal-justice process. The term refers primarily to a decision by police not to advise prosecution — for whatever reason — though prosecutors may also in effect unfound claims by themselves deciding not to carry through on a case. Police unfound about one-fifth of the rape complaints they receive, for a variety of reasons that often "are not relevant to whether or not a rape has been committed. They are, however, relevant to the chances of obtaining a conviction in court" (Le Grand 1973, in Chappell, Geis, and Geis 1977, pp. 71–72). While a great many specific factors can lead to unfounding, it invariably involves a conclusion that the charge will not hold up — a conclusion commonly based on an overall inference from the woman's background and/or the circumstances surrounding the alleged rape that her complaint of forced intercourse is not to be believed. In one way or another, the reasoning goes, this woman "brought it on herself." As Clark and Lewis point out, there are categories of women who are simply not deemed credible rape victims (Clark and Lewis 1977, pp. 91–94). These women who "cannot be raped" have traditionally been held to include prostitutes, other women of "poor reputation," women alleged to drink or be mentally unstable in any way, divorcées, unmarried mothers, women previously acquainted with their attackers or who were attacked while on dates, and of course wives — when they have been attacked by their husbands.

The frequently voiced thesis of *victim precipitation* encourages this way of thinking. Camille Le Grand notes, however, that "as a post facto conclusion . . . a finding of victim precipitation depends upon the perspective of the largely male police, prosecutors, and judges who appraise the case. The concept of victim precipitation hinges primarily on male definitions of expressed or implied consent to engage in sexual relations, and is shaped by traditional restrictive stereotypes of women" (Chappell, Geis, and Geis 1977, p. 72). Unfortunately, social scientists may sometimes have reinforced common stereotypes by employing this concept in an insufficiently cautious manner. (See discussion by Clark and Lewis 1977, chap. 10). A major study, which analyzed all rapes reported to the Philadelphia police in 1958 and 1960, made heavy use of the precipitation theme, even though the researcher himself classified less than one-fifth of the rape situations as falling into that category (Amir 1971). As Clark and Lewis cogently note, investigators may conclude — after the fact, for if there had been no rape there would have been no rape-precipitating behavior, even if the women had acted in the same ways — that some demeanor or action invited rape. Yet actually it would be at most the offender's alleged interpretation that might account for the assault, not the behavior in the abstract (Clark and Lewis 1977, p. 153).

To credit such interpretation may be to imply that under certain circumstances — if, for example, they picked them up in bars, or were out on dates with them — men have a right to rape women. The likelihood of sexist assumptions underlying uses of the precipitation concept is seen in one analysis of rapes of hitchhikers, where the authors in part conclude that "further study should be done regarding the reasons that women place themselves in such vulnerable positions" (Nelson and Amir 1973, in Chappell, Geis, and Geis 1977, pp. 288–289). It is one thing to recognize that if a given woman had not hitchhiked, she would not (in that circumstance) have been raped; it is quite another to imply that she should not have been free to hitchhike or that by doing so she actively precipitated an assault. Failure to meet unwarranted burdens of self-protective behavior should not become a basis for impugning a person's basic character or for considering their reports to be untrustworthy.

The result of the tendency to discredit rape victims is seen in the poor record of the criminal-justice system in dealing with the offenders. Typical is the state of affairs referred to in one recent report as "the almost complete immunity rapists in New York City have enjoyed from effective prosecution. In no recent year have more than 8 percent of rape arrests resulted in rape convictions" (Chappell and Singer 1977, p. 246). Until recently, the legal requirements for proving rape placed special evidentiary burdens on the prosecution, making convictions extremely difficult to obtain. These requirements included especially an explicit requirement of independent corroboration of the complainant's rape claim and a virtual requirement (implicit in permitting extensive defense cross-examination on the topic) that the victim establish a history free of sexual "impropriety" and the absence of any rape-precipitating behavior on her part in the immediate rape situation. Under severe challenge, these burdens are now being eased: "Very few jurisdictions now retain special corroboration requirements for forcible rape, and increasingly the permissible scope of defense questioning about the prior sexual behavior of a victim of forcible rape is being circumscribed" (Chappell 1976, p. 17).

Legislated rule change is not likely, however, to eliminate immediately the deeply entrenched outlooks that dominate responses to rape. Juries remain extremely reluctant to convict rape defendants. Chappell quotes an experienced prosecutor on this matter: "Unless her head is bashed in or she's 95 years old or it's some kind of extreme case, jurors just can't believe a woman was raped. There's a suspicion that it was her fault, that she led the guy on, or consented — consent is the hardest thing to disprove. It's just his word against hers" (ibid. p. 21). One interview study found that even judges may be "far less impartial than is frequently supposed." Noting that judges too focused heavily on the issue of victim credibility, this researcher found certain "cases which may be rape according to law, but which they classify as consensual intercourse." She cites as one example. "when a woman meets a man in a bar, agrees to let him drive her home, and then alleges he raped her. Judges have several graphic ways of describing this situation: 'friendly rape,' 'felonious gallantry,' 'assault with failure to please,' and 'breach of contract' " (Bohmer 1974, in Chappell, Geis, and Geis, eds., 1977, pp. 162, 164).

Despite the considerable persistence of sexist victim-blaming outlooks the women's movement has managed over the last decade to bring about some important changes with respect to rape. Discussion among themselves in consciousness-raising groups, and public "speakouts" in which rape victims gave personal testimony, helped to rapidly mobilize women on the rape issue (Connell and Wilson 1974, pp. 3–55). Activist efforts led to increased media coverage of a previously taboo subject and to some growth in public awareness of the need for change (Largen 1976). Rape hot lines and crisis centers to help victimized women sprang up around the country under the sponsorship of the movement, and even in some police departments new rape investigation-and-assistance units were established, staffed at least partly by female officers (Keefe and O'Reilly 1976). Programs in self-defense for women proliferated. Working groups drafted model rape laws (see Connell and Wilson 1974, pp. 164–169), and lobbying for legislative change was reasonably successful—so that many jurisdictions now have laws on the books that are more impartial in at least some respects.

In attempting to build on this far-from-negligible record of success, the women's movement continues to face significant obstacles. One is the complex overlay of interracial fears, tensions, and hostilities that continues to affect thinking about rape, even though systematic research indicates that most rapes are in fact intraracial. (See Curtis 1976.) Another is the persisting concern, on civil liberties grounds, that false rape charges could lead to a railroading of innocent defendants. The specter of notorious cases in which black men were wrongly convicted of raping white women, as well as systematic evidence in states that make rape a capital offense showing disproportionate imposition of the death penalty on blacks (Wolfgang and Reidel 1977) contribute to such uneasiness. Yet the civil liberties issue reflects more than just a desire to ensure the rights of black defendants. It expresses a more general concern that the evidential burdens will be tipped so far away from the earlier distrust of the complaining woman that the defendant's basic presumption of innocence until proven guilty will be cast aside (Herman 1977; Sagarin 1977). Current practice in our courts suggests, however, that we are very far from reaching the point where that could become a widespread danger.

Without any doubt, the biggest obstacle to further change in this area is the general persistence within our society of sexist attitudes and practices. To that extent, rape activists will have to continue to rely heavily on the resources of the women's movement itself. Neither blacks nor the poor are likely to adopt rape as a major political concern, since there are other issues to which they accord higher priority. Nor can the political left be expected to rally to the cause. According to Susan Griffin, it was the student left's lack of interest in the matter that led to the need for a separate women's effort on rape: "In their rhetoric, the issue of rape, which seemed to be central to us—at the core of something which we could not fully explain, perhaps our being—was an epiphenomenon, a spin-off several generations away from the real cause, which was division of labor" (Griffin 1979, p. 26). Not even all factions within the recent women's movement seem fully in agreement as to the precise priority to be given to rape, but at the very least it should remain one of the major women's issues for some time to come.

EXAMPLE 6. *Corporate Crime: Maintaining Immunity*

If deviantizing involves an assertion of social power, so too does the avoidance of stigma that others might seek to impose. The success of those who — while engaged in widespread problematic behavior that could be defined as serious "trouble" — nonetheless manage to keep from being treated as deviant, is thus the other side of the social-reactions or definitional thesis regarding deviance. Corporate crime is without doubt the most glaring example in contemporary American society of systematic immunity from deviance-defining by those who commit major social harms. As well as showing how concentrated power can help shield wrongdoers from legal control, it illustrates the fact that both stigma and nonstigma outcomes reflect the same basic self-fulfilling mechanism in official deviance processing through which power is confirmed and reinforced. In the legal response to much ordinary street crime, it is low socioeconomic power that is reinforced: the already-disadvantaged defendant (who often has a prior criminal record) is deemed a "poor risk" and on that very basis is apt to incur harsh penalties. The same kind of self-propelling cycle is at work (only in reverse) when the "good risk" executive charged with corporate crime escapes negative sanctioning. As one observer comments, "Lawmakers and judges see businessmen as 'respectable' because they have rarely been convicted of crimes; however, they have rarely been convicted of crimes because they are regarded as respectable" (Conklin 1977, p. 113).

It is widely recognized that the economic cost (benefit, to the offenders) of corporate and other business-related crime is enormous. One review notes, "The financial losses from fraudulent business transactions are probably many times as great as the financial losses from burglary, robbery, and ordinary larceny" (Sutherland and Cressey 1978, p. 24). In the late 1960s, the President's Crime Commission — a rather conservative body composed largely of public figures — acknowledged a range of substantial white-collar crime costs:

> The exact financial loss to the Government caused by tax fraud is difficult to determine but undoubtedly enormous. Estimates of the amount of reportable income that goes unreported each year ranges from $25 to $40 billion. . . . The financial loss to the public caused by a single conspiracy in restraint of trade may be untold millions in extra costs paid ultimately by the buying public. It is estimated the cost to the public annually of securities frauds . . . is probably in the $500 million to $1 billion range. A conservative estimate is that nearly $500 million is spent annually on worthless

or extravagantly misrepresented drugs and therapeutic devices. Fraudulent and deceptive practices in the home repair and improvement field are said to result in $500 million to $1 billion losses annually; and in the automobile repair field alone, fraudulent practices have been estimated to cost $100 million annually. [President's Commission on Law Enforcement and Administration of Justice 1967, pp. 103–104]

Direct and indirect physical costs of corporate violations are without any question also huge, although they cannot always be easily or adequately documented. Such violations include marketing of inadequately tested drugs, thereby causing illness or even death; unsafe work conditions that lead to injuries and deaths; environmental pollution producing long-term health hazards; and the marketing of harmful food products. Additional social costs, in terms of widespread public cynicism and a generalized hostility among the poor and the exploited, are likewise incalculable.

Over the years, sociologists and social critics have regularly stressed the sharp discrepancy between this record of substantial wrongdoing and the weakness of official response to it. A pathbreaking effort in this connection was Edwin Sutherland's study, *White Collar Crime* (1949, 1961). As part of a more general attempt to frame a comprehensive theory of crime causation, Sutherland sought to document the fact that criminality was not limited to the lower socioeconomic classes. Defining white-collar crime technically as "a crime committed by a person of respectability and high social status in the course of his profession," he focused especially on the criminality of large corporations. The common notion that crime is a lower-class phenomenon, Sutherland insisted, reflects misapprehensions that stem from contrasting public and official reactions to the criminal behavior of the different classes. In studying court and administrative decisions against 70 of the largest American corporations, he found that over the years there had been a total of

980 such decisions, or an average of 14 per corporation. Major patterns of criminality included antitrust violations, illegal rebates, patent, trademark or copyright violations, advertising misrepresentation, unfair labor practices, various financial manipulations, and violations of special wartime regulations. Though many of the decisions were administrative ones, 60 percent of the corporations had received criminal convictions — some individual corporations incurring as many as four. Even in the criminal cases, however, the imposition of major sanctions was a rarity. In a companion study of the largest power and light corporations, private utilities supposedly operating in the public interest, Sutherland again found that the corporations had violated laws with "great frequency" but that actual convictions and criminal penalties had hardly ever resulted. The preference for imposing administrative sanctions did not, however, according to Sutherland, mean that these crimes were any the less real. Rather, he concluded, an important class of criminals was using its power and prestige to secure preferential treatment. He cited a number of specific techniques — ranging from legitimate lobbying to openly illegal means of influence — that helped the corporations achieve favorable outcomes.

In some degree it may be true, as radical criminologists have charged, that American criminology since Sutherland's time has tended merely to pay lip service to the significance of upper-class and corporate crime, concentrating instead on the more heavily stigmatized offense categories and largely studying the officially processed individual offenders. Even if this has until recently been the case, the current interest in social reactions and definitions should focus new attention on corporate wrongdoing. Recognition of power and conflict as key factors in deviance-defining, increased study of societal-level deviance categorizing, and the very recognition that immunity from stigma is the other side of the deviantizing process all work in that direction. Furthermore, the ever-increasing role of large-scale organizations in our society has meant that sociology must pay attention to the corporation as a major violator of crime laws (Ermann and Lundman 1978; Schrager and Short 1978).

At any rate, corporate crime represents one significant area of potential deviance-defining in which the radical critique's thesis of ruling-elite domination does hold up well. We have already seen that in most deviance situations, the selection and reaction to individual deviators will typically be affected by considerations of socioeconomic status. Often, however — particularly in such areas as illicit drug use, alcoholism, behavior treated as sexually deviant, and mental and physical disabilities — the relation between economic stratification and the broad categorizing and overall social response to potential deviance is indirect or uncertain. Here, the direct tie-in with collective socioeconomic power is unquestionable. This is not surprising, since, to begin with, the problematic condition consists precisely of the economic elite's own behavior. When issues arise regarding the means corporations use in the everyday pursuit of profit, it is only reasonable to expect that the corporations will take advantage of all the power resources at their command in seeking favorable outcomes. The prospect of being defined as criminal on these grounds strikes at their most basic interests. And they are, of course, in a position of unusual strength in defending themselves against such a threat.

The unparalleled magnitude and concentration of economic power that corporations hold greatly facilitates the defense of what are essentially economic interests. That is quite obvious. Since definitions of crime and the ways in which they are applied are — unlike less institutionalized forms of social stigmatizing — formally dependent on the legal system, the corporate elite's close links to that system also provide great benefit. Even if we were to assume the complete political independence and impartiality of the judiciary, which assumption may not be fully warranted, the close ties between big business and other major policymakers — both legislative and administrative (Mills 1957;

Domhoff 1971) — would ensure substantial influence on corporate crime policy. While his statement no doubt glosses over variations and exceptions, Quinney is probably correct by and large in asserting that "the makers of criminal policy are members of or representatives of big business and finance, including the legal establishment which is tied to corporate and financial wealth" (Quinney 1974, p. 59). Thus, it is one thing for the public leaders who made up the Crime Commission to profess a concern about white-collar crime. It would be quite another for policymakers who have close links with the corporate world to actually legislate and administer a program that aimed at significantly curbing such behavior. Nor can such inhibitions be attributed solely to direct or indirect economic interest. The very centrality of the corporation in modern American life — our society's deep commitment to the idea of capitalist enterprise and widespread acceptance of "the business of America is business" outlooks — implies favorable evaluations of corporate activity and generates among many persons, including some policymakers, a sincere belief that legal intervention would be undesirable.

In shielding themselves from severe stigma and criminal sanctions, the large corporations have been very successful in sustaining their favored social definitions of crime and of corporate activity. They have derived benefit from, and have sought to perpetuate, a number of common ideas that together encourage people to feel that corporate crime is not "real" crime. The more direct and immediate fears people have of physical violence and other face-to-face crimes against individuals divert them from the recognition that they are victimized by corporate wrongdoing. As one observer properly emphasizes, business offenses are "rarely dealt with as part of 'the crime problem' " (Conklin 1977, p. 2). The treatment of corporate crime in Charles Silberman's much praised book, *Criminal Violence, Criminal Justice* (1978), illustrates this point. Notwithstanding the special focus implied by the title, this book clearly purports to be a comprehensive discussion of America's most serious crime problems. Yet, despite the author's concern throughout the book in exposing double standards and hypocrisy, and although he notes in passing that "well-bred people steal far larger sums than those lost through street crime" (ibid. p. 45), approximately six pages of this large volume are all that he devotes to white-collar crime. Such treatments of crime not only reflect, but also reinforce, differential public reactions to lower-class and upper-class criminality. Other reinforcing factors are the FBI's exclusion of such offenses from its list of major "index crimes" — statistics for which are continuously publicized — and the fact that business crime often is played down by the media — for example by being reported in the financial section of a newspaper rather than as part of the general news. Corporate control of, and influence on, the media helps to ensure such a diversion of public attention (Conklin 1977, pp. 1–2, 116–117).

Citizen acquiescence in victimization by corporations persists in part because most people see neither the offenses nor the offenders as posing a personified threat. There is certainly no dearth of victims, even if they themselves don't always realize it or do anything about it.

> Employees, consumers, and the general public are potential partisans [protesters] with respect to organizational activity in ways determined *by their relationship to the production of goods and services*. Employees are directly affected by the process of production within the workplace; consumers, by products purchased in the marketplace; and the general public, by substances from this process which are introduced into the environment. [Schrager and Short 1978, p. 413]

Part of the problem of mobilizing these victims for protest purposes has to do with the hidden and sometimes merely statistical nature of the injury. It is difficult to get people to do something about corporate violations that increase the statistical probability of their eventually dying from cancer, even when this probability may in fact be higher than that of being violently assaulted by a robber. Similarly, with respect to financial victimization, consciousness of the social harm or its full dimensions may remain low.

> . . . the injury to an *individual* consumer from a price-fixed or deceptively advertised product is very small, perhaps $50, perhaps only a few cents. On the other hand, the aggregate injury to the *class* of all consumers who purchased the product may amount to millions of dollars. Because the injury is so minor, the consumer probably will not even perceive that it has occurred. It is an "invisible injury," or "invisible tort" as a consumer lawyer might refer to it, and modern technology has given rise to mass production of these invisible torts. [Moore 1970, p. 305]

It is not surprising that another legal commentator offering prescriptions for "How to Make Crime Pay," lists as his first rule: *"Steal from large numbers of people as indirectly as possible.* Individuals are afraid of crimes directed specifically at them: their person or property. The threat disappears when the crime is impersonal, the loss indirect — the more impersonal and indirect, the better" (Gillers 1978).

"Types of persons" thinking and also common outlooks regarding types of offenses militate against a strong response to corporate crime. Many people mistakenly believe that only certain kinds of persons can be criminals. In this stereotyped view, crime offenders are often taken to be biologically or psychologically warped in some way, or at the very least they are pictured as a distinct class of persons set apart socially from the ordinary workings of "respectable" society. As noted above, the conceptualizing of some kind of homogeneous category of deviators is an important element in the depiction of threat. Not only can the "type" be reacted to uniformly — with all possible variations obscured through its use — but it is the "type" more than any concrete individual that generates fear and stigmatizing response. This social stereotype of the alleged criminal was one of the major targets of Sutherland's exposé; yet the tendency he showed to be unwarranted continues to have strong appeal.

Here again, we see the self-confirming nature of "respectability" and "nonrespectability." Only those offenders who can be conceived of as criminals become criminals (through official processing). Furthermore, response to the offense and to the offender come together in the common feeling that ordinary business activity, pursued by ordinary-looking and ordinary-acting people, cannot constitute "real" crime. This judgment not only directly affects public policy; it also confirms the corporate violator's favorable self-conceptions and hence may provide a rationalization for continuing criminality. According to the President's Crime Commission, "There is strong evidence that many white-collar offenders do not think of themselves as criminals" (President's Commission on Law Enforcement and Administration of Justice 1967, p. 108). If they do not, it is because they are making subtle and distorted distinctions. This is seen in the following testimony of a Westinghouse executive during hearings (connected with the electrical price-fixing conspiracy cases of 1961) before the Senate Subcommittee on Antitrust and Monopoly:

> Committee Attorney: Did you know that these meetings with competitors were illegal?
> Witness: Illegal? Yes, but not criminal. I didn't find that out until I read the indictment. . . . I assumed that criminal action meant damaging someone, and we did not do that. . . . I thought that we were more or less working on a survival basis in order to try to make enough to keep our plant and our employees. [Quoted in Geis 1967, p. 144]

Similarly, when questioned about the ethical issues raised by recent disclosure of widespread foreign bribery by American corporations (see Conklin 1977, pp. 48–50), several top executives

> expressed frustration over the unwillingness of critics to make appropriate distinctions in "payout" situations. Not all payouts are "payoffs" . . . those countries where governments manage

the details of economic life tend to be corrupt societies where there is a price for a favorable decision. The executives themselves drew distinctions among *extortions*, *"grease"* or *"speed" money*, *gifts*, and *bribes*. [Walton 1977, p. 181]

Obscurity and diffusion of personal responsibility for corporate offenses further limit and undermine the public stigmatizing and official processing of violators. People do not always know precisely whom to blame, and prosecutors may not always be certain who should be prosecuted. The complexities of modern business transactions and also of the corporation's internal structure and division of labor pose problems in this regard. Christopher Stone uses as an example a Los Angeles incident in which a freeway bridge under construction collapsed killing six workers and in which criminal prosecution was not recommended because of difficulty in pinning down the responsibility. He asks, "How does one locate (much less prove in a court of law) what, exactly, went wrong, and which of the countless companies involved — contractors, subcontractors, suppliers, suppliers' subcontractors — did it?" (Stone 1975, pp. 105–106). Differentiation of tasks and departments within today's large corporations make it very difficult to know which person or unit initiated a given action, on whose orders, and with whose knowledge.

While it might seem logical to hold top management responsible for systematic criminality of the corporation, more often than not establishing direct responsibility at that level is not easy — whether because of intentional actions by management or simply as a result of organizational structure and procedure. Indeed, as Conklin notes, "The delegation of responsibility and unwritten orders keep those at the top of the corporate structure remote from the consequences of their decisions and orders, much as the heads of organized crime families remain 'untouchable' by the law" (Conklin 1977, p. 65). Although sometimes a corporation will want to shield middle-level executives from public exposure in order to protect the organization from embarrassment (J. Katz 1977), when wrongdoing is exposed, it is on those middle-management individuals that the burden of sanctioning often will fall. The extent to which the corporation itself will endorse or back up such action is likely to vary. Following the 1961 electrical price-fixing cases, one of the corporations involved, Westinghouse, supported and retained in its employ persons directly implicated in the conspiracy. General Electric, on the other hand, reacted in a much more punitive fashion, insisting that its employees had violated basic company policy as well as federal law and therefore deserved severe punishment. "The company's action met with something less than wholehearted acclaim; rather, it was often interpreted as an attempt to scapegoat particular individuals for what was essentially the responsibility of the corporate enterprise and its top executives (Geis 1967, p. 146).

When the burden of punishment does fall on the top executives, it is unlikely to do so with great severity. Conklin reports:

> Most of the 21 business executives who pleaded guilty during 1973 and 1974 to making illegal [political] contributions continued to preside over their companies and were not treated as pariahs by fellow businessmen; a few were living in semi-retirement by 1975 as a result of their illegal actions. Only two had been in jail, and these had served only a few months. Most had paid small fines of one or two thousand dollars. . . For the most part they retained their wealth and their power in the business world. (Conklin 1977, pp. 124–125.)

Although one might hope that the legal fiction of the corporation as "a person" would encourage officials to hold it criminally liable, reluctance to apply severe criminal sanctions for corporate crimes remains strong. In a way, this fiction seems only to complicate matters further.

> . . . organizations are not shamed by labeling, nor can they be jailed. Instead they are fined—in amounts that are often no greater for criminal than the civil convictions. Rather than having a direct impact on those individuals responsible for the illegal

actions, fines are absorbed by innocent parties such as stockholders or consumers. [Schrager and Short 1978, pp. 410–411]

More specifically, Stone notes:

> Ford lost an estimated $250 million on the Edsel; sales of the Mustang, in the first twenty-seven months alone, may have netted Ford $350 million. When considered against those figures, a $7 million fine for EPA [Environmental Protection Agency] violations is significant, but no more so than a lot of things management has to worry about, and indeed far less so than others. [Stone 1975, p. 40]

It is now widely accepted that corporate crime is one area in which the deterrent effect of severe punishment — especially a convincing threat of imprisonment — is likely to be strong. Yet, such punishment is rarely, if ever, imposed, and hence the deterring threat is not credible. (The jailing of executives in the 1961 electrical price-fixing cases — seven sentences were served; and twenty-seven other sentences were imposed but suspended — constituted such an exception to the general practice that they are unlikely to have exerted much deterrent influence.) The threat of imprisonment does usually remain in the picture, as a kind of background warning, but there is a strong preference for proceeding in most cases under administrative provisions and for imposing administrative sanctions (Ball and Friedman 1965). This preference reflects, along with the general reluctance to brand businessmen as criminals, difficulty in prosecutors establishing criminal intent (Edelhertz 1970), and also the possible advantages of by-passing various other procedural encumbrances, as well as the desire to avoid the substantial delays and draining of legal resources that are likely in connection with a lengthy criminal trial. The last point has special pertinence with respect to proceedings against the most powerful corporations; it may account for the directing of a high proportion of governmental action against smaller ones. Thus, a recent news account quotes an official of the Justice Department's tax division as asserting, "Any criminal case is war" and

"A criminal case against a major corporation is all-out global war. Corporations use every weapon they can afford, and they can afford a lot" (Taubman 1979b, p. 29). The report goes on to note that the major weapon is expert defense counsel, consisting of lawyers "who have years of experience handling corporate cases and who can frustrate the Government at every turn." A specific example is described as follows: "In litigation of a case involving illegal tax havens . . . defense attorneys, invoking the Freedom of Information Act, asked for an index of thousands of pieces of documentary evidence collected by the Government. It took 30 Government lawyers and investigators six weeks to prepare the index (ibid.).

Reliance on administrative procedures also reflects the very fact that an enormous body of administrative machinery for regulating business is available. The close ties that exist between the regulatory agencies and the industries under their jurisdiction are frequently cited as a reason for lack of severity in sanctioning corporate wrongdoing. One investigator asserts:

> The existence of permanent respresevatives of industry in Washington, a political advantage the general public does not possess, has helped cause the corporate acculturation of Washington agencies by the industries they supposedly regulate. Most important decisions are made in the middle levels of the bureaucracy; it is at this stage that policy is the most malleable, and it is at this stage that industry has both formal and informal input. [Fellmeth 1970, p. 247]

The same writer goes on to describe the following major patterns of influence: informal contacts — primarily, entertainment by industry of agency personnel; formal advisory groups — set up by the agencies and consisting chiefly of industry representatives; public lobbying; job interchange — personnel shifts in both directions between agencies and industry are commonplace; and political influence over agency appropriations and appointments (ibid. pp. 248–252). Between the strong tendency of both agencies and prosecutors to accept various types of settlement in lieu of actual trials and the inadequacy of continuous monitoring and controlling procedures, many of the worst corporate abuses persist free of interference. This widespread failure of regulations has been a major reason for the recent growth of public-interest organizations, undertaking research, public education, and lobbying in such areas as consumer and environmental protection.

That governmental commitment to effective regulation is unclear is illustrated by the Carter administration's apparent willingness to back away from an earlier strong stand against overseas bribery by American corporations. According to a *New York Times* story, a White House task force recommended — in the wake of "intense lobbying" by big business — "immediate weakening and eventual abandonment of key provisions" in the Foreign Corrupt Practices Act, which, "the business community has complained . . . puts American multinational corporations at a competitive disadvantage abroad" and which, "costs the United States $1 billion annually" (Taubman, 1979a). Even if government prosecutors and regulators were able and willing to apply available control methods comprehensively and vigorously, it is not clear that they could come close to eliminating corporate crime. As Christopher Stone emphasizes, legal sanctions are most effectively employed after the fact, whereas often—as in the case of drugs or environmental pollution that will produce long-term genetic damage—steps should be taken in advance to ensure that the harm never does occur (Stone 1975, p. 94). Furthermore, effective control of corporate wrongdoing often requires the power to make changes in the organization's internal structure or procedures. A fine or other penalty for a specific incident of proven harm will not by itself eliminate the possibility that the harmful conduct will continue (ibid. pp. 31–33).

Given the current climate in business-government circles and the fact that the mobilization of public pressure for corporate accountability remains slight, it seems unlikely that we can soon expect corporations — on their own or under pressure — to adopt the organizational changes (reform of internal structure and lines of communication, public directorships, self-scrutiny, and the like) that might deal with some of these problems. Nor is the motivation for adequate self-policing clearly present. A long-time business journalist no doubt speaks for many corporate advocates in asserting that "the most important cause of darkness over the corporate scene is the inherent difficulty of communicating an activity as complex and as fast-changing as modern business" (Ways 1977, p. 111). Mobil Corporation now devotes substantial resources to an "educational" effort, employing widely circulated newspaper advertisements, which state its general philosophy and positions on specific public-policy issues. In one of these ads, for example, Mobil assailed, not unexpectedly, "all those regulators in 'activist government' who want to impose their often-inexperienced righteousness on the most complex economy on earth. They have been careening from one costly blunder to the next, while the dollar weakens and the nation's economic strength drains away" (Mobil Corporation 1978).

On balance, the indictment by radical sociologists and social critics — of corporations for committing widespread "crimes of economic domination" (Quinney 1977, pp. 50–5.001) and of the legal system that permits this situation — seems well founded. Certainly the official processing of crime offenders provides an inadequate basis for conceptualizing the true dimensions of criminality in our society. (See Schwendinger 1975.) Whether by intent or indirection, differential response to upper-class and lower-class crime does function "to further enhance the hegemony of the privileged through the creation of a criminal stereotype" (Krisberg 1975, p. 62; also, Pearce 1976, pp. 81–82). The dismal record of governmental control may, furthermore, justify the conclusion that negative sanctioning represents tokenism, or even the interpretation that "the State may be pressured either nominally or effectively to prosecute the wealthy if their criminal practices become so egregiously offensive that their victims may move to overthrow the system itself" (Gordon 1971, 1976, p. 204).

Collective action by these victims, however, remains weak at the level of mere protest, let alone as any kind of approach to a radical break with "the system." Of course, most of the factors enhancing corporate power and legal immunity that were discussed above function at the same time to limit the strength and effectiveness of collective opposition. According to Conklin, the public does not really condone business crime. "Rather, people feel powerless and unable to combat the powerful and wealthy corporations which influence the direction of legislation and law enforcement in this country" (Conklin 1977, p. 109). Yet even if certain specific business offenses violate widely professed norms and ideals, the omnipresent role and broad acceptance of the corporation in modern American life work against dramatic change. So too does the dominant individualistic ethic. What Mills called the higher immorality (Mills 1957, chap. 15) in many respects reflects values that are endemic to our social system.

To revert to our earlier terminology, the modern corporation's deviance seems virtually uncontainable, although the token response that occurs when it exceeds certain limits (noted by Gordon) may represent one kind of containment. The concentrated power of big business is so great, one suspects, that if it "wished" to control dominant definitions in various other substantive deviance areas it might even be able to do so. As we have seen, usually there is no clear reason why such control — with respect to behaviors that do not directly threaten corporate interests as such — would be desired. While corporations may indeed indirectly benefit from a range of deviance policies, their overriding goal must be to maintain the social definitions under which their own economic wrongdoing is differentiated from "real crime." At this time, only the very beginnings of a serious challenge to their success in that effort are apparent.

References

Adam, Barry D. 1978. *The Survival of Domination.* New York: Elsevier North Holland

Amir, Menachem 1971. *Patterns in Forcible Rape.* Chicago: University of Chicago Press.

Aubert, Vilhelm, and Sheldon L. Messinger. 1958. "The Criminal and the Sick." *Inquiry* 3: 137–160.

Balbus, Isaac D. 1977. *The Dialectics of Legal Repression.* New Brunswick, N.J.: Transaction Books.

Ball, Harry V., and Lawrence M. Friedman. 1965. "The Use of Criminal Sanctions in the Enforcement of Economic Legislation." *Stanford Law Review* 17: 197–223.

Bell, Alan P., and Martin S. Weinberg. 1978. *Homosexualities: A Study of Diversity Among Men and Women.* New York: Simon and Schuster.

Bohmer, Carol. 1974. "Judicial Attitudes Toward Rape Victims." *Judicature* 57 (February); as reprinted in Duncan Chappell, Robley Geis, and Gilbert Geis, eds., *Forcible Rape.* New York: Columbia University Press Pp. 161–169.

Brodsky, Carroll M. 1976. "Rape at Work" In M. J. Walker and S. L. Brodsky, eds., *Sexual Assault.* Lexington, Mass.: Heath. Pp. 35–51

Brownmiller, Susan. 1976. *Against Our Will.* New York: Bantam.

Burgess, Ann Wolbert, and Lynda Lytle Holmstrom. 1974. "Rape Trauma Syndrome." *American Journal of Psychiatry* 131: 981–986; as reprinted in Chappell, Geis, and Geis, eds., *Forcible Rape.* Pp. 315–328.

Burgess, Ann Wolbert, and Lynda Lytle Holmstrom. 1976. "Rape: Its Effect on Task Performance at Varying Stages of the Life Cycle." In Walker and Brodsky, eds., *Sexual Assault.* Pp. 23–33.

Chappell, Duncan. 1976. "Forcible Rape and the Criminal Justice System." In Walker and Brodsky, eds., *Sexual Assault.* Pp. 9–22.

Chappell, Duncan, and Susan Singer. 1977. "Rape in New York City," In Chappell, Geis, and Geis, eds., *Forcible Rape.* Pp. 245–271.

Chappell, Duncan et al. 1977. "A Comparative Study of Forcible Rape Offenses Known to the Police in Boston and Los Angeles." In Chappell, Geis, and Geis, eds., *Forcible Rape.* Pp. 227–244.

Clark, Lorenne, and Debra Lewis. 1977. *Rape: The Price of Coercive Sexuality.* Toronto: The Women's Press.

Cohen, Albert K. 1974. *The Elasticity of Evil.* Oxford University Penal Research Unit. Oxford: Basil Blackwell.

Conklin, John E. 1977. *Illegal But Not Criminal.* Englewood Cliffs, N.J.: Prentice-Hall.

Connell, Noreen, and Cassandra Wilson, eds. 1974. *Rape: The First Sourcebook for Women.* New York: New American Library.

Conrad, Peter, and Joseph W. Schneider. *Deviance: From Badness to Sickness.* St. Louis: C. V. Mosby, forthcoming.

Curtis, Lynn A. 1976. "Rape, Race and Culture." In Walker and Brodsky, eds., *Sexual Assault.* Pp. 117–134.

G. William Domhoff. 1971. *The Higher Circles.* New York: Vintage.

Edelhertz, Herbert. 1970. *The Nature, Impact, and Prosecution of White-Collar Crime.* Washington, D. C.: Government Printing Office.

Edelman, Murray. 1977. *Political Language.* New York: Academic Press.

Edgerton, Robert B. 1967. *The Cloak of Competence.* Berkeley: University of California Press.

Emerson, Robert M., and Sheldon L. Messinger. 1977. "The Micro-Politics of Trouble." *Social Problems* 25 (December): 121–134.

Ermann, M. David, and Richard J. Lundman, eds. 1978. *Corporate and Governmental Deviance.* New York: Oxford University Press.

Fellmeth, Robert C. 1970. "The Regulatory-Industrial Complex." In Bruce Wasserstein and M. J. Green, eds., *With Justice for Some.* Boston: Beacon Press. Pp. 244–278.

Freidson, Eliot. 1971. *Profession of Medicine.* New York: Dodd Mead.

Geis, Gilbert. 1967. "White Collar Crime: The Heavy Electrical Equipment Antitrust Cases of 1961." In M. B. Clinard and Richard Quinney, eds., *Criminal Behavior Systems.* New York: Holt, Rinehart & Winston.

Gillers, Stephen. 1978. "How to Make Crime Pay." *New York Times,* February 16, p. A23.

Gordon, David M. 1971, 1976. "Class and the Economics of Crime." *The Review of Radical Economics* 3; as reprinted in W. J. Chambliss and Milton Mankoff, eds., *Whose Law? What Order?* New York: John Wiley. Pp. 193–214.

Gottfredson, Michael R. et al., eds. 1978. *Sourcebook of Criminal Justice Statistics — 1977*. Washington, D.C.: Government Printing Office.

Gould, Leroy et al. 1974. *Connections*. New Haven: Yale University Press.

Griffin, Susan. 1971, 1977. "Rape: The All-American Crime." *Ramparts* 10 (September): 26–36: as reprinted in Chappell, Geis, and Geis, eds., *Forcible Rape*. Pp. 47–66.

Griffin, Susan. 1979. *Rape: The Power of Consciousness*. New York: Harper & Row, Pub.

Gusfield, Joseph R. 1966. *Symbolic Crusade*. Urbana: University of Illinois Press.

Gusfield, Joseph R. 1967. "Moral Passage: The Symbolic Process in Public Designations of Deviance." *Social Problems* 15 (fall): 175–188.

Gusfield, Joseph R. 1978. "Political Ceremony in California." *The Nation*, December 9.

Hawkins, Richard, and Gary Tiedeman. 1975. *The Creation of Deviance*. Columbus, Ohio: Chas E. Merrill Pub.

Herman, Lawrence. 1977. "What's Wrong With the Rape Reform Laws?" *Victimology* 2 (spring): 8–21.

Hindelang, Michael J., and Bruce J. Davis. 1977. "Forcible Rape in the United States: A Statistical Profile." In Chappell, Geis, and Geis, eds., *Forcible Rape*. Pp. 87–114.

Katz, Elihu. 1960. "The Two-Step Flow of Communication." In Wilbur Schramm, eds., *Mass Communications*. 2nd ed. Urbana: University of Illinois Press Pp. 246–365.

Katz, Jack. 1977. "Cover-Up and Collective Integrity." *Social Problems* 25 (October): 3–17.

Keefe, Mary L., and Henry T. O'Reilly. 1976. "Changing Perspectives in Sex Crime Investigations." In Walker and Brodsky, eds., *Sexual Assault*. Pp. 161–168.

Krisberg, Barry. 1975. *Crime and Privilege*. Englewood Cliffs, N.J.: Prentice-Hall.

Largen, Mary Ann. 1976. "History of Women's Movement in Changing Attitudes, Laws, and Treatment Toward Rape Victims." In Walker and Brodsky, eds., *Sexual Assault*. Pp. 69–73.

Lasswell, Harold D., and Abraham Kaplan. 1950. *Power and Society*. New Haven: Yale University Press.

Lazarsfeld, Paul; Bernard Berelson; and Hazel Gaudet. 1948. *The People's Choice.* New York: Columbia University Press.

Lee, Alfred McClung, and Elizabeth Bryant Lee. 1939. *The Fine Art of Propaganda.* New York: Harcourt Brace Jovanovich.

LeGrand, Camille E. 1973. "Rape and Rape Laws." *California Law Review* 61 (May); as reprinted in Chappell, Geis, and Geis, eds, *Forcible Rape.* Pp. 67–86.

Lehman, Edward W. 1977. *Political Society.* New York: Columbia University Press.

Lindesmith, Alfred R. 1965. *The Addict and the Law.* Bloomington: Indiana University Press.

Lippmann, Walter. 1922. *Public Opinion.* New York: Macmillan.

Lofland, John. 1969. *Deviance and Identity.* Englewood Cliffs, N.J.: Prentice-Hall.

MacKinnon, Catherine A. 1979. *Sexual Harassment of Working Women.* New Haven: Yale University Press.

Medea, Andra, and Kathleen Thompson. 1974. *Against Rape.* New York: Farrar, Straus & Giroux.

Melani, Lilia, and Linda Fodaski. 1974. "The Psychology of the Rapist and His Victim." In Connell and Wilson, eds., *Rape: The First Sourcebook for Women.* New York: New American Library. Pp. 82–93.

Merton, Robert K. 1957. *Social Theory and Social Structure.* Rev. ed. New York: Free Press.

Millett, Kate. 1971. *Sexual Politics.* New York: Avon.

Mills, C. Wright. 1957. *The Power Elite.* New York: Oxford University Press.

Mobil Corporation. 1978. "The Capitalist Revolution. 4. The Free Market: Radicalism for the '80s" (advertisement). *New York Times,* July 20, p. A21.

Moore, Beverly C., Jr. 1970. "The Lawyer's Response: The Public Interest Law Firm." in Wasserstein and Green, eds., *With Justice for Some.* Pp. 299–333.

Nelson, Steve, and Menachem Amir. 1973. "The Hitchhike Victim of Rape." In Israel Drapkin and Emilio Viano, eds., *Victimology.* Lexington, Mass.: Heath; as reprinted in Chappell, Geis, and Geis, eds., *Forcible Rape.* Pp. 272–290.

Pacht, Asher R. 1976. "The Rapist in Treatment." In Walker and Brodsky, eds., *Sexual Assault.* Pp. 91–97.

Pearce, Frank. 1976. *Crimes of the Powerful*. London: Pluto Press.

President's Commission on Law Enforcement and Administration of Justice. 1967. *Task Force Report: Crime and its Impact — An Assessment*. Washington, D.C.: Government Printing Office.

Quinney, Richard. 1974. *Critique of Legal Order*. Boston: Little, Brown.

Quinney, Richard. 1977. *Class, State, and Crime*. New York: D. McKay.

Ross, Robert, and Graham L. Staines. 1972. "The Politics of Analyzing Social Problems." *Social Problems* 20 (summer): 18–40.

Rossi, Peter H. et al. 1974. "The Seriousness of Crimes." *American Sociological Review* 39 (April): 224–237.

Russell, Diana E. H., and Nicole Van de Ven, eds. 1976. *Crimes Against Women: Proceedings of the International Tribunal*. Millbrae, Calif.: Les Femmes.

Sagarin, Edward. 1971. "From the Ethnic Minorities to the Other Minorities." In Sagarin, ed., *The Other Minorities*. Lexington, Mass.: Ginn. Pp. 1–19.

Sagarin, Edward. 1977. "Forcible Rape and the Problem of the Rights of the Accused." in Chappell, Geis, and Geis, eds., *Forcible Rape*, Pp. 142–160.

Sagarin, Edward, ed. 1971. *The Other Minorities*. Lexington, Mass.: Ginn.

Schrager, Laura Shill, and James F. Short, Jr. 1978. "Toward a Sociology of Organizational Crime." *Social Problems* 25 (April): 407–419.

Schur, Edwin M. 1962. *Narcotic Addiction in Britain and America*. Bloomington: Indiana University Press.

Schur, Edwin M. 1971. *Labeling Deviant Behavior*. New York: Harper & Row, Pub.

Schur, Edwin M. 1979. *Interpreting Deviance*. New York: Harper & Row, Pub.

Schwendinger, Herman, and Julia. 1975. "Defenders of Order or Guardians of Human Rights?" In Ian Taylor, Paul Walton, and Jock Young, eds., *Critical Criminology*. London: Routledge and Kegan Paul. Pp. 113–146.

Silberman, Charles E. 1978. *Criminal Violence, Criminal Justice*. New York: Random House.

Spector, Malcolm, and John I. Kitsuse. 1977. *Constructing Social Problems*. Menlo Park, Calif.: Cummings.

Stone, Christopher D. 1975. *Where the Law Ends*. New York: Harper, Torchbooks.

Sutherland, Edwin H. 1949, 1961. *White Collar Crime*. New York: Holt, Rinehart & Winston.

Sutherland, Edwin H., and Donald R. Cressey. 1978. *Criminology*. 10th ed. Philadelphia: J. B. Lippincott.

Taubman, Philip. 1979a. "Carter Unit Recommends Easing of Bribery Law." *New York Times*, June 12, Pp. D1, D15.

Taubman, Philip. 1979b. "U.S. Attack on Corporate Crime Yields Handful of Cases in 2 Years." *New York Times*, July 15, Pp. 1, 29.

Turner, Ralph H. 1969. "The Public Perception of Protest." *American Sociological Review* 34 (December): 815–831.

Waller, Willard 1936. "Social Problems and the Mores." *American Sociological Review* 1(December): 922–934.

Walton, Clarence C. 1977. "The Executive Ethic: View From the Top." In Walton, ed., *The Ethics of Corporate Conduct*. Englewood Cliffs, N.J.: Prentice-Hall. Pp. 173–211.

Ways, Max. 1977. "A Plea for Perspective." In Walton, ed., *The Ethics of Corporate Conduct*. Pp. 173–211.

Wolfgang, Marvin E., and Marc Reidel. 1977. "Race, Rape, and the Death Penalty." In Chappell, Geis, and Geis, eds., *Forcible Rape*. Pp. 115–128.

Zurcher, Louis A., Jr., et al. 1971. "The Anti-Pornography Campaign: A Symbolic Crusade." *Social Problems* 19 (fall): 217–238.

4
chapter

Mobilizing Protest

"The aggregates of incumbents of positions with identical role interests are at best a potential group. . . . Interest groups are groups in the strict sense of the sociological term; and they are the real agents of group conflict. They have a structure, a form of organization, a program or goal, and a personnel of members."

> Ralf Dahrendorf,
> Class and Class Conflict in Industrial
> Society *(1959)*

BUILDING ON LATENT
INTERESTS

Because consensus on norms and values is incomplete, the struggle over deviance-defining is, in one sense, an implicit and continuous feature of the ordinary everyday workings of our society. However, for such struggle to become explicit, to take the form of an openly engaged-in collective politics of deviance, there must be intentional organizing and campaigning by and among those individuals who are especially concerned. The processes through which that occurs and the problems encountered in such efforts are probably much the same whether the attempted crusade aims to impose or expand deviantizing (in whatever substantive area), or on the contrary, seeks to overturn stigma-laden definitions and reactions. Yet, as we have already seen, the heavier burden with respect to mounting a concerted campaign clearly lies with those who wish to change the currently dominant meanings and policies; those who support them start with a definite advantage. Partly for this reason, and also in view of the recent widespread activity within our society by those who oppose various kinds of deviantizing, the main focus in this chapter will be on problems facing deviance "liberation" movements. Most of the general points developed here, however, would apply equally well in any consideration of problems faced by the "other side."

Consciousness and Cohesion

The mere existence of a good many individuals in similar situations and with similar problems does not, by itself, make for a real conflict group or active political force. Without certain necessary conditions and efforts, these individuals will remain at most "potential partisans" (Gamson 1968, p. 32) who can perhaps be described as comprising a "community of latent interests" (Dahrendorf 1959, p. 187). Dahrendorf further points out that for such a potential constituency to become a true interest or conflict group, there must be organizers, founders, and leaders; political conditions must permit organizing activity to occur (under totalitarianism such groups must work underground); and above all, "social conditions of organization" must be met (ibid. pp. 182–189). Among the most important of the social conditions is the development of collective consciousness.

Gamson, who suggests the term *solidary group* for an intermediate stage of development — between the mere potential suggested by Dahrendorf's "quasi-group" (see the epigraph) and the fully organized interest group — mentions four major elements that will promote solidarity: "symbolic expressions of the group as a collectivity" (including a special group name or slogan); "treatment as a group by others"; "a common style of life, norms, and values"; and "a high rate of interaction." (Gamson 1968, pp. 32–36). As we have seen, treatment by others as a group, or at least as a homogeneous category, lies at the very heart of the deviantizing process. By the same token, deviance typing implies special group names, though from the stigmatizers' standpoint, ones imbued with opprobrium. But at least this sets the stage for a contest — as part of the renaming and problem-depiction struggles referred to in the last chapter — over alternative designations of the persons subject to stigma. Thus we find the effort to establish the use of *gays* in place of *homosexuals*, *the handicapped* instead of *cripples*, and *working women* in place of *whores* or even *prostitutes*. In much the same way, the term *blacks* was promoted as a substitute for the stigma-associated *Negroes*, let alone the common anti-black epithets. Pictorial symbols, such as those adopted by the gay liberation movement and in organized efforts to promote the interests of the physically handicapped, represent additional symbolic expressions that may be solidarity enhancing, functioning in much the same way as have special "black power" salutes and handshakes.

The other elements in Gamson's list are much more problematic. Because of the complicated ways in which imposed deviance categories intersect with other bases for social and attitudinal differentiation — socioeconomic status; racial, ethnic, and religious affiliations; age and gender categories; geographic location; general political orientations and allegiances, and also any relevant major personality patterns — the sharing of a common style of life, norms, and values by individuals in any one stigmatized grouping is at most incomplete. We saw early in this book that no person is ever just "a deviant" (of whatever alleged type), despite the insidious effort to depict offending individuals in that way. Immersion in a special lifestyle and, likewise, degree of interest in, or commitment to, a deviance-related "cause" are bound to vary considerably. Although the gay community does come close to offering a general style of life, involvement of individual homosexuals in this communal life varies; nor are even the most fully involved likely to be in complete agreement on all norms and values.

Similarly, there is no guarantee that those on the receiving end of a given deviance attribution will have a high rate of interaction with one another. Geographical dispersal and social heterogeneity work to limit interaction, though some of the isolating, segregating, and other containing responses to the stigmatized may promote it. The relative success of the gay liberation movement (but see example 7 in this chapter for a discussion of some problems it faces) may be partly attributable to the geographical concentration and high-interaction rate of the "gay ghetto." On the other, the noteworthy advances made by the recent women's liberation movement suggest that if a potential constituency is large and powerful enough, wide dispersal and attentuated contact need not prevent success in mobilizing for political action. The main importance of interaction lies in its influence on collective consciousness. Direct interaction and communication encourage people to recognize problems and interests held in common and to see that many of their experiences have socially institutionalized rather than individual causes. As a result, the likelihood is increased that a strong group consciousness and sense of identification will emerge.

While most of the sociological and political theorizing about collective consciousness of this sort has to do with socioeconomic class consciousness and its relation to political revolution, many of the general themes emerging from this work are relevant to deviance protests as well. For any "subordinated class," including deviantized groups, collective consciousness concerns, essentially,

> the extent to which members understand that their situation is crucially affected by an institutional contradiction, that social change is required to realize their class interests, and that certain forms of collective action are requisite to achieving the necessary

transformation. Another component is the degree to which members are personally committed to participating in the appropriate political efforts. [Useem 1975, pp. 38–39]

In their analysis of poor people's movements, Piven and Cloward note three aspects of the transformation of consciousness needed for the emergence of a protest movement:

> First, "the system" — or those aspects of the system that people experience and perceive — loses legitimacy. . . . Second, people who are ordinarily fatalistic, who believe that existing arrangements are inevitable, begin to assert "rights" that imply demands for change. Third, there is a new sense of efficacy: people who ordinarily consider themselves helpless come to believe that they have some capacity to alter their lot. [Piven and Cloward 1979, pp. 3–4]

This statement draws on Gamson's earlier discussion of "trust" as a major source of inactivity. As that writer succinctly stated, "A combination of high sense of political efficacy and low political trust is the optimum combination for mobilization — a belief that influence is both possible and necessary" (Gamson 1968, p. 48).

For protest groups developing around deviance issues the primary target or opposition, as noted earlier, will not always be the public authorities or the overall existing political system. Yet something very much like this distrust and withdrawal of legitimacy must nonetheless occur, and it will take the form of a repudiation of the deviantizing and deviantizers, an unwillingness by the stigmatized any longer to acquiesce in their own disvaluation and subordination. Piven and Cloward cogently state, "It is the daily experience of people that shapes their grievances, establishes the measure of their demands, and points out the targets of their anger" (Piven and Cloward 1979, pp. 20–2.001). Those subjected to the social stigma of "inferiorization" (Adam 1978; also Mitchell 1973), on whatever substantive grounds, will more likely be drawn to protest — much as the poor people with whom Piven and Cloward were concerned — by the oppressive conditions governing their everyday experience than because of some abstract political ideology. Indeed, this point is particularly important for our purposes, because in many if not most stigma contests the potential partisans do not share any overarching ideology or belief system — of the sort that often lies behind more overtly political protests and revolutions. Frequently the only explicit goal held in common among persons who might band together to combat a particular kind of deviantizing is the overturning of that quite specific type of oppression. But even if neither the prevailing political-economic system nor those holding official power can easily be seen as direct ideological enemies, protest mobilization requires at least that so-called normals, conformists, or straights be seen as implementing, facilitating, or implicitly supporting oppressive reactions and policies.

Again, as in the case of mobilizing persons in support of stigmatization, personifying of the threat is probably necessary in some degree so that specific groups can be identified and earmarked as targets for protest. Among individuals who have been subjected to severe deviantizing, there may be serious obstacles to developing this awareness of, and active response to, external enemies. For one thing, the deviantized frequently have struck various less-than-satisfactory accommodations with their oppressors (see Schur 1979, chap. 5; also Goffman 1963; and Adam 1978, chap. 4), thus trying to make the best of a bad situation. These accommodations — passive acquiescence in the face of slurs and mistreatment, willingness to accept partial segregation, modifying behavior so as not to give public offense, and so on — become socially entrenched in ways that may inhibit the organizing of militant protest. Stigmatized persons may be reluctant to risk whatever degree of tolerance or limited domain of freedom from interference they have been "granted" in the hope of achieving a more complete freedom, which they themselves may have come to believe is unattainable. For them to try to break out of the various social containments may greatly increase the likelihood of their incurring the full-fledged and potentially devastating wrath of the stigmatizing forces.

Other aspects of the deviantizing process also work against politicizing efforts. The low self-esteem that frequently afflicts persons who have been heavily stigmatized militates against involvement in collective activism. It is very likely true that such involvement, when it does occur, will have a favorable impact on the stigmatized individual's self-conceptions. As Adam points out, "Solidarization tends to mark increasing abandonment of guilt-based responses for self-affirmation. Sense of self, understanding, and effectiveness may indeed be enhanced through this process" (Adam 1978, p. 122). Yet an inadequate sense of self-worth — even when it has been caused primarily by systematic social rejection — may prevent such involvement from occurring in the first place. As we have already seen, the tendency in deviantizing is to depict the "problem" or "deficiency" as residing in the perceived offender, thereby encouraging low self-esteem. (This is why efforts to depict the alleged problem differently, as noted in the last chapter, represent such an important tactic for protest organizers.)

Whatever the specifics of the presumed nature and causes of the "deviance," this widespread tendency to blame the victim (Ryan 1972; also Gaylin et al. 1978) may be internalized by the stigmatized themselves. To the extent that they accept the societal judgment that the "problem" consists of some deficiency within themselves, it becomes difficult for them to recognize and act against its real sources in the outside world. This was the major impetus for, and problem confronted by, the consciousness-raising groups that have played such an important part in the women's movement (Dreifus 1973). Although the chance to get together and to speak openly about their personal experiences and problems has for many women been emotionally satisfying and has also served to increase their self-assertiveness, the most important development has been political. According to Juliet Mitchell, in the most effective of these groups there is

> the changing awareness that women's problems are not private and personal, so, neither is their solution, or, to put it another way, it reflects the change from personal self-awareness (in the psycho-therapeutic sense) to group consciousness or the oppressed person's equivalent to "class-consciousness." The small group permits the transition from the personal to the political and simultaneously interrelates them. [Mitchell 1973, p. 59]

In addition, an extensive national network of these local groups has helped the women's movement to surmount the aforementioned problem of mobilizing protest in the face of great geographical dispersal. Provided they develop a clear focus on the specific social sources of collective oppression, consciousness-raising groups among persons stigmatized in other ways could similarly function as an important catalyst promoting political action.

Efforts by outside professionals to establish "jurisdiction" over an alleged problem (discussed briefly above) can also have important consequences affecting politicization efforts. In particular, a version of the individual-deficiency theme may be promoted by those who would "help" or "treat" the stigmatized, thus confronting organizers with an externally imposed "anti-politics" definition. Edelman goes on to suggest that this tactic may even be used when those in power must deal with overtures toward unwanted change. "Whenever a political issue threatens to produce conflict or an impasse or a result unacceptable to elites, some will define and perceive it as inappropriate for politics: as calling for specialized expertise rather than political negotiation and compromise" (Edelman 1977, p. 136). Some of its radical critics have attacked the recent sociology of deviance itself for focusing its studies on the officially established "offenses" and for viewing the individual as being a passive recipient of labeling processes. According to these critics, this approach diverts attention from the systematic sources of oppression and underestimates the possibility of active resistance (Gouldner 1968; Liazos 1972; Thio 1973). Ironically, the Marxian class-conflict model toward which some of these critics lean could also, when applied in an inflexible or reductionist manner, work against the organization of directly concerned persons around specific deviance issues. Thus, a rigid insistence on economic determinism as the exclusive explanation of all oppression, or a tendency to see economic-class consciousness as the only kind of collective consciousness that is needed, can amount to "a brittle orthodoxy immune to the manifest permutations of domination" (Adam 1978, p. 127; see also Greenberg 1976).

The Evolution of Protest

A number of characteristic difficulties must be overcome, then, even in the early stages of raising consciousness and recruiting members to participate in deviance-protest campaigns. Defining potential partisans as those persons who are affected "in some significant way" by a given or prospective decision, Gamson suggests that "significant" implies a *threshold* concept (Gamson 1968, p. 33). If this notion applies to the initial emergence of potential partisans from among the more general population, it is probably also applicable to the subsequent stages of mobilizing protest. At each stage of potential and actual organization, it may be possible to discern conditions under which stigmatized individuals who had previously acquiesced in their own subordination, or at least had been unwilling or unable to do anything about it, reach a point where they will no longer put up with such a situation. This threshold possibility represents a counterpart to the role of *tolerance limits* in determining the behavior of persons and groups whose developing percepions of threat may lead them to active and organized deviantizing efforts. That there may be successive thresholds, on either side of a potential deviance dispute, is consistent furthermore,

with the "value-added" thesis regarding the general development of social movements; namely, the idea that the reaching of
each stage in a movement's development is dependent on the
existence of certain precedent conditions and the occurrence of
certain prior developments (Smelser 1963). Finally, it highlights
the processual nature of deviance situations, referred to in the
opening chapter of this book. On both sides of stigma contests,
and at the collective level as well as the interpersonal one, the
elaboration and "organizing" of "trouble" (Emerson and Messinger 1977) involves sequential processes —including various
points at which one or the other party concludes that new types
or degrees of action have now become necessary.

As this notion of process implies, the growth of deviance-
protest movements — like that of any other social
movements — reflects the continuous interaction between protesters and opposition forces. Each action provokes a counter-
reaction, which in turn produces a modified situation — a new
basis from which decisions regarding subsequent action must be
taken. Despite efforts to delineate major stages in this sequential evolution of social movements (Smelser 1963) and social
problems (Spector and Kitsuse 1977; also Mauss et al. 1975, pp.
61–70), the precise course of development of any one collective
stigma contest is difficult to predict. This is so because at any
stage each party is likely to have some degree of freedom to
choose among several lines of response. At the very least, however, we can see that interaction with opposing groups —
whether official authorities or private partisans — will condition
such choices. The opposition can rarely be ignored. It is the
specific nature and direction of the response, not whether there
will be one, that is variable or uncertain.

In some ways, an interactionist view of deviance situations
seems to imply the likelihood of cycles of increasingly intense
hostility and activism among competing groups. Thus, Lemert's
important formulation of deviance-defining as a process of differentiation involved this idea: "Most frequently there is a pro-

gressive reciprocal relationship between the deviation of the individual and the societal reaction, with a compounding of the societal reaction out of the minute accretions in the deviant behavior, until a point is reached where ingrouping and outgrouping between society and the individual is manifest" (Lemert 1951, p. 76). Presumably, a similar process may be at work if we view the situation from a collective rather than an individual standpoint. Yet it is not entirely clear what the political ramifications of progressive "outgrouping" are likely to be.

The consequences of this process could include increased cohesiveness and collective militancy on the part of the stigmatized. As we have seen, however, the process also can result in a breaking of morale, an acceptance of accommodation, and self-protective isolation, a fragmentation that would tend to undermine organization efforts. A leading writer on conflict asserts that, in general,

> Outside conflict unites the group and heightens morale, but whether it will also result in centralization depends on the structure of the group itself as well as on the nature of the conflict. . . . conflict between groups or nations has often led to anomie rather than to an increase in internal cohesion. . . . The degree of group consensus prior to the outbreak of the conflict seems to be the most important factor affecting cohesion. If a group is lacking in basic consensus, outside threat leads not to increased cohesion, but to general apathy, and the group is consequently threatened with disintegration. [Coser 1956, pp. 92–93]

Referring primarily to severe social-control response to protest movements by public authorities, Wilson has suggested a number of ways in which such measures are likely to have a dampening effect on protest mobilization. They "seem to generate distrust among protest movement members . . . which seriously impairs the ability of the movement to co-ordinate its work"; they may be "a source of emotional stress," even "creating intolerable tension — unless the movement develops coping structures"; they may intensify the need for "better coordination and compliance procedures" and impose "administrative demands on a movement organization — it must respond to social control agencies in terms dictated by those agencies" (Wilson 1977, pp. 476–478). These practical problems compound the still more basic definitional impact of official control, which, as we have already seen, can represent "a denial of the political status of acts and affirmation of their deviant character" (ibid. p. 475).

Whatever the developing interplay with opposing forces, deviance protesters must push well beyond the raising of consciousness and individual commitment in order to further their cause. Leadership, organization, and concerted actions of various kinds are necessary ingredients of effective protest. While the term *mobilization* is most often used in referring to the early stages of protest, in a sense the entire course of protest consists of a continuous mobilization effort — as one writer puts it, "the orientation of resources toward the instigation of social change" (Useem 1975, p. 29). In addition to the articulation of grievances, the drafting of agendas for change, and the activation and organization of protest groups (ibid.), mobilization involves the development and implementation of "a repertory of successful strategies and tactics" designed to enhance organizational strength and influence (Mauss et al. 1975, p. 56). The details of strategy and tactics will, of course, vary greatly and will reflect the specifics of the problem and the surrounding social context. But the need to act, by one means or another, remains. As we saw earlier, power is realized in the desired outcomes it enables the group to achieve. Among the most important general kinds of action by the protest group will be outward-reaching efforts to "press claims" (Spector and Kitsuse, 1977, p. 145) and inward-reaching attempts to preserve group cohesiveness, maintain high morale and commitment, and impose necessary coordination.

With respect to claims-pressing activities, a particularly important issue may have to do with whether, or to what extent, the protesters ought to work within the established political system. The inevitable strain between maintaining credibility and some degree of legitimacy, on the one hand, and maximizing member commitment and group militancy, on the other, has been a key problem for virtually all social-protest organizations. The stance a particular group adopts will be influenced by the nature of its claims, the identity of the most crucial targets of opposition, the group's actual goals and expectations, and the specific options among which it can choose. Although the danger of being co-opted is always present, when a group has relatively narrow claims to press and is not in direct opposition to the prevailing political order working within the system may make sense and may at times even be distinctly advantageous. Thus we saw that some abortion-reform activists attributed much of their success to their ability to capitalize on existing political contacts and experience with standard political techniques. On the other hand, there may be situations in which — as Piven and Cloward suggest of the urban poor — "collective defiance" becomes necessary (Piven and Cloward 1979, p. 5).

When alternative means are not available, protest may of course erupt into overt violence. Commenting on the Watts (Los Angeles) riot by blacks in 1965, Lewis Coser states, "Where political structures are incapable of accommodating all political demands there is an ever-present chance that violence will be resorted to by those who feel that they cannot get their voice heard, as well as by those who have a vested interest in suppressing this voice" (Coser 1967, pp. 106–107). The prisoners whose protests we considered in example 3 are in roughly the same kind of situation, although as we saw, some limited possibilities for nonviolent action may be emerging. In his study of fifty-three "challenging groups" that mounted social protests in America between 1800 and 1945, Gamson found those that used violence to have a higher-than-average success rate, in terms of the gaining of acceptance and the securing of "new advantages" (Gamson 1975, pp. 79–82). In many deviance-related protests, however, it may be true overall that

> violence is usually detrimental to the cause. Strategies and tactics in movements are generally those which we associate with any political action in our system: the seeking and forming of alliances, lobbying, picketing, fundraising, speechmaking, pamphletering, broadcasting in the media, and so on. Sometimes a successful tactic can consist of no more than a skillful reaction to an unplanned *precipitating incident*. [Mauss et al. 1975, p. 56; see also Smelser 1963]

This last point is well illustrated by several pivotal incidents affecting recent gay liberation mobilizing efforts, as discussed later in this chapter.

Internal cohesion is also a significant problem for most deviance-protest movements and organizations. Whereas a group's organizers will continuously be attempting to "increase its constituency's connectedness" (Useem 1975, p. 43), concerted effort will frequently be undermined by the development of internal factions. Particularly in broad, socially heterogeneous movements—as the recent examples of civil rights, women's liberation, and gay liberation (see below) make clear—factionalism is very difficult to avoid. Gamson found that "factional splits" (formal schism) had occurred in 43 percent of the protest groups he studied and concluded further that "the sorry reputation of factionalism is a deserved one. It is especially related to the achievement of new advantages; less than one-fourth of the groups that experience it are successful, in contrast to 70 percent of those that escape it" (Gamson 1975, p. 101). However, it should be noted that Gamson's study covered very specific organizations (such as the American Birth Control League, the Church Peace Union, the German American Bund, and the League of Deliverance.)

While broader social movements — within any one of which there may emerge a number of more specific protest organizations — are precisely because of their breadth highly susceptible to factionalism, they may also for that same reason be better able to accommodate internal differences and to succeed in attaining overall goals despite them. Gamson's study showed that, among specific protest organizations, decentralized ones were more likely than centralized ones to develop factional splits and to be hurt by them. He also found, however, that some decentralized groups,

> if they are able somehow to manage their internal differences . . . do quite well in spite of their lack of centralized power. One reason that they do well is that they have another organizational attribute that promotes success — bureaucratic organization. Only eight decentralized groups were able to win new advantages, but six of these were bureaucratic. [ibid. p. 105]

Coordination of some sort, then, seems essential if a broadly based movement — which may, in effect, be a less-than-tightly-knit network of component protest organizations — is to hold together its collective power and wield it effectively in the public arena.

CONSTITUENCY AND COALITION

As Spector and Kitsuse properly note, "Other things being equal, groups that have a larger membership, greater constituency, more money, and greater discipline and organization will be more effective in pressing their claims than groups that lack these attributes" (Spector and Kitsuse 1977, p. 143). Gamson found that a specific organization's size in terms of reported membership may not have much bearing on the advantages it can secure (Gamson 1975, pp. 50–54). At the same time, it seems likely that nationwide collective protest efforts will start with an edge when there is a very large potential constituency on which to draw for membership and support. The civil rights and women's liberation movements, and to a more limited extent the gay rights movement, clearly derived benefit from having sizeable potential or base constituencies. Current efforts to combat the deviantizing of the handicapped and the elderly similarly carry the built-in advantage of this kind of potential strength. By contrast, a group seeking to oppose deviance-defining in a situation where the stigmatized comprise a very small segment of the total population — for example, transsexuals or transvestites — cannot mobilize a large "natural" constituency, and must instead rely heavily on generating outside support.

As we noted earlier, protest groups often will seek to maximize the potential constituency by trying to effect a definition of the situation in which the specific problem is viewed as a working-class issue, a women's issue, or (as urged at the opposite end of the political spectrum) an issue of "decency," patriotism, or one that involves threat "to our entire way of life." It seems clear that a movement for change on any specific deviance issue will be greatly assisted by whatever prospects it may have for being held to fall under some such umbrella constituency. Several of our specific examples have shown how the women's movement provides one of these widely encompassing, somewhat free-floating constituencies. Table 2 (to which, no doubt, some further additions might be made) indicates a large range of deviance issues with respect to which partisan groups may especially be able to draw on the collective strength of engaged womanhood. While the comparable working-class-issue umbrella could potentially also encompass a very broad range of specific issues, we have seen that current working-class consciousness in our society does not provide an adequate basis for the wide recognition of indirect social linkages that that would require. The case of the women's movement, in relation to numerous specific deviance issues and protests, seems to be similar to what Smelser has in mind when he notes that general social movements will sometimes "provide a backdrop from which many specific norm-oriented movements emanate" (Smelser 1963, p. 273). However we conceptualize the causal relation between the general women's movement and these more specific stigma-contesting efforts, there can be little doubt

TABLE 2

The Women's Movement as an Umbrella Constituency

MAJOR WOMEN'S ISSUES	OTHER DEVIANCE ISSUES OF SPECIAL INTEREST TO WOMEN:
Abortion	Mental illness (definitions of women as "disturbed")
Prostitution	Lesbianism (and gay rights movement more generally)
Rape	Treatment of the elderly (ageism)
Woman battering	Deceptive advertising and consumer fraud
Child abuse	Welfare rights
Pornography	Environmental pollution
Female "delinquency"	
Out-of-wedlock children	

that a significant interrelationship does exist. One possible consequence of such interrelation could, of course, be a fragmentation and dissipation of the broader movement's energies through being spread too thin. In other words, some movement-related deviance-protest efforts would always be made at the expense of others. Although that is in some degree inevitable, it seems more likely that the overall tendency has been for the general movement and the specific protests to nurture and strengthen each other. From that standpoint, each victory of the women's movement — in whatever area — potentially contributes to all movement-related deviance efforts that will follow. (It might be added that women, every bit as much as men, have some interest in deviance issues not included in the table — alcoholism and drug addiction, suicide, corporate crime, and so on. With respect to the umbrella-constituency prospect, however, many of those issues do not have a similarly compelling special appeal.)

The umbrella constituency is of special value too because of the added leverage it provides in efforts to develop coalitions. In collective efforts to overturn stigma, the problem of obtaining outside support and allies becomes especially pressing — precisely because of the extent of social disapproval or imposed isolation. The umbrella movement provides an overarching system of beliefs and broad social goals that may be absent in some of the more specific protest areas. Prostitutes, to cite just one example, would be hard put to project any kind of convincing political ideology that would help attract powerful allies, in the absence of the women's movement. (A certain limited success would be achieved by emphasizing civil liberties arguments; perhaps some additional appeal, likely only to enlist minimal support, could be made to other groups of stigmatized individuals — on the very ground of similar victimization.) Finally, the umbrella constituency has great importance for what it implies with regard to ability to confer benefits (votes, reciprocating support, and the like) in exchange for support received. The umbrella constituency can deliver, in a way that its component parts cannot.

The Web of Cross-Pressures

Both in seeking out group alliances and in generating commitment and support among individuals, deviance-protest movements confront significant cross-pressures (Lazarsfeld, Berelson, and Gaudet, 1948) that stem from overlapping social positions and intersecting and competing values and interests. The potential for internal factionalism and also the tendency toward accommodation that can limit militancy, noted above, in part reflect the effects of that kind of complexity. Cross-pressures among deviance protesters represent, furthermore, the other side of the picture in which multiple interests similarly keep stigmatizing "control" from ever becoming uniform or absolute.

Earlier in this book deviance-defining was described as constituting or producing a kind of moral stratification. Since this system of distributing socially valued and disvalued statuses and identities overlaps and intersects with other dimensions of social and economic standing in our society, when the deviance-related and other dimensions are experienced or examined together they will often present a special type of "status inconsistency" (Lenski 1966, pp. 86–88) or at least a confusing multiplicity of statuses. Among the potentially organizable categories of stigmatized persons themselves, this complexity undoubtedly affects recruitment and protest participation. Each such category is made up, after all, of individuals who — apart from the general commonality of shared stigma — are quite diverse socially, economically, and politically. Degrees of commitment to movement goals and organizing efforts are bound to vary accordingly. It cannot simply be assumed that all former mental patients, or all alcoholics, or all homosexuals, or all physically handicapped persons, will share a common sense of purpose or display an equal indignation and motivation to act collectively. On the contrary, raising consciousness of the primacy of the deviance issue — particularly among those who, because of otherwise fortunate circumstances, have achieved a tolerable accommodation or have not experienced the full impact of deviantizing — is a major task for protest organizers.

Among those individuals who are not so directly involved in the dispute, but whose support might be solicited, similar cross-pressures again come into play. Those individuals have multiple or inconsistent statuses too. On the one hand, there is some evidence suggesting that persons displaying status inconsistency may be especially likely to support liberal or radical political movements (ibid.). On the other hand, it seems equally probable that in many collective stigma contests such complexity may make individual allegiances and commitments uncertain, variable, and diffuse. A relatively affluent middle-class black woman, for example, may find her response split with respect to supporting an effort to improve the situation of (primarily poor, female, and black) streetwalkers. Gender and race will push her in one direction, economic status in another. Even the lower-class black woman, whose statuses are more consistent (i.e., all relatively "low"), is not without multiple interests and frames of reference—in this instance and also more generally. While she may not experience a split along liberal-conservative lines, she may nonetheless still be torn and her political energies dispersed among possible commitments to class-based, gender-based, and racially based causes. (Of course, many such persons may instead be totally alienated and politically apathetic.)

Essentially the same problem exists with respect to seeking alliances with organized groups that are in a position to either enter the dispute or stand apart from it. Such groups may have multiple goals and interests, some but not all of which may favor an alliance. Often an outside group's failure to support or to support wholeheartedly will reflect not any ideological reluctance but simply a determination or a sense that its organizational priorities will not permit the expenditure of such effort in the desired direction. Some organizations—for example, the American Civil Liberties Union—may have a broadly based concern that dictates attention to (certain aspects of) a wider range of deviance issues; yet, even in such cases, organizational resources are far from inexhaustible, and decisions must be made regarding specific priorities and relative emphases.

A purely instrumental coalition, in which an outside group provides support despite its ideological indifference or even opposition, is another conceivable possibility. But given the unpopularity of many deviance causes and the typically low power of deviance-protest movements, the kinds of payoff that would motivate such a move will usually be absent. If and when such a coalition were to occur, it would most likely be half-hearted and short-lived. It is primarily such alliances of expediency that Coser has in mind when he writes that "coalitions resist transformation into more permanent groups. They are the simplest form of unification issuing from conflict because they contain an irreducible minimum of unifying elements. Permanent bonds would require the participants to relinquish some freedom of action in the pursuit of group interests" (Coser 1956, p. 145). The same writer also points out that uniting to combat "a common enemy" promotes such coalitions. With respect to current deviance issues, we might for example find gay liberation groups and prisoner rights organizations forming a temporary alliance in joint opposition to some specific measures advocated by a conservative coalition favoring law and order, antipermissiveness, and "the reassertion of decency in American life." But as Coser notes, more than a common enemy is needed for a coalition of convenience to evolve into a yet-more-unified action group.

Another type of cross-pressure that may arise in connection with deviance disputes also deserves mention. Sometimes a deviance-protest issue presents individuals and groups with a forced choice between two highly prized, but now directly competing, values. Two protest campaigns (see Dullea 1970; Stokes 1979) — in which efforts to curb exploitation of stigmatized groups have clashed with First Amendment free-speech, free-press guarantees — illustrate this possibility. One continuing campaign has involved feminist antipornography activity, organized through such groups as Women Against Pornography and Women Against Violence Against Women. This campaign has focused on derogatory depictions of women (as sex-objects, especially through depictions with sadomasochistic overtones) not only in pornographic books and movies but also in popular-music lyrics, on jackets for phonograph records, and even in a type of high fashion advertising sometimes termed brutal chic (Dullea 1979; also London 1977). While almost uniformly deploring the unhealthy associations and exploitative themes being promoted in these depictions, liberals have found themselves struggling with the hazy but important line between protest and censorship. The apparent willingness of some feminists to support overt censorship has been repudiated by various civil liberties advocates, who are not fully persuaded by statements like the following, attributed to the women's movement activist Susan Brownmiller: "Nowhere is it written that you can exploit a woman's body because of the First Amendment" (quoted in Dullea 1979).

Much the same sort of value conflict was posed when gay activists in New York sought to protest the filming in Greenwich Village of a motion picture, *Cruising*, which they held would disseminate misleading and derogatory depictions of gay life. (See example 7, immediately following this section.) In this instance, the active street protests that took place and the efforts that were made to convince gay men who were being hired as extras not to cooperate in the filming were less controversial than the attempt by some activist groups to get city hall to withdraw all support (permits, and so on) from the project. The activist contention that this was not an effort at censorship but simply a request that the city not cooperate in the filming did not convince civil libertarians (Stokes 1979). Even the gay activist forces were divided on the issue, as an article opposing censorship by the well-known novelist John Rechy indicated (Rechy 1979).

In seeking to minimize the negative effects of all these common types of cross-pressure, deviance-protest organizations and movements must expend considerable effort. And they must aim this effort both at maintaining internal cohesion and at marshalling the broadest possible support from outside forces. Central to this effort will be the struggle over definitions, which we considered in the last chapter. How individuals and groups resolve the cross-pressures they experience will not depend solely on the relative strengths of the competing interests —

measurable in some supposedly objective way. Perceptions and priority judgments will prove to be crucial in this connection. Thus, again, social definitions are ultimately at stake. Protest organizers must actively seek to influence conceptions regarding the nature of the "problem," the justness of their cause, the necessity of their tactics, the consistency of the movement's own priorities. Activists must thus advance claims about the very process of claims-pressing itself. Perceptions of means as well as ends, and of justifications as well as ramifications, will strongly influence people's ordering of priorities and decisions regarding support.

EXAMPLE 7. *Generating and Sustaining Protest: Gay Activism*

Gay liberation organizers must overcome substantial obstacles in order to promote collective consciousness and commitment to political action. Some of these difficulties are the standard ones that confront all protest movements. Others reflect special features of the homosexual's situation under conditions of social stigma and legal harassment. Considering the usual treatment of gay people in our society, it is not surprising if many of them want simply to be left alone and have little inclination to stand up and be counted. While it is true that to an extent the common lifestyle and high interaction rate that the gay subculture offers might (as per Gamson's analysis) encourage group solidarity, there are also aspects of this quasicommunal existence that work against the development of political interest and the sustaining of organized collective effort.

To begin with, because "homosexuals are to be found throughout the entire nation in all social strata" (Hoffman 1969, p. 33), there is great variation among gay persons regarding their overall social situations, the kind of oppression they experience, their corresponding levels of indignation and/or alienation, and their general social and political attitudes and commitments. In particular, social-class, racial, and gender cleavages within the gay population make for cross-pressures that impede unified organizatoin and render individual allegiances problematic. Some of these differences, furthermore, are closely related to the types of social accommodation available to gay persons. As a result, homosexuals in certain strata may have little inclination toward, and run considerable risks through, open political involvement.

At the heart of this complex situation is the fact that, since homosexuality need not be immediately evident to the observer, "passing" as heterosexual in at least some situations (Schur 1979, pp. 289–290; Goffman 1963) is an important option for most gay persons. Although increased openness about homosexuality and the growth of the gay liberation movement lessen the necessity for recourse to this option, it is nonetheless still true that a great many homosexuals continue in some degree to compartmentalize their lives — for example, by keeping their sexual orientation covert at work or in other heterosexually dominated situations. Thus a major survey in 1970 in the San Francisco Bay Area (where gay militancy is relatively high), which employed volunteer respondents, noted the persistence of this pattern of adaptation: "Despite the expectation that homosexual men and women who volunteer for studies of this kind would be relatively overt, we found that the majority were relatively covert" (Bell and Weinberg 1978, p. 67).

Although the situation of professed homosexuals has further improved since 1970, disvaluation, discrimination, and the possibility of legal interference continue to dominate the gay person's life situation. It is still true today that "the average homosexual has ample cause to fear arrest" (Humphreys 1972, p. 19) and that gay people, more generally, remain "perpetual outlaws" (Young 1977, p. 14). While legal protection of gay rights continues to advance, the professed homosexual still faces roadblocks in many fields. Thus the recent ACLU report on the rights of gay people includes a listing of over three hundred occupations covered by licensing restrictions in one or more states (Boggan et al. 1975, pp. 211–235 and chap. 3). Most of these statutes have provisions (e.g., requirement of "good moral character") that have been used in efforts to bar gay applicants.

In the light of continuing debasement and persecution, it is understandable that many gay persons have unfavorable self-conceptions (Schur 1965, pp. 97–102), negative feelings about homosexuality generally, and little sense of the collective identification needed for concerted political action. One observer notes, "To have a community one must have members who will acknowledge to themselves and to others that they are members of that community" (Dank 1971, p. 195). Many gay individuals not only accept limited social accommodations but also develop personal outlooks involving an "escape from identity," psychological as well as social withdrawal, "compensatory conservatism," and even "in-group hostility" (Adam 1978, chap. 4). According to another perceptive commentator on gay liberation, gay self-hatred reveals itself in the strong hostility many homosexuals have for any kind of gay political movement. Such movements "threaten too closely the manner in which most homosexuals have arranged their lives" (Altman 1973, p. 63).

Self-esteem and sense of group identification, furthermore, probably vary along with the extent to which an individual's major mode of adaptation is overt (or, conversely, covert). Research indicates that "self-hatred is much stronger among those covert passing homosexuals than for overt gays" (Humphreys 1972, p. 69), and one writer even asserts, "Homosexuals in positions of influence . . . may seek to protect themselves by excluding their fellows. 'Closet queens' often present themselves as the first to endorse the homophobic ideology" (Adam 1978, p. 89). The distribution of these outlooks also may reflect the relation between the compartmentalizing of work and leisure and the hierarchical patterning of occupational opportunities for homosexuals. Though this relation, too, is currently undergoing change, studies have long shown that covert adaptation tends to be associated with high-status jobs and overt adaptation with low-status ones (Leznoff and Westley 1956; also Humphreys 1972; and Bell and Weinberg 1978, p. 68).

Particularly, then, among gay persons who do not choose to reveal widely their deviantized sexual orientation, personal outlooks as well as practical considerations may militate against open and active protest involvement. Gay individuals would, in any case, presumably run the gamut of possible political orientations; these other factors simply make the probability of radical commitment smaller. In interviewing men who had engaged in homosexual encounters in public restrooms, Laud Humphreys found that many held quite conservative attitudes on social and political matters. He attributed this to a more general "breastplate of righteousness" or "protective shield of super-propriety," in which "the covert deviant develops a presentation of self that is respectable to a fault. His whole lifestyle becomes an incarnation of what is proper and orthodox. In manners and taste, religion and art, he strives to compensate for an otherwise low resistance to the shock of exposure" (Humphreys 1970, pp. 135–136). The same author concluded that, notwithstanding the considerable recent politicization of gay issues, "for the vast majority, the unsoon deviants, the breastplate of righteousness replaces the offensive weapons of all but the most conservative political action" (ibid. p. 147).

In Bell and Weinberg's large-scale survey of homosexual experience and attitudes, most respondents (black and white, male and female) described themselves as "liberal" or "moderately liberal" on "most issues of the day." (Bell and Weinberg 1978, p. 368). However, only 39 percent of the white homosexual males and smaller proportions in the other respondent categories reported "relatively high" political involvement (ibid. p. 369). Asked whether their homosexuality had affected them politically in any way, 58 percent of the white homosexual males said it had not, and much larger percentages in the other categories gave negative responses — 84 percent of black homosexual males, 82 percent of white homosexual females, and 88 percent of black homosexual females (ibid. p. 370). Of the 42 percent of white males who said they had been affected politically, 34 percent reported that being homosexual had made them more liberal. On the other hand, 20 percent of the same respondents reported no effect on their political activism, while 17 percent said that being homosexual had made them "more active" (ibid. pp. 371, 373).

Certain other aspects of homosexual subculture, besides the highly prevalent desire to preserve anonymity, may serve to limit the development of political consciousness and involvement. One is the sheer preoccupation with sexual behavior and imagery, which psychiatrist Martin Hoffman terms sex fetishism. According to him, "The most striking thing about gay life in general, which differentiates it from the straight world, is that its participants devote an inordinate amount of time to sexual matters" (Hoffman 1969, p. 75; see also Delph 1978). Though framing their specific explanations in rather different terms (in the one case psychoanalytic, in the other political), both Hoffman and gay activist Dennis Altman attribute this tendency to the impact of stigmatization and oppression. Responded to by straights almost entirely on the basis of their sexual orientation, gays too have become almost totally preoccupied with it. Although the shared pattern of having experienced oppression could facilitate the development of a collective consciousness, the resulting sex preoccupation is an obstacle to political organizing in its own right and also obscures true liberationist goals. Altman comments, "For the homosexual, the new affirmation involves breaking away from the gayworld as it has traditionally existed and transforming the pseudocommunity of secrecy and sexual objectification into a genuine community of sister/brotherhood" (Altman 1973, p. 227).

Intense involvement in allegedly distinctive gay cultural forms may also detract from political awareness and commitment. According to one observer, gay persons must make a partial transition from the "world of Americanism" to "another world with its own (potentially alienative) symbolic universe." She asserts, as key aspects of this symbolic universe, gay knowledge, gay vocabulary, gay legends and literature, and gay ideology (Warren 1974, chap. 5). While all subcultures — by definition, "cultures within a culture" — to some extent exhibit symbolic features of this sort, in the case of the gay community the symbolic trappings of, and claims regarding, a supposedly distinctive way of life are extremely far-reaching. The proliferation of special gay establishments now extends well beyond gay bars and baths to include gay-oriented clothing stores, restaurants, nightclubs, theatres, art galleries, bookstores, and churches and synagogues. There are now also numerous gay periodicals as well as special legal-service organizations, social and discussion groups, and therapy programs. Even more significant, there is a strong belief within the homosexual community in the importance of what one knowledgeable writer recently described as gay style, gay sensibility, even a gay aesthetic (Kopkind 1979).

Conceptions of cultural distinctiveness and gay separatism no doubt in part reflect a defensive adaptation to stigmatizing by, and exclusion from, the heterosexually oriented world of "respectability." As we have seen too, in the case of the black power movement and to a more limited extent in the case of the recent women's movement, such themes can at times serve a useful political purpose. They may in this instance encourage feelings of "gay pride," and they probably help stigmatized individuals to develop a new sense of social solidarity and collective security. Their more directly political implications are, however, unclear. It could be that the notion of distinctive gay culture will usefully contribute to organized militancy by providing an alternative to the "assimilationist" path that one writer describes as a major obstacle to gay liberation (Adam 1979). On the other hand, excessive preoccupation with "gay style" and "sensibility" could easily lead to apolitical outlooks and to a comforting, but also limiting, immersion in a self-enclosed social world. This could be so whatever the specific content of the separatist culture—for example, whether it is built around "feminine" themes (thus perhaps representing an internalizing or acting out of heterosexual stereotypes of gays) or instead around "supermasculine" ones (reflecting an effort to overturn such stereotypes). Time and personal resources are always limited, and if they are heavily devoted to fashion, mannerisms, "aesthetics" — and, as just noted, sexuality as such — there may be little left over to devote to larger issues and political endeavors. It is precisely this kind of encapsulation of the individual that the women's movement has been fighting: the limiting of women to their "special" role, and also their ultimate acceptance of their own sexual objectification and immersion in "women's culture."

We know that despite all these difficulties, the gay liberation movement has made striking gains in recent years. Actually, as Jonathan Katz has indicated, "American Gay history includes a long and little-known tradition of resistance" (Katz 1978, p. 505). His interesting collection of historical documents describes various precursors of the gay liberation movement and notes that in 1924 the state of Illinois chartered "the earliest documented homosexual emancipation organization in the United States" — the Chicago Society for Human Rights (ibid. p. 581). Through personal interviews with Henry Hay, a former Communist Party member who founded the first Mattachine Society (the prototype of the early "homophile" groups), Katz uncovered a number of early manifestoes. A 1950 one asserted that "encroaching American Fascism . . . seeks to bend unorganized and unpopular minorities into isolated fragments" and cited the organization's aim to provide a "collective outlet for political, cultural, and social expression to some 10% of the world's population" (ibid. pp. 615, 616). One journalist, discussing the potential for militancy suggested by this early organizational effort (which took place in Los Angeles, and in the face of McCarthyism) presciently suggested that eventually such groups "might swing tremendous political power" (ibid. p. 626). Throughout the 1950s, however, the homophile organizations by and large played a very moderate role. (See Sagarin 1969; Martin and Lyon 1972, chap. 8; Humphreys 1972, chap. 3). They provided assistance to individuals and sought to improve group morale and only gradually became involved in political efforts designed to promote significant change. The more recent considerable success achieved by gay liberation forces reflects in part the emergence of a new kind of organization, differing ideologically as well as programmatically from these early homophile groups. Altman chronicles the progression from moderation to activism as follows:

> The earliest groups tended to act as mutual-support groups for homosexuals who half-believed the stereotypes about themselves; during the sixties there was a development toward more open demands, even confrontation of and protest against social discrimination. But gay liberation represents a new self-affirmation and a determination that if anyone will be "cured," it is those who oppress rather than those oppressed. [Altman 1973 p. 119]

In attempting to achieve this last stage, however, the movement has continuously faced difficulties both in maintaining internal cohesion and in enlisting outside support. The aforementioned heterogeneity of gay people has ensured, from the outset, not only great variation in individual commitment but also a high degree of factionalism within the movement. One account, by the founders of Daughters of Bilitis, the major lesbian organization, refers to a dispute (over allowing straights to be present) at one of their first gatherings:

> That marked the beginning of a long series of arguments about rules and regulations, about the degree of secrecy we had to maintain, about mode of dress and behavior, about dealing with straights as well as gay men, about the possibility of publishing

pamphlets explaining our cause. The arguments eventually led to an ultimate rift. . . .

Only recently have we realized that the DOB split was along worker/middle class lines. The blue-collar workers who left DOB wanted a supersecret, exclusively Lesbian social club. The white-collar workers, however, had broadened their vision of the scope of the organization. [Martin and Lyon 1972, pp. 240–241]

Similarly within the male homosexual organizations, dissension and internal splinterings have been common. The existence of many gay groups, varying as they do in social composition and degrees of militancy, has perpetually blocked the consolidation and unified direction of the movement at the national level. Humphreys describes efforts at the 1970 San Francisco meeting of the North American Conference of Homophile Organizations (NACHO) to forge a coherent national unit as bogging down in endless dispute over petty procedural issues. He comments:

NACHO's dissolution in San Francisco illustrates the futility of attempting to impose old organizational forms upon nascent social movements. . . .

There were too many in NACHO who wished to "proceed like the members of any other large national organization." Closely defined goals and selective admission may be functional for Rotary International or the Masons; the very forms that help provide legitimacy for most voluntary associations, however, may throttle change organizations and render them ineffectual. [Humphreys 1972, p. 109]

By the late 1960s and early 1970s, factionalism within the gay movement had developed to such an extent that one participant-observer could discuss the contrasting political goals and styles of "two major 'radical' gay groups in New York, the civil libertarian Gay Activists Alliance and the revolutionary Gay Liberation Front" (Altman 1973, p. 122). Indeed, according to Altman, dissatisfaction with even the more radical Liberation Front "led to a number of breakaway groups. Women, youth,

Third World and transvestite organizations have all been set up, part of gay liberation as a movement but distinct from the GLF" (ibid. p. 126).

Notwithstanding the emergence of, and competition among, a great many specific gay organizations, the major split within the movement continues to be between moderate and radical elements. According to one writer, the primary ideological division is "between radical 'movement' gays, whose roots in radical politics and cultural criticism lead them to stress societal liberation, and gay professionals who, probably reflecting the desire of the truly silent majority of gays, do not wish to appear threatening to society's institutions" (Ross 1977, p. 527). The reference to "gay professionals" suggests that disagreement over goals and tactics may be associated partly with socioeconomic differences. A further complexity in the web of interests at play on gay issues is seen in explicit claims to the effect that certain homosexuals may have a direct economic interest in preserving the status quo. Thus Adam (1979, p. 296) refers to "gay capitalism," and Altman asserts: "In a sense, there is a 'gay establishment,' which, like the black establishment, benefits economically from the present system of (liberal) oppression—even after paying for protection, gay bars/baths are profitable investments" (Altman 1973, p. 132).

Although at times one or another gay organization claims to speak for all homosexuals, in fact there is no unified and fully coordinated national movement. Recently, however, when specific incidents and issues believed to be of special significance have ignited strong direct protest and been widely publicized, at least a temporary solidarity has been forged in which factional differences have largely been set aside. Without question, the most striking example was the nationwide furor that arose in the spring of 1977 when residents of the Miami, Florida, area voted in a special referendum to overturn a previously enacted gay rights ordinance (Ayres 1977a and 1977b; Schur 1979, pp. 424–425). An acrimonious contest over this referendum had produced a considerable marshalling of gay support nationally, in an attempt to offset the campaign led by singer Anita Bryant. Arguing that homosexuality was immoral, she helped form the antigay organization Save Our Children and led the (eventually successful) crusade to overturn the rights ordinance (Ayres 1977a). The subsequent Miami vote provoked large demonstrations across the country and led gay leaders to plan an expansion and strengthening of various political efforts (Ayres 1977b). Similar referenda votes in several other cities heightened concern about antigay backlash, and the increased media coverage of gay rights issues that these events triggered may have conferred a degree of legitimacy on movement efforts that also helped to promote solidarity.

Pivotal issues and incidents since then have included the following: In 1978 California voters defeated the Briggs Initiative, which would have banned homosexual teachers and homosexual advocacy in the public schools (Gusfield 1978). In 1979, an outspokenly antigay former policeman and city supervisor assassinated both the mayor of San Francisco and a supervisor who was an acknowledged gay activist. Even more inflammatory than the murders was the short prison sentence subsequently imposed for the crimes. (See Ireland 1979.) Most recently, the dispute over the film, *Cruising*, in New York City not only raised the First Amendment dilemma noted above but also elicited major street demonstrations by gays. A commentator on one of these demonstrations noted, "The march itself, which paused at bar after waterfront bar to summon the patrons inside, seemed to be a way for gay people to signal each other that the time had come to stop flaunting fetishism." As the same writer went on to point out, factional differences were largely surmounted in developing this protest: "Even though an ad hoc committee [of radical activists] sponsored this campaign, its impetus came from the movement's moderate wing—especially the National Gay Task Force. The Militant Gay Activist Alliance call this 'The National Gay Tom Force,' but both organizations rely on each other's presence, though they revile each other's ideology" (Goldstein 1979, p. 18).

If the welding together of an internally cohesive gay movement has presented serious problems, so too has the enlisting of outside support and the forging of specific alliances. One important source of potential support is the predominantly heterosexual women's movement, but mobilization has been very uneven. Lesbianism, in fact, has been one of the major issues over which serious factionalism has erupted within that movement. Much as in the case of prostitution, heterosexual women often find lesbianism a personally confusing and threatening topic. Furthermore, leaders of the women's movement frequently have argued that a focus on lesbian rights would divert effort from what they saw as more urgent organizational priorities, and also they have feared that the movement would be smeared by its enemies as being lesbian dominated. (See Hole and Levine 1971, pp. 93–94; Martin and Lyon 1972, chap 9.) These factors led one analyst to refer to the "long record of the women's movement's hostility toward lesbianism," and to comment also that this "has resulted in some instances in returned hostilities of lesbians toward the women's movement" (Simpson 1977, p. 52). Overall, then, notwithstanding the claims by some gay activists that they represent one major strand of a single battle against sexism (Altman 1973, chap. 3; Young 1977, p. 29), efforts to produce a close and stable alliance have been ineffective.

Despite the recognition by many within the gay liberation movement of the "need for alliance with other alienated groups" (Altman 1973, p. 120) and the general commitment by some gay activists to radical politics, there has been no significant success in enlisting large-scale support among either the working class or the oppressed racial and ethnic minorities. These constituencies and organizations have their own priorities, which do not usually call for a heavy focus (if any) on problems relating to sexual orientation. Orthodox Marxists, furthermore, are likely to perceive the oppression of gays primarily as a secondary by-product of the capitalist system and to call for militant opposition to that overall system as the first order of the day. Indeed, from the standpoint of gays themselves, the attractiveness of an alliance with orthodox leftist forces may be limited. As one writer comments, "The traditional left, both Old Left and New Left, has been as oppressive to homosexuals as has establishment America" (Young, 1977, p. 22).

The mobilization of gay protest, then, continues to prove difficult. In addition to all of these cross-pressures, variations in commitment, and problems in developing external alliances, what might be called the internal alliance between homosexual males and homosexual females is itself shaky. (See Jay and Young 1977, esp. pp. 290–293.) Some current gay activist organizations are gender neutral while others are gender based, and among the latter there exist varying outlooks on gay unity. Perhaps the most potent resource the gay liberation movement has is the sheer size of its potential base constituency. Together with the recently increased support for, and indeed approval of, gay openness and assertiveness — at least within the homosexual community itself — this ensures a substantial core of continuous protest and activism. To the extent "passing" remains necessary in certain circles, commitment and involvement will be somewhat weakened, and individual concern over the implications of acknowledged organizational membership (Boggan et al. 1975, chap. 1; Humphreys 1972, p. 95) will persist. But the conviction that the broad current of social change favors their cause and the enhancing of morale through a slow but steady achievement of successes in asserting and advancing gay rights are likely to sustain the movement in its already impressive efforts to overcome stigma and collective oppression.

References

Adam, Barry D. 1978. *The Survival of Domination.* New York: Elsevier North Holland.

Adam, Barry D. 1979. "A Social History of Gay Politics." In M. P. Levine, ed., *Gay Men*. New York: Harper & Row, Pub. Pp. 285–300.

Altman, Dennis. 1973. *Homosexual: Oppression and Liberation*. New York: Avon.

Ayres, B. Drummond, Jr. 1977a. "Miami Debate Over Rights of Homosexuals Directs Wide Attention on a National Issue." *New York Times*, May 10, p. 18.

Ayres, B. Drummond, Jr. 1977b. "Miami Vote Increases Activism on Homosexual Rights." *New York Times*, June 9, p. 1.

Bell, Alan P., and Martin S. Weinberg. 1978. *Homosexualities: A Study of Diversity Among Men and Women*. New York: Simon and Schuster.

Boggan, E. Carrington et al. 1975. *The Rights of Gay People*. New York: Avon.

Coser, Lewis A. 1956. *The Functions of Social Conflict*. Glencoe, Ill.: Free Press.

Coser, Lewis A. 1967. *Continuities in the Study of Social Conflict*. New York: Free Press.

Dahrendorf, Ralf. 1959. *Class and Class Conflict in Industrial Society*. Stanford: Stanford University Press.

Dank, Barry M. 1971. "Coming Out in the Gay World." *Psychiatry* 34 (May): 180–197.

Delph, Edward W. 1978. *The Silent Community*. Beverly Hills, Calif.: Sage Publications, Inc.

Dreifus, Claudia. 1973. *Woman's Fate*. New York: Bantam.

Dullea, Georgia. 1979. "In Feminists' Antipornography Drive, 42d Street is the Target." *New York Times*, July 6, p. A12.

Edelman, Murray 1977. *Political Language*. New York: Academic Press.

Emerson, Robert M., and Sheldon L. Messinger. 1977. "The Micro-Politics of Trouble." *Social Problems* 25 (December): 121–134.

Gamson, William. 1968. *Power and Discontent*. Homewood, Ill.: Dorsey Press.

Gamson, William. 1975. *The Strategy of Social Protest*. Homewood, Ill.: Dorsey Press.

Gaylin, Willard et al. 1978. *Doing Good*. New York: Pantheon.

Goffman, Erving. 1963. *Stigma*. Englewood Cliffs, N.J.: Prentice-Hall.

Goldstein, Richard. 1979. "Why the Village Went Wild." *Village Voice*, August 6, pp. 1, 16–18.

Gouldner, Alvin W. 1968. "The Sociologist as Partisan." *The American Sociologist* 3 (May): 103–116.

Greenberg, David F. 1976. "On One-Dimensional Marxist Criminology." *Theory and Society* 3: 610–621.

Gusfield, Joseph R. 1978. "Political Ceremony in California." *The Nation*, December 9.

Hoffman, Martin. 1969. *The Gay World*. New York: Bantam.

Hole, Judith, and Ellen Levine. 1971. *Rebirth of Feminism*. New York: Quadrangle/The N.Y. Times.

Humphreys, Laud. 1970. *Tearoom Trade*. Chicago: Aldine.

Humphreys, Laud. 1972. *Out of the Closets: The Sociology of Homosexual Liberation*. Englewood Cliffs, N.J.: Prentice-Hall.

Ireland, Doug. 1979. "Lambda Under Siege." *Village Voice*, June 25, pp. 80–82.

Jay, Karla, and Allen Young, eds. 1977. *Out of the Closets: Voices of Gay Liberation*. New York: Harcourt Brace Jovanovich.

Katz, Jonathan. 1978. *Gay American History*. New York: Avon.

Kopkind, Andrew. 1979. "Present at the Creation." *Village Voice*, June 25, pp. 61–66.

Lazarsfeld, Paul; Bernard Berelson; and Hazel Caudet. 1948. *The People's Choice*. New York: Columbia University Press.

Lemert, Edwin M. 1951. *Social Pathology*. New York: McGraw Hill.

Lenski, Gerhard E. 1966. *Power and Privilege*. New York: McGraw Hill.

Levine, Martin P. 1979. "Gay Ghetto." In Levine, ed., *Gay Men*. Pp. 182–204.

Leznoff, Maurice, and William A. Westley. 1956. "The Homosexual Community." *Social Problems* 3 (April): 257–263.

Liazos, Alexander. 1972. "The Poverty of the Sociology of Deviance." *Social Problems* 20 (summer): 103–120.

London, Julia. 1977. "Images of Violence Against Women." *Victimology*, 2, 510–524.

Martin, Del, and Phyllis Lyon. 1972. *Lesbian/Woman*. New York: Bantam.

Mauss, Armand L. et al. 1975. *Social Problems as Social Movements.* Philadelphia: J. B. Lippincott.

Mitchell, Juliet. 1973. *Woman's Estate.* New York: Vintage.

Piven, Frances Fox, and Richard A. Cloward. 1979. *Poor People's Movements.* New York: Vintage.

Rechy, John. 1979. "A Case for 'Cruising.' " *Village Voice,* August 6.

Ross, Ken. 1977. "Gay Rights: The Coming Struggle." *The Nation,* November 19, pp. 526–530.

Ryan, William. 1972. *Blaming the Victim.* New York: Vintage.

Sagarin, Edward. 1969. *Odd Man In.* Chicago: Quadrangle.

Schur, Edwin M. 1965. *Crimes Without Victims.* Englewood Cliffs, N.J.: Prentice-Hall.

Schur, Edwin M. 1979. *Interpreting Deviance.* New York: Harper & Row, Pub.

Simpson, Ruth. 1977. *From the Closets to the Courts.* New York: Penguin.

Smelser, Neil J. 1963. *Theory of Collective Behavior.* New York: Free Press.

Spector, Malcolm, and John I. Kitsuse. 1977. *Constructing Social Problems.* Menlo Park, Calif.: Cummings.

Stokes, Geoffrey. 1979. "The First Amendment Bullies." *Village Voice,* August 20, pp. 14–15.

Thio, Alex. 1973. "Class Bias in the Sociology of Deviance." *The American Sociologist* 8 (February): 1–12.

Useem, Michael. 1975. *Protest Movements in America.* Indianapolis: Bobbs-Merrill.

Warren, Carol A. B. 1974. *Identity and Community in the Gay World.* New York: John Wiley.

Wilson, John. 1977. "Social Protest and Social Control." *Social Problems* 24 (April): 469–481.

Young, Allen. 1977. "Out of the Closets, Into the Streets." in Jay and Young, eds., *Out of the Closets: Voices of Gay Liberation.* Pp. 6–31.

Conclusion:
The Persistence of
Stigma Contests

Political efforts to contest and influence deviance-defining constitute a major social phenomenon of our times. Although overt politicizing of stigma issues frequently involves the use of standard political processes and techniques, this should not be seen as an arbitrary or undesirable importing of the stuff of politics into some supposedly abstract and settled "moral" realm. On the contrary, deviance situations are — at the same time — both moral and political in nature. Deviantizing as a mode of defining and reacting, a way of characterizing people and their behavior, incorporates and imposes moral judgments and determines the distribution of moral propriety. By the same token, however, since both the deviantizing of individuals and the collective definition of deviance amount to put-downs of some persons by others, they necessarily involve the exercise of power, reflect preexisting power differentials, and influence the subsequent distribution of power.

Social diversity and normative conflict underlie both deviantizing and deviance disputes, and the widespread persistence of these conditions within modern societies makes contests over stigma inevitable. Lack of absolute consensus on norms and the impossibility — especially within a democratic system — that absolute coercion or control can be imposed by those in power (even assuming they would want to exert it on all matters, which is not the case), ensure the emergence of disagreements and disputes as to what is acceptable and what is offensive. Not even the totalitarian regime can maintain complete and monolithic control over its citizenry in such a way that officially imposed norms will be fully agreed upon and complied with. Within democratic systems as well as under totalitarianism, the absence of overt conflict and the surface appearance of attitudinal consensus may often mask deep-seated latent conflicts of value and interest.

We have seen also that perceptions or feelings of threat underlie deviantizing definitions and reactions. At all levels, deviance situations reflect some people's response to other people's behavior as being troublesome, offensive, problematic, or unsettling — as being, in one way or another, personally or socially threatening. Who will feel threatened by whom or what, and under what conditions, are not always readily predictable. The perceived threat may be direct or indirect, patently economic or largely symbolic, and grounded in rational assessment, irrational response, or mistake. What is most important in setting off or sustaining stigmatizing reactions is the perception itself, or the sensing of a threat, on whatever grounds. Because of the varied bases for perceiving threat and experiencing disadvantage, and also for perceiving and actually deriving benefit from particular deviance outcomes, there usually is — with respect to any given deviance issue — a large array of individuals and groups whose potential interests may be activated. As a consequence, collective deviance struggles will typically involve not only direct antagonists but also potential and probable allies on either side, as well as a wide range of persons and organizations who in varying degrees may stand to gain or lose from one or another "solution" to the disputed problem.

In these conflicts, as in all social conflicts, preexisting power is an important determinant of every outcome. But given the substantive diversity of perceived deviance problems, the relevance of sheer economic power varies considerably. It is easy to see that, in one way or another — either because oppressive living conditions drove them to crime or because their low status adversely influenced their treatment by the police and the courts — the incarceration of many criminal offenders is largely "due to" their preexisting poverty. Likewise, it is clear that economic power is crucial in insulating corporate crime — both by protecting individuals who might otherwise be subject to stigma and in the maintenance of collective definitions treating it as a relatively benign offense. However, in other major areas of deviantizing — such as alcoholism, mental illness, homosexuality, physical disability — the relationship between economics and stigma outcomes is, as we have seen, much more tenuous. Even here, at the individual level, personal vulnerability to severe deviantizing will tend to vary according to socioeconomic status. But the collective definition of these conditions is not easily explained in economic terms. And the fact that the distribution of persons exhibiting them cuts across all of the socioeconomic strata within our society implies situations in which the politics of deviance are not entirely class based. Because of this complex intersection of the moral stratification of deviantizing with other standard dimensions of stratification, any theory that attributes all deviance defining to the allegedly monolithic power wielding of some economic elite must ultimately fail. Similarly, as we saw, explanations of deviance that rest exclusively on coercion and control by the state are equally untenable. In many deviance issues the direct interests of those holding ultimate political power are simply not at stake. For some of these same reasons, it is virtually impossible to conceive of a type of socioeconomic system within which deviance and deviance disputes would not be present.

It follows from all this that in collective deviance struggles a variety of factors besides economic power can help to produce desired outcomes. Political skills and contacts, overall strategies and specific tactics, credibility as a legitimate political force, and timing can all be very important. Timing can matter greatly in at least two ways. As we have seen, specific pivotal incidents may facilitate protest mobilization or be otherwise capitalized on by participants in a deviance dispute. Even more significant, though, is the long-term aspect of timing. Some specific deviance contests grow out of, as well as contributing to, broader currents of social change within a society. Thus we found, in several of our detailed examples above, that a specific deviance issue was being pressed as part of—and largely as a result of—the wider movement for women's liberation. While no conscious attempt was made to have these examples comprise a representative sampling of current deviance contests, it is perhaps not surprising that three of the seven (abortion, rape, prostitution) involve major women's issues, and another (psychiatry and mental illness) also poses questions of strong interest to the women's movement. That reflects the fact that the very state of being a woman has until recently in effect been deviantized. The current collective efforts of the women's movement in large measure aim to overturn the many manifestations of that stigma.

By definition, however, those who attempt to undo current patterns of deviance-defining are, at least by virtue of the existing stigma, in a have-not position. They must shoulder in their collective opposition a special burden of activism that the supporters of the stigmatizing do not bear. In a way, this is the implication of the institutional politics of deviance discussed early in the book. Since deviance-defining usually reflects the structures and values of a society's major social institutions, groups that aim to change existing definitions typically confront more than just their recalcitrant opponents. Even when the general social trend seems to favor their cause, deviance-protest movements often must deal with deeply entrenched patterns and values that make for considerable resistance to change. We saw this tendency at work in the persisting sexism that constitutes the gender politics of abortion, rape, and prostitution; in the strong persistence of ideas and values relating to business and crime that help to keep corporate crime from being more severely stigmatized; and in the prestige and power of psychiatry that allow it to cut across and affect a range of specific deviance issues.

More generally, the organizers of a collective deviance-protest effort face all the basic tasks and difficulties that confront a protest movement of any kind. As we saw, these include generating and sustaining collective consciousness, developing and preserving internal cohesion, maintaining external credibility and internal morale, mobilizing group membership for concerted collective action, and seeking specific alliances and more general outside support. In all of this activity, a large and powerful potential constituency of persons directly concerned obviously provides a substantial advantage. And, as just reemphasized, the umbrella constituency of a wider social movement can also be a great help. At the same time, the complex web of intersecting statuses and interests that in general compounds the relation between social class and deviance also means that even within a movement's potential base constituency cross-pressures will produce great variability in degrees of individual commitment and a strong likelihood that internal factions will develop.

The emphasis throughout this book on the complicated network of statuses and interests relevant to most deviance issues should in no way be taken to imply that deviance-defining displays a benignly pluralistic give-and-take through which socially desirable outcomes usually emerge. Our specific examples make quite clear that this is not the case. Deviance protesters are not engaged in some kind of political game the fruits of which invariably serve to vindicate "the American way." The social welfare and even the lives of real people are crucially at stake in these stigma contests. There is little indication, overall, that the composite pattern of deviance-defining in present-day American society is either rational or just. That this is so no doubt in large measure reflects the oppressive conditions and distorted priorities of a society that is dominated by capitalist, racist, and sexist values and institutions. By itself, however, such as assertion explains everything and yet nothing. The specific ways in which the workings of this all-encompassing "system" come to be implicated in concrete deviance situations remain complex, however appealing it may be to assert some sort of generalized conspiratorial "explanation" of deviance-defining. Acknowledging the complexity of contested deviance issues is not necessary only for analytical purposes. It is a prerequisite, as well, to the realistic and effective organization of collective action to overcome oppression.

Index

235